MILES TO GO...

MILES TO GO...

One Man's Recover Journey

MILES WALCOTT

iUniverse, Inc.
Bloomington

Miles to go . . .
One Man's Recover Journey

This is a work of fiction. All of the characters, names, incidents, organizations, and dialogue in this novel are either the products of the author's imagination or are used fictitiously.

iUniverse books may be ordered through booksellers or by contacting:

iUniverse
1663 Liberty Drive
Bloomington, IN 47403
www.iuniverse.com
1-800-Authors (1-800-288-4677)

ISBN: 978-1-4759-8913-7 (sc)
ISBN: 978-1-4759-8914-4 (ebk)

Library of Congress Control Number: 2013907981

Printed in the United States of America

iUniverse rev. date: 05/06/2013

For My Children, Family
and the Still Sick/Suffering Addict

Special thanks to my children for encouraging me to write, even when I was discouraged. I would also like to acknowledge my Sister Lizan and my friends Lisa G., Pam B., Vivian D. and my many FBF's for supporting me during this sometimes painful process.

CONTENTS

Hi, my name is Miles and I'm recovering from the disease of addiction and the emotional pain of trauma. About ten years ago, my first sponsor suggested that I write a book about my interesting journey through life. I dismissed the idea as nonsense at the time, but the farther I traveled down my path, the more compelled I felt to tell my story. After many years in the process of recovery, I realized that it would be the epitome of selfishness if I didn't! For how can one possess hope, and not share it? I learned from attending 12 Step meetings that we can only keep what we have by giving it away.

I am on a mission to spread hope. Hope for the addict who may not believe that he or she can break free from the shackles of trauma and/or addiction. Hope for the person who is watching a loved one destroy their life through active addiction. Hope for the man or woman who finds themselves in the revolving door of the Dept. of Corrections as a direct result of their addiction and the unhealthy, impulsive choices we sometimes make.

My experiences and the experiences of others that I know personally have shown me that without hope, a person who seeks recovery is doomed. Now that I have hope, I feel morally and spiritually obligated to spread that hope and let others know that no matter what happened to you in the past, no matter your age, race, sexual identity, religion or lack of religion or socio-economic background, regardless of what your situation is now . . . freedom from trauma/addiction is possible for anyone. Whether you are addicted to drugs, sex, violence or even Ben & Jerry's ice cream, freedom from that which is causing unmanageability in your life is possible!

Many survivors of trauma share common beliefs and behaviors, such as feelings of low self-worth and substance abuse. Once caught up in the vicious cycle of addiction one may feel like freedom from addiction is a hopeless endeavor. I am her to show you that freedom from active addiction and the pain of past trauma is possible. This is the story of how I gained my freedom.

Prologue

Nuremberg, West Germany circa 1985

"Damn Shorty, I'm high as a kite!" I said out loud as I wiped the sweat from my brow with the back of my left hand and puffed on a fat Bob Marley looking joint with my right. It was a hot August afternoon and I'd been drinking all day at my Army unit's company party. My home-boy "Shorty", from New Jersey, his cute, German girlfriend, "Milla" and I had just snuck away from the party to smoke a hash-lace joint together. "Puff, puff, pass, man!" Shorty admonished, prompting me to stop hogging the jay, as I took my third long pull. Shorty was about 5'4" but no one took his small frame for granted. If you were in a fight, this was the guy you wanted to have your back. "Hold up, man", I said, taking one last pull.

After we finished the jay, Shorty and his girlfriend returned to the party, but I had to get home and get some sleep because I had guard duty in about 6 hours. I staggered along the narrow bike path and struggled to keep my 6'3" tall, dark and handsome frame from veering off into the bushes! Five years of regular exercise had me in top physical condition, but I was no match for warm brandy and hash on a hot summer's day.

I looked up and saw two fine German girls jogging up the trail towards me wearing skimpy halter-tops and tight shorts. It was almost as if they were jogging in slow motion as I noticed their breasts rising and falling with each successive stride! I attempted to straighten myself up and think of something witty to say, because no matter how lame your line was, most German girls would stop and talk to a "brotha" whether they spoke English or not. As long as he wasn't rude and obnoxious, a young black man could at least get some conversation whether his swag was smooth or not!

Young black men were in high demand in this land of fair skinned Europeans, and I was more than willing to do my part to supply that demand! There was a myth that all black men were well "endowed" and there was no shortage of local girls who were curious to find out how true this was!

I was wearing a pair of sky blue khakis with a matching sky blue polo shirt and a brand new pair of white Nike sneakers. I tipped my white, "snap-back" NY Yankees baseball cap to the ladies and said, "Good affer noon laydeesh", in what I thought sounded like my smoothest "Billy Dee Williams" voice. They looked at each other, giggled something in German, and rolled their eyes as they continued jogging down the path. Apparently, they were not interested in the drunken American soldier with the slurred speech! As I turned around in mid stride to check out their behinds, I stumbled, fell and landed on my ass with my hands and feet in the air! As I lay there on my back, I was relieved to look up and see that my lit Newport and half bottle of E & J brandy I was carrying were still intact. I got up, dusted off the seat of my pants, mumbled something about "stuck up bitches" and continued on my way.

Suddenly, the sound of dirt bikes filled the air and although I was drunk and high as hell, I figured it might be a good idea to get out the way. Three white dudes, dressed in black, revved their engines as they passed me, spraying gravel all over my clothes. I quickly stumbled to the side of the path to avoid being hit and shouted, "Geez, you almost ran me da fuck over!"

The dirt bike riders sported green Mohawk haircuts, black eye liner and had tattoos creeping up their necks from beneath their black tee-shirt collars. They were wearing dusty, black leather boots with silver buckles and although it was a hot summer's day, the long, black leather coats they sported flapped in the wind as they raced up the path. "Faggot-assed punk rockers," I shouted, as I continued on my way. Back then, the word "Faggot" had nothing to do with someone's sexuality; it was just an insult we used for people we didn't like.

Suddenly, their dirt bikes slowed, and they spun around to face me; revving their engines. I could feel my heart rate increase as they stared at me from about 50 feet away, shouting over the sound of their engines to each other in German.

"*Look at you*", said that familiar voice in my head "*Don't just stand there like a little bitch . . . DO SOMETHING!*" I flicked my cigarette away, but held on to my bottle of liquor as they revved their engines one more time and began to speed towards me.

As they made another pass, they shouted insults at me in English. "Go back to America, Nigger Boy", one of them shouted as they began their approach. I could see that these weren't the kind of punk rockers that I used to see hanging around Toads Place when me and the fellas would go downtown New Haven to "hit" on the "Yale Chicks". These dudes had swastikas emblazoned on their coats and a tough look in their eyes that said," We ain't here to pass a hash joint around with you or share your bottle!" "They must be some of those skinheads I've heard about", I said to myself as I began to emerge from my drug and alcohol induced fog.

FUCK YOU, American Nigger!" another one yelled, as they continued to taunt me. "Hmm . . . never been called an AMERICAN nigger before" I chuckled, as I quickly became aware that this shit was about to get ugly.

The year was 1985 and I was a 23 year old Army private from the 3/5 Field Artillery Battalion which was headquartered in Nuremburg, West Germany. I had just left my unit's company picnic at the Dutzendikes, and I was high as hell from drinking E&J Brandy all day and smoking some of that potent red hash that I had copped from the "Turk" the day before.

"Fuck you too!" I yelled, as another s passed me. I was beginning to get nervous because with each pass, they came closer and closer to mowing me down with their dirt bikes. He and his two buddies had been harassing me for the last hundred yards or so, shouting racial slurs at me and spitting at me each time they passed.

"Is "fuck you too" the best you can come up with?" said my sarcastic, inner voice. Fear and adrenalin raced through my veins as I quickly began to sober up and wonder how I was going to hold my own against these three menacing skinheads. I was having flashbacks of the white guys who jumped me when I was a kid and I'd be damned if THESE guys were gonna hurt the "little boy" trapped in this grown mans body!

On their next pass, a well placed "hock" spit found its mark smack dab in the middle of my face and that was enough to convert me in the blink of an eye from a drunk, frightened young soldier into a vicious sociopath who would stop at nothing to protect "Little Miles". It was as if a switch had been flipped in my brain and suddenly, I was ready to inflict as much pain as necessary to stop these guys from harassing me. I consciously decided that I was going to "go off". . . . damn the consequences. It wasn't so much of an impulsive, drunken decision as it was an acutely calculated, fine tuned choice.

Instead of flying into a rage, I stopped walking and acted like I was just standing there wiping my face with my left hand and smearing the disgusting phlegm on my pants leg, but in my mind, I was carefully planning my attack. No longer feeling the effects of the hash and alcohol, the adrenalin had taken over. My senses became fine tuned and I began to formulate my course of attack. My Dad always said," The best defense is a damn good OFFENSE!

With my head tilted down, I continued to wipe my face but I was peeking through my fingers, carefully timing the moment that the next skinhead would come within arms reach. It was as if the sun had become brighter and my sense of hearing became acutely intense. I could hear them speaking loudly in German, and although I didn't understand what they were saying, I knew they meant business. It was time to take action or become a victim. I could see one of them approaching as I wiped the vile smelling spit from my face, I heard him "hock" up another load of spit and at the precise moment he reared his head back to unload another repulsive spit bomb on me. I took three quick steps towards him, swung the E&J bottle with all my might and caught him square in the face. He didn't even see it coming! The impact of my blow shattered the bottle and created a shower of glass and liquor. I held on to the sharp, jagged bottleneck that remained and watched as my attacker flew off his dirt bike and landed on his back, slamming his head into the pavement. The momentum of his dirt bike caused him to slide about twenty feet until he came to rest in a motionless, bloody heap, on the ground.

His rider less dirt bike crashed into a bush with its rear wheel still spinning and his buddies jumped off of their bikes to tend to him. When they saw how badly he was injured, they cursed loudly in German and turned their attention to me. Not giving them a chance to formulate an attack, I immediately pounced on them and began wildly punching them both with my fist and the broken remains of the E&J bottle while screaming at the top of my lungs," Leave me alone! Leave me alone! Leave me the FUCK alone!"

I had made a conscious decision that today I would NOT get my ass kicked like I did in the past! The days of Miles Walcott getting his ass kicked were over, and I was willing to do whatever it took to protect myself. The switch that I had turned on in my mind was becoming increasingly hard to turn off! It was as if all the rage that had been building up inside me since childhood suddenly came flooding out in an uncontrollable torrent.

As the second skinhead lay, bleeding on the ground holding the side of his face to stem the flow of blood from his gaping facial wound, I stood over the third, holding his collar with my left hand and the broken bottle neck in my right . . . deciding whether or not to stab him in the neck with it or just slam his head into the concrete. As the German police began to arrive on the scene, I felt a wave of relief and began to let my guard down until I realized they were not here to rescue me.

CHAPTER 1

My Earliest Memories

As a child, I lived in the Brookside housing project. It's so ironic that the places our society houses its poorest citizens in have such affluent sounding names such as Elm Haven, Brookside, Rockview Circle, Westville Manor etc. Our particular "project" was aptly named Brookside. The reddish brown, brick, two story buildings did border a quiet rolling brook but only thing was; on the other side of the brook was the city dump! Even as a six-year-old child, I found it quite odd that I lived so close to the dump. I can remember the other kids and I hopping the fence between Brookside and the brook to go "exploring" in the small stand of trees that we called "The Woods".

"The Woods" was actually a small plot of undeveloped land that acted as a sort of buffer between the Projects and the Hamden City Dump. It was here that we would sort through society's refuse, in search of something useful. They say," One mans trash is another mans treasure" which is especially true if you are a poor kid growing up in public housing. "This bike only has a ripped seat!" one of us would proclaim, excited at our latest find. It was amazing to us at what folks would throw away! "Check out this lamp" another might say." I bet my momma's boyfriend can fix this with some of that black tape" said another. Although our parents forbade us from going beyond "The Brook", we were drawn to the dump like so many roaches to sugar!

I began to wonder in my young, impressionable mind, why I lived next to a dump. How come my friends and I wear jeans with holes in the knee and raggedy sneakers on our feet? Why are so many of the cars where I live old and damn near broke down? When my Dad took us to school in our old station wagon with the wood accents on the exterior, we would pass by the dump on our way into town. After the dump, we would drive by Southern Ct state College and pass by what seemed to a little kid from the PJ's, as majestic homes along Crescent St. They were actually modest middle-income homes, but to me, "That's where the rich folks live!"

I became aware, at an early age that I was poor and I didn't like it! Unbeknownst to me, my all ready fragile self-esteem was being slowly eaten away by my own false perception of reality. I thought I was poor because that's what I deserved. I began to think of myself as," Not good enough". In spite of the love I received from my family, I always had this nagging feeling that I was "less than".

My parents instilled pride in their children and taught us to take care of what little we had. Although we lived in the projects, we kept our home and our yard spotless. "The Projects is where we live, not who we *are*" Ma always said. We all had chores, and although our furniture may have been a little old and worn, our home was always clean. Although we had old clothes, we were taught to wash, fold and iron them. I can remember my mother putting those iron-on patches on the knees of my Lee jeans when I wore them out.

Even though our car was old, my brother Chris and I still helped Dad wash it after Saturday morning chores. My dad also taught how to check the oil and do basic maintenance.

I was one of the few kids who had a Mom *and* Dad in the same house! They were both hard workers, so we weren't entitled to food stamps. My Dad was a proud man and could have easily had my Mom, Barbara, lie on the food stamp application, but Charlie Walcott would have none of that! He even told the truth on the free lunch application at school so we had to pay for lunch while a lot of my classmates ate for free.

Charles Christopher Walcott Jr., my Dad, was about 5'5". Not a very tall man, but he had a "presence" that made him larger than life. He was stocky in stature and walked with a confident stride. His skin was the color of coffee with just a drop of cream. Dad's looks reminded me of Fred G. Sanford from the hit show Sanford & Son probably because of the stubbly salt & pepper gray hair that framed his face and head. But that was where the resemblance stopped. He was a proud man who worked hard to keep a roof over his family's head and food on the table. He did his best to teach me what being a man was all about and if it wasn't for him, I wouldn't be half the man that I am now!

My mother, Barbara Sarah Walcott, was one of the most beautiful women I have ever seen! Her good looks rivaled those of Lena Horne! She was very light skinned as a result of her mixed heritage of Irish and African American. She always dressed in a style that showed she had class and carried herself like a lady at all times. My mom taught me skills that I use to this very day. She taught me how to mend clothing, cook and was the best English teacher I ever had, always correcting me when I mangled the language." No one is going to hire you for any job, talking like that" she would gently admonish me when I used words like "aint" or other slang. My mother was the sweetest woman in the world and everyone loved her. My father would often joke after one too many Johnny Walker Reds on the rocks that he loved her so much he would drink her dirty bathwater if she asked him to! I used to wonder if he was joking or not!

My Mom and Dad were hard working folks. At the time, "Ma" as we affectionately called her, worked as a mail handler for the US Postal Service and Dad worked for the New Haven Housing Authority as an administrator. Eventually, they both attained supervisory positions in personnel and maintenance at the Post Office, and were able to send my four siblings and me to St Martin De Porres; a Catholic School located smack dab in the middle of the hood. St. Martin de Porres was the black patron saint of blah blah blah, but I always felt like they just named it that because the school was located in a black neighborhood.

Most of the nuns there were sweet, kind white women who are probably in Heaven as we speak, because of their tireless crusade to educate poor underprivileged inner city kids. There was this one nun though, Sister Rita, who made Archie Bunker look like a sweet old man! Sister Rita was a disciplinarian who, in spite of her short stature, carried a "presence" with her that made even the classroom bully quiver in his shoes! She had this all white hair that was coiffed into a neat hairdo under her "Habit" and these piercing blue eyes that could make you cry when she told you that if you didn't behave, you would go straight to hell immediately following your demise! So between Sister Rita and "The Black Leather Belt" I became quite motivated to become an academic scholar and behave myself! Of course I loved the positive attention I got from my parents when I bought home good grades, but it was the fear of an ass whooping and going to hell that kept me on the straight and narrow!

Dad always told us that if we wanted a good life, education was the key! Anytime I asked him the definition of a word or what something meant, he would say," look it up!" Mom & Dad had purchased a set of World Book encyclopedias along with dictionaries and a wide variety of books that covered a wide array of topics on our bookshelf. This bookshelf became my "Internet" and the encyclopedias were my "Google" I remember trying to read "The Prophet" by Gabril Kahan at 10 years old . . . it was way too "deep" for me at ten, but what I walked away with was the knowledge that the Catholic Church was only ONE religious point of view. There are many spiritual beliefs and only I could choose my spiritual path!

The food we ate at home was bought with hard earned cash, and it was a cardinal sin to waste even a helping of black-eyed peas! Nothing was wasted and it wasn't uncommon to find a left-over chicken leg or a pork chop incorporated into a pot of spaghetti sauce. I remember one night; I learned two very valuable lessons. I don't recall the whole meal, but black-eyed peas were one of the items on the menu. Our family ate most of our meals together at the table, but this particular night it was just my younger sister Lizan and I at the table. My older brother Chris, had teasingly told me that black eyed peas came from the eyes of dead black folk, so there was no way I was gonna eat them! Chris was always "yanking our chain" by telling us crazy stuff like, "You aren't a real Walcott. Some one left you at the door in a basket and Ma & Dad decided to keep you cuz you were so cute". In spite of his weird sense of humor, Chris was my protector and I always looked up to him. You could mess with me if you wanted to, but if Chris found out; that was your ass!

I quietly scooped one portion of black-eyed peas at a time onto my fork and placed them on the floor underneath me, so that our German Sheppard "Rerun", who would always happily eat any scraps that I didn't eat, could get them! We named him Rerun after a character from the

70's black sit-com "What's Happening'", that featured an overweight buffoon named Rerun. As a puppy, Rerun was the cutest lil fat puppy you ever wanted to pet! When my Dad came into the kitchen to check my progress, I looked him straight in the eye and answered," Yes, I ate ALL my black eyed peas!" Little did I know that "Rerun" hated Black Eyed Peas just as much as I did, and although he ate the scraps of fat that I also placed under the table, he politely left the peas in a neat little pile under the table! Of course I hadn't noticed this, but Dad did! After a whooping' with the infamous" Black Leather Belt", I was made to endure a lecture on telling the truth! "Nobody likes a liar" Dad scolded me. "I'd rather you steal my money than lie to me, because when you lie to me you are stealing my reality!" "You are trying to make me believe some shit that's not even REAL!" The two lessons I learned that evening were that Dogs don't eat Black Eyed Peas and if you are going to lie, make sure you cover your tracks!

I'll always remember the pained look on my Moms face whenever I got a "beatin". She would be sitting in a chair reading and when I passed by her she would wipe my tears and say something sweet, in a soft, low voice so that Dad didn't hear. God forbid she get caught, "Babying that boy". Back then, you were supposed to take your ass whuppin' like a man, even if you were only ten years old!

Barbara Walcott wasn't your typical loud, outspoken, "in your face" Black woman. I use the term "typical" because many a night I would hear other black women "cussing their men out" for one thing or another, berating their men at the top of their lungs, emasculating them with their hurtful words. Barbara Sarah Walcott on the other hand was the sweetest, most demure woman in the world and I can count on one hand the times I ever heard her raise her voice and still have some fingers left over! She left corporal punishment to my Dad, whose style of discipline was; kick ass and ask questions later! If he came home from work and found one dirty dish in the cupboard, we were all awakened with an ass whuppin and made to wash every dish in the cabinet over.

Don't get me wrong, he was a sweet, loving man most of the time, he spent time with us, took us on family vacations and was a great provider. I never saw him hit my Mom or "call her out her name". He instilled a work ethic in me that has lasted to this very day. Charles Walcott also taught us other values such as integrity, loyalty, family etc., but once you pissed him off, you could forget about it! When Charlie Walcott was upset, everyone within earshot knew it!

I took this particular trait with me into adult hood, and of course, in true addict form, I took it to the extreme, and as a result, accumulated an extensive police record of domestic violence! As an adult, in "active addiction", I fought men *and* women, but in my culture men didn't call the police when they fought other men . . . you either took the ass whuppin' or plotted your revenge, but you never called the police! A lot of women, on the other hand were taught to not take any shit from a man, because "most men aint shit anyway". If your man pisses you off, cuss him out, slap him or throw something at him, and if he really pisses you off . . . throw his shit outside, but if he hits you back . . . call 911!

At this point I must say that I don't condone domestic violence at all! A mature adult handles conflict in an appropriate way, but unfortunately many men (including myself, at the time) had missed that e-mail! As kids, we were taught that if someone . . . *anyone* hits you, you hit him or her back! When you are growing up in "The Hood" your "Rep" would be destroyed if anyone found out Sally or Sam hit you and you didn't do anything back! Fear of appearing soft to my peers was a driving force in me that kept me on edge during confrontations. I learned at an early age to overcompensate during arguments in hopes that my loudness and threats would intimidate you into backing down. As a young adult, I expected the women in my life to behave like my mother did and yield to my wishes, and when they didn't, I resorted to threats and physical violence because I wasn't emotionally equipped to handle confrontation.

CHAPTER 2

Racism 101

By the late sixties/early seventies, my big brother Chris had become involved with the Black Panther Movement. He was quite the Black History scholar and I shared his interest in history in general and Black history in particular. I was appalled by the fact that not too long ago, black folks were slaves in the very country whose flag I pledged allegiance to the every morning in class! I found it unbelievable that during my own lifetime "Colored" folk weren't even allowed to drink out of the same water fountains as white folk!

Chris's interest in Black history sparked my own quest to find out all I could about the horrors of slavery and the plight of the Black Man in America. I read all sorts of books in my teens from Tom Sawyer to The Hon Elijah Muhammad's "Message to the Black man" (which scared the crap out of me with talk of white men being devils and such.)

One of my favorite stories was that of Nat Turner, the runaway slave who started a violent slave uprising, killing scores of slave owners during his rampage. If not for the teachings of Martin Luther King and Charlie and Barbara S. Walcott, I may have followed the radical path and began shouting," Death to Whitey" along with the rest of the disenfranchised, uninformed folks in the "struggle". My Dad taught me "All white folk aint bad . . . and all black folk aint good!" "You gotta judge folk by the way they act". Kinda like M.L.K's ". . . content of their character" speech! Fortunately for me, my folks had white friends also. One of Dads best friends (I can't remember his name) was a white guy and they used to laugh and drink Johnny Walker Red in our living room whenever he visited. I used to call them "I Spy"; after the Bill Cosby and Robert Culp television show. It was the first show I can remember that starred a black and white guy where the "brotha" wasn't a pimp, gangster, drug dealer, servant or a buffoon! Even though my studies emphasized the horrors of slavery by "Whitey" upon the Blackman, I also learned about the abolitionist," White folk" who helped us and advocated for our freedom. To this day, I teach my children racial tolerance and love and I denounce racism of any sort. I remember one day when I was in my thirties, my 8 year old son referred to white people as "Crackers". After I enlightened him about our family tree, I enjoyed the look of awareness come over his face as he said," That would make me a cracker too huh Daddy?" Trevor, my son, now has friends of all races and he loves his God Father, "Uncle Marky" to death! Uncle Marky happens to be a white man and one of my best friends!

One time though, shortly after Alex Hailey's novel "Roots" came out, I witnessed a horrible beating where about ten black kids seemed to come out of no where, and commenced to whipping this one white guys ass so bad that he needed to be taken away in an ambulance! Someone shouted," That's for Kunte Kinta, motherfucker!" as they kicked and stomped the poor guy

I remember feeling an overwhelming sense of shame and embarrassment that the very people who I identified with and was once trying to emulate, would act in such a horrific, barbaric way. I caught a lot of flak from the fellas for not participating in the melee, and was even called a "pussy" for not joining in on similar atrocities such as throwing rocks at cars with white occupants or going a few blocks up the road into Hamden to look for some "white boys" to jump! Being from a family that had white folks in their family tree, and parents who taught us that you only fought if someone hit you first or looked like they were *about* to hit you, I just couldn't buy into fighting people for sport or just because of the color of their skin.

Another one of my encounters with racism was in the winter of '75. Back in the day, there was an ice skating rink at Edgewood Park. Edgewood Park was a gorgeous place that was in the Westville section of town; kind of like a mini Central Park. There was a duck pond, playground and plenty of grass and trees and paths for a kid to go "exploring" in. In the warmer months, Ma & Dad would take Lizan and I there to feed the ducks. Sometimes we would bring tuna sandwiches, Kool Aid and potato chips and have little picnics by the duck pond.

During the winter months the highlight of the park was the ice skating rink. Adjacent to the ice skating rink was a building where you could rent skates. It was built like a Swiss chalet. It had a vaulted, high cathedral ceiling and a huge fireplace where folks could come sit and get warm. It opened up to a large skating rink where folks of all colors would come and enjoy themselves.

I can't remember ever seeing a fight or anything there and it was here that I realized that it was possible for folks of all colors to co-exist without violence. I remember having a crush on this cute white girl named Molly, who took the time out to teach me to skate. Molly had long red hair and a freckled face that turned an adorable shade of red when the cold air hit it. Molly and I used to have a cup of hot chocolate after skating before I would walk her halfway home. She lived on Ellsworth Ave which was an affluent neighborhood on the way to my street and she said she would get in trouble if her folks saw her walking with a boy, so I would say goodbye at the corner and watch her walk down the street to her home wondering if she would get in trouble if she was seen walking with a "white" boy.

Well, one particular day, after skating and hot chocolate, Molly and I were walking home when we were accosted by a group of white boys who were a few years older and bigger than me. Apparently, the black boys from the hood weren't the only ones who would harass people of another race when they walked through their hood! I remember the biggest one asking Molly if I was giving her any trouble. When she said no, he punched me in the face anyway and said, "That's for the niggers who jumped my brother last week!" I jumped up off the ground and tore into him like a Tasmanian devil, but he was too strong and his buddies would knock me down every time it looked like I was getting the best of him. Eventually, they tired of kicking my ass and went running down the street laughing hysterically. Molly was crying and was trying to dab my facial wounds with her hanky but I was so angry and embarrassed that I yelled at her to leave me alone and went running down the street. When I got home, Ma cleansed my wounds and put a bandage on my ear where one of the kids had kicked me while I lay face down in the snow waiting for the beating to stop.

When my brother Chris got home, he was furious! He demanded to know where the guys who did this to me lived but I had no idea where they were from. He made me walk up and down Ellsworth Ave. with him trying to find my assailants till it got dark. Even Chris knew that it wasn't a good idea for two black guys to be in this part of town after dark! I didn't go skating for a couple of weeks due to my embarrassment and fear of running into them "white boys" again. When I did finally muster up the courage to go back, I saw Molly and this white kid skating, so I went up to her and tried to say hi but she acted like she didn't even know me! When I asked what was wrong, her eyes darted back and forth between me and a stern looking white man who was standing on the side of the rink with his arms crossed looking at us with an angry look on his face. My Momma didn't raise any dummies, so I knew the deal and walked away with tears in my eyes at the realization that apparently, Molly was only allowed to fraternize with white boys now. The pain I felt inside was greater than any ass whipping anyone could have inflicted on my body! Again, I was feeling less than and not worthy.

A few days later, after one of those nasty New England Nor'easters, I was shoveling snow in the predominantly white neighborhood of Beaver Hill. Everyone knew that most black folks didn't pay others to shovel their snow, and if they did, they didn't pay much, so you had to go to the "white" neighborhoods if you wanted to make any real money As I said earlier, my Dads work ethic was already deeply engrained in me and a snowstorm was the perfect opportunity to make some serious cash for an eleven year old! Not only did I make forty or fifty bucks per snowstorm (which was big money for a kid back then) but the folks who let me shovel their walk for five or ten bucks would invite me in for hot chocolate and cookies! Some would even offer me dinner but I was taught not to accept food from strangers; cookies and hot chocolate didn't count!

On this particular day, after making a nice piece of cash, I was on my way home when I spotted the same group of white boys that had whipped my ass a few of weeks ago. They didn't see me because they were too busy frolicking in the snow in the driveway of this really nice colonial style house. I ran as fast as I could to Whalley Ave, which was the closest main thoroughfare, and stepped into a phone booth outside of Pegnataros supermarket to call home. "Please Chris, answer the phone," I said out loud as I listened to the phone ring. Brrrrring . . .

brrrring. "Hello?" It was Chris! "Those fuckin white boys who jumped me are right here on Ellsworth!" I screamed into the phone. "Don't move! I'll be right there," Chris said. As I waited for my big brother to come, I could feel the anxiety building in my chest as my heart began to race, anticipating my revenge! Chris is ten years older than me so that would make him at least five years older than my assailants. When he arrived, we just started walking towards where I saw the dudes who had jumped me. We didn't speak at all; we just walked purposefully towards Ellsworth Ave.

As we approached them, I could see the frightened look in their eyes as they watched the kid they had jumped a couple of weeks ago approaching with this militant looking older black guy with the black beret and boots with bullets in the leather loops. We walked into the driveway where they were standing and Chris said," Which one of you motherfuckers hit my brother?" No one said a word. "Somebody is gonna pay for hitting my brother" said Chris as he approached the group of five or six white boys. The big one who had punched me in my face pulled out a small pocket knife and said, "How much you wanna bet, nigger?"

Suddenly, Chris got this crazed look on his face that I had never seen before. He reached into his jacket and pulled out this big assed rusty old sickle with a sharp point on it that he must have grabbed from the basement." I bet you your *life* mother fucker!" Chris screamed. The rest of their crew scattered, screaming, "Oh my God! This nigger's crazy!" It looked like they were attacking us as they scrambled towards us, so I raised my shovel in a defensive posture but they were running *away* from us! The driveway was sloped on both sides and the only way out was past us. The big guy lay on the ground whimpering. "Please don't kill me!" he pleaded as my brother stood over him menacingly. Chris raised the sickle over his head and it looked like he was about to really kill this dude. "No Chris, stop!" I screamed, as I tried to grab his arm; I wanted revenge, but I wasn't ready to murder any one!

Chris instructed me to "Kick this mother fucker in the head like he did you!" I turned and kicked home boy in the head with all my might, but as soon as my boot made contact with his head, I felt remorseful. Here I was feeling sorry for this racist bully who not only kicked my ass but embarrassed me in front of Molly!

"Look at you, you lil pussy", a voice inside me said mockingly. Chris told me to kick him again, but I said," Let's go!" Suddenly, I didn't want revenge anymore. Chris stomped him in the head with his combat boots and I heard a sickening crack as the big guys head snapped sideways and hit the cold, hard driveway. We took off running down the street and didn't stop until we got home, except when Chris threw the sickle into a dumpster behind Franks Package Store.

When we got home, we burst through the front door only to see two official looking white men in trench coats and dress shirts and ties talking to Ma. As we stood there with shocked looks on our faces, wondering how in the hell these two "detectives" knew where we lived, Ma said," Take those boots off before you come in the house". "Chris, Show these men to the basement while I check on dinner". Come to find out they were just furnace salesmen! Later on that evening, we cracked up laughing together as we recalled the scared look on each other's faces when we thought we were about to be arrested!

CHAPTER 3

Movin' Up!

After we moved out of the Projects, my parents brought a three family house on Sherman Ave. It was a really nice brown and yellow 3 family house in a pretty nice, middle-class neighborhood that had a mixture of renters and owners. I'll never forget the proud look of accomplishment on my Dads face when he pulled the For Sale sign up and tossed it in the garbage. I was about eleven or twelve years old now, and I was learning from my folks that if you worked hard and saved, you could improve your living conditions considerably. Now that we weren't in a cramped Project apt, we would have big family dinners where all my Aunts and Uncles would come over. After dinner, my cousins and I would shoot baskets on my very own basketball hoop that my Dad and I put up in the back yard, while the grown-ups would sit around the kitchen and living room playing cards, drinking liquor and having a good ole time.

Living on Sherman Ave was cool! Now that he was a landlord, Pop was responsible for the upkeep and repair of the house. No longer did we have the luxury of calling the maintenance man when something was broken. When a door needed replacing or a wall needed repairing, I was Pops apprentice; fetching a flat head or Phillips screwdriver from the basement or holding wood while Pop cut it with the circular saw. I got immense pleasure from working with my dad. When we were doing a job together, Pops would explain every step of a task whether it was measuring and cutting wood or mixing cement for post holes while putting up a fence. All the while, holding a Benson & Hedges menthol cigarette in the corner of his mouth with that long ash that never seemed to fall off! It was during these times that I felt closest to my father. Dad had a way of making me feel like he couldn't have gotten the job done without me (even though all I did was stand there and hold the end of a board!)

In the work I do now as a Mental Health Caseworker, a recurring theme with a lot of adults with substance abuse issues is the lack of a positive male role model in their lives while growing up. I had many friends with that dilemma but, MY Dad was there for me all my life! He took us on summer vacations to the Cape, where some of my fondest memories are of the whole family rolling down the sand dunes or eating out at a seafood restaurant before retiring to our quaint little cottage that we would rent for the week. Other trips included New York, Atlantic City, Philly and when my first niece Kiante was born in D.C., Dad packed us all up and we spent a week down there admiring the newest addition to the Walcott family and visiting historic sites such as the Lincoln Memorial, the Washington Monument and the White House. Because of this, not having a father wasn't an excuse I could use to explain away my drug use and self-destructive life style.

My Dad instilled a strong work ethic in me by example. He went to work every day and when he retired from the Postal Service, he had over one thousand sick time hours saved up! Dad was a great provider and he taught me the value of a buck! He would never just *give* me money; if I wanted something, I had to earn it. Rake the yard, sweep the stairs, or straighten up the basement. He was teaching me that if you wanted anything in life, you had to work hard for it. I could go on and on about the good father I had and the loving home I came from but the point I am trying to make is that in spite of having a good father in my life, I still chose to use drugs.

CHAPTER 4

Who wants to become . . . a drug addict?

Many people have blamed broken homes and absentee fathers as an excuse to use drugs, but the bottom line is that I was curious about drugs at an early age. I saw the older kids smoking and giggling and eating sweets as they got the "munchies" and I couldn't wait to smoke my first joint! Drug use was almost a rite of passage for a lot of us growing up in the early 70's.

We were bombarded with images of Cheech and Chong in that smoke filled van, George Clinton on stage with that fat assed joint. Rick James was singing about Mary Jane, Eddie Hendrix was on acid, Flower Power, Free Love etc. Hell, I even had a poster on the wall in my bedroom of the Jolly Green Giant with red, half closed eyes lying on the ground while the little green guys were carrying a big joint. The caption of the poster read; "I get high with a little help from my friends"!

My first time smoking weed was when I was 12 years old and my family went to Washington, D.C. to visit my new-born niece, Kianti. The birth of my niece was a special occasion for the whole family. I remember standing in awe as I touched her cute little hands and looked into her beautiful eyes. Kianti was the first child born to any of my siblings and I felt extra special because I was now an uncle! There was something about becoming an uncle that made me feel like I was on a higher level of maturity than before. None of the uncles in my family ever spent any time with me and I must say that in retrospect, besides my mom's brother, who lived all the way in Virginia, all of my uncles were either alcoholics and/or drug addicts. Besides my dad and my big brother Chris, I didn't have many positive male role models in my family to look up to. I vowed to be the kind of uncle that took his niece to the park and spent time with her, a sharp contrast from what I was used to.

My oldest sister Candace shared an apartment there with her fiancée, Major. I viewed Major as the intellectual type because he spoke very eloquently and articulately as he quoted Malcolm and Martin DuBoise etc with ease. He wore a brown, tweed sports jacket with the suede elbow patches and sported a cool pair of black "Ray Bans" that made him look like a cool college professor. Major had strong opinions on the plight of the Black Man, but also offered solutions to the Black Mans dilemma . . . these were qualities that really appealed to my young impressionable mind.

Ma & Dad were taking Kandi, as we affectionately called my sister, out to buy baby stuff the next day and Major offered to watch me as there wasn't much room in the car with the baby seat and all. He took me to a local park and read a book while I shot baskets with the other kids. Afterwards, we returned to their apartment and Major began rolling a joint. I felt privileged to be a witness to the whole process because I had seen folk smoke weed before, but never saw how a joint was actually rolled. Incense smoke filled the air while Earth Wind & Fire played on the turntable in the background. "Shining star for you to see . . . what your life could truly be".

I watched, fascinated, as he poured some weed on an empty album cover and expertly sifted it, making the seeds fall onto the table while the crushed buds remained on the album cover. Next, he removed the stems, until he had a uniform pile of weed in front of him. He then pulled out a book of "Bambu" rolling papers and commenced to rolling the most perfect joint I had ever seen! It resembled one of the filter-less Pall Malls my mom smoked! I was quite intrigued at the whole process. After taking a few pulls on the joint, Major looked over to me and casually asked me, "Do you smoke lil man?" Not wanting to appear like a lame, I answered, "Of course I do" and proceeded to take a few pulls off of what was probably some very excellent weed. In retrospect, my virgin lungs would have probably caught a buzz off of a few hits of oregano!

Even at the tender age of twelve, I felt an overwhelming need to "fit in" and to be accepted. My only memory of my first high is of me lying on the couch, spellbound and amazed by the lava lamp that sat on top of the book shelf. My next memory is of being awakened by the smell of sausage cooking as my Mom and Kandi prepared a spaghetti dinner in the kitchen. When it was ready, I tore into that spaghetti with a ravenous abandon, eating as if I hadn't eaten for days. I remember the quizzical look on Dads face as I guzzled grape Kool Aid and continued to stuff spaghetti and garlic bread into my face as I enjoyed my first case of the munchies! Later on that evening, my father pulled me to the side and said, "Are you ok Chief?" I told him everything was fine, but all I could think about was eating some of the brownies that were cooling off on the counter. My first time getting high and I was already lying about my drug use!

Years later, after Kandi and Major broke up, I found out that he had become a heroin user and had died from an overdose. Little did we know back then that marijuana could act as a gateway drug that could lead to other more "hardcore" drugs.

CHAPTER 5

The Terrible Teens!

It's a well-known fact that when a person begins abusing drugs at a young age, their emotional growth is retarded or stunted. I'm sure there is a scientific explanation for this, but the bottom line is, most 30-year-old men who have been getting high since the age of thirteen, have the emotional maturity of a thirteen year old! So if you fast-forward this story to my adult years, that bit of info should help you understand why I reacted in such a childish way to most of life's situations.

Mom and Dad were now on their second home, a quaint, one family house on Tilton St. Tilton St was a relatively quiet street that was two blocks away from the biggest housing project in New Haven. Elm Haven Housing Project consisted of five 10-story "High Rises" and about fifteen "Low Rise" buildings that were spread over a ten-block radius. I quickly became friends with the kids there because we all went to the same school and played ball together at one of the five or six basketball courts that were scattered throughout the project. Dad would playfully tease me that, "You can take the boy out of the projects, but you can't take the projects out of the boy!" because I spent most of my time hanging out in the PJ's. Elm Haven was located down the hill from Tilton St and some of the kids didn't like me because of my "Up the hill" status, as if living "up the hill" made me somehow better than them. The bottom line was that other than the fact that we lived in a house, we were all lower to middle class kids whose parent(s) were struggling to make ends meet. I guess I wasn't the only one dealing with self-esteem issues.

We had a dog named Ishmael, named after the character in the novel, Moby Dick" Ishmael was a white Siberian husky who had the sweetest temperament I have ever seen in a dog. He would walk with me with no leash and if he saw a cat or a squirrel he would just stop, lower his head and growl while the hairs on his back stood up. He never attacked anyone or anything and the folks in the neighborhood knew him well.

One day, while taking "Ishey" for a walk, we passed by Big Al's house around the corner. Big Al was the neighborhood bully who was about 3 or 4 years older than me but was the size of a grown assed man! He never really gave me any trouble because I kept my distance and he knew Chris was my brother. On this particular day, Big Al was on his porch fixing a bike with a couple of his boys as Ishmael and I came walking by. Ishmael started to take a crap, like dogs usually do, on the curbside grass in front of his house. Besides the crap from Big Al's dog, there was an assortment of broken forty oz. bottles, candy wrappers and Stateline potato chip bags that had accumulated over time (they never cleaned in front of their house!)

Before my dog could begin doing his business; this bastard hurled a pair of, silver adjustable grip pliers at him, hitting him square in the side. Ishmael let out a loud yelp and took off down the street headed towards our house.

"Da fuck you do THAT for?" I screamed, suddenly realizing that yelling at the neighborhood bully certainly was not the smartest thing I had done all day. In spite of the fact that this 'wanna be' Tiny Lister outweighed me by at least fifty pounds, I was in a rage because Ishmael was like a little brother to me.

As I stood there on the sidewalk and glared at Big Al with my fists balled up, I detected the look of fear in his eyes and immediately bounded up the stairs of his porch, picked him up over my head and threw him over the bannister. One of his boys made a move towards me and I gave him a quick round-house kick to his temple as I leapt over the bannister to finish off Big Al. Not taking any chances, I whipped out a pair of black nun chucks and began spinning them and switching them from hand to hand and around my waist like Bruce Lee did in Enter the Dragon! The neighborhood bully and his friends stood in awe as I stood there with my "chucks" tucked under my right armpit and extended my left arm in front of me and beckoning him to come on with my forefinger.

As my momentary fantasy faded away, I could slowly hear Big Al's voice come back into focus, demanding that I bring him his pliers. I can vividly remember the intense range of emotions that were coursing through my body at that moment, but what enraged me the most was the fact that this asshole and his friends were getting such a kick out of my dogs' pain.

I knew I had no chance of winning this fight, but I had to do something and without even thinking, I snatched the pliers from the ground and threw them as far as I could down the street. Big Al was furious! He jumped over the railing of his porch and headed towards me. I started to run, but he was too fast for me. He caught me by the back of my shirt and whirled me around to face him." Go get my fucking pliers or I'm gonna bust your little punk ass" he said. "Fuck you!" I screamed. "Get off me! You shouldn't a hit my dog!"

My defiance only added fuel to the fire and Big Al began to shake me violently while holding my collar with both his hands. The more I struggled to get free, the tighter he held me. I realized that I was no match for his strength so out of desperation; I slammed my forehead into his face as hard as I could, splitting his lip *and* causing his nose to bleed.

At first, everything became silent and for a moment, all you could here was the locust's high-pitched screech cutting through the thick summer air. Everyone including myself stood in wide-eyed shock that someone had the balls to head-butt this Neanderthal in the face! Somebody shouted," Ohhhh SHIT!" as Big Al's face began leaking blood. The desperate look in his eyes slowly changed from fear of "losing face" in front of his friends to a look of anger.

He suddenly let go of my collar and punched me in the mouth so hard that my front tooth was pushed back and my top lip was split down the middle. I still have the scar under my moustache to this very day! I ran home holding my face and I can remember the horrified look on Ma's face when she saw all the blood. My Mom pleading with my Father and brother not to go around the corner and retaliate," Just call the police, Charles" My father replied angrily that the police didn't care if we all killed each other as long as we didn't bother any white folks.

I'll handle this myself!" he said calmly as he escorted me to the car. Chris couldn't do anything because he had been arrested at a Black Panther rally for refusing to cease taking pictures of the police as they kicked the shit out of the protestors and couldn't risk violating probation. Dad remained composed and took me to the E.R. where I received stitches and the doctor straightened my tooth out. The doctor said my tooth would tighten up eventually.

Later on that evening, Dad was sitting on the porch with a glass of Johnny Walker Red on the rocks, tapping his little chrome plated .25 caliber pistol against the side of his leg, looking very serious. "How ya feelin Chief ?" he asked me, using his special nickname for me that he only used when I was feeling down or sick with a cold." I'm ok" I said, not wanting to sound weak. "Real men don't show pain . . . they suck it up" was one of the myths that I subscribed to back then. In there was hose days there was an unwritten rule that if you admitted pain, you were weak. My father got up and put his pistol in his back pocket and looked me straight in the eye. "Don't leave this porch no matter what!" he said, and started down the steps and began walking around the corner to Big Al's house.

Dad wasn't by any means a gangster or a thug, he was a quiet, family man, but he believed in protecting his family by any means necessary. I sat on the porch as instructed and waited a couple of minutes until my father disappeared around the corner. Unable to contain my curiosity any longer, I ran into our backyard and hopped the fence that separated our house from Big Al's. As I crept down the alley that separated the two houses I expected to hear gunshots any minute now because I knew my Dad was upset about my face being all busted up by a teenager who was twice my size. As I approached the front of Big Al's house, I stooped behind a bush and listened. I could hear my Dad speaking in low, yet adamant tones that didn't diminish the seriousness of the conversation.

Big Lou had tears in his eyes as my Father calmly confronted his dad. I could see the terrified look in Big Lou's dad's eyes as my father spoke calmly yet firmly into his ear. Every couple of sentences, my Fathers voice would raise an octave or two and I could hear bits and pieces of what he was saying. ". . . I swear to God I will . . . if he EVER touches my son again . . . !" As I peeked through the bushes, I could see my Dads hand holding his pistol by his side in plain sight for everyone to see. He wasn't pointing it at anyone but it was implied that he would use it if necessary. It became abundantly clear that my Dad meant business and he had everyone's attention. No one pulled out a pistol unless they were ready to use it! The next thing I remember is my Dad firmly saying, "Let's go" as the three of them began walking back towards my house. I scrambled back down the alley and hopped the fence just as they rounded the corner and began walking towards my house. As they approached, Dad yelled out, "Go get your Mother!" Not wanting to miss a thing, I just rang the doorbell over and over till Ma came to the door. The three of them stood on the sidewalk in front of our house and when Ma stepped onto the porch, Big AL's dad began profusely apologizing to her. Afterwards he looked at his son and said," Well?" After a moment or two, Big Al looked at me and reluctantly offered a half-assed "Sorry". His father smacked him solidly in the head and said," Say it like you mean it, got dammit!" Big Al mumbled another half assed apology and he and his father walked back around the corner. I don't know exactly what my Dad said to them when he went to their house, but for the next week or two, Big Al was at our house raking leaves and cleaning the dog shit out of our yard every day after school; much to my delight!. After that, Mr. Greene, his dad, was always extra nice to me when I walked by and I never had a problem out of Big Al again!

I held on to the resentment I had against Big Al well into adulthood, and one day when I was home on leave from the Army, I bumped into him as he sat, drunk, on a bench at the Canal St basketball court. By now he was no longer "Big Al". I was at least a foot taller than him and about a hundred lbs. heavier. I was in top physical shape from being in the Army, and now I was able to give him a "fair one". He looked a hot mess sitting there in dirty clothes looking like he hadn't bathed in days.

"Remember me, bitch?" I said to him in my "I'm a grown assed man now" voice. Big Al snapped out of his drunken stupor and looked up at me puzzled. "Nah man, who are you?" he said as he struggled to recognize me. "Do I owe you money or somethin?" he asked. I could feel the anger that I had for him slowly dissipate as I realized he had turned into a feeble drunk. There was a small voice in the deep recesses of my heart that said," Let it go man, his condition is revenge enough" but I ignored the small voice and listened to the deafening roar that said, *"Payback is a BITCH!"*

"Oh, wait a minute, you dat lil nigga that used to live on Tilton St., right?" he mumbled as his memory came back to him. "That's for my lip you son of a bitch", I said as I punched him square in the face with all my might. He fell off the bench and onto the ground from the force of my blow. As he lay there on the ground, I kicked him in his stomach and shouted, "And that's for my fuckin' dog!" He vomited all over the ground and curled up into a fetal position as I walked away. The revenge I had waited so many years for was somehow very unfulfilling. He was no longer "Big Al", just Drunken, Pathetic Al.

Once again, I felt sorry for someone who had inflicted bodily harm upon me. Many years later, I would learn to listen to that quiet, non-violent voice that told me to let it go, but at this point in my life, the anger that had built up inside me for years was too overwhelming for me to hear or listen to anything else except for the angry, malevolent voice that wanted to wreak havoc.

Back then, it was nothing for me to go to the package store and buy liquor. Even though I was like 13 years old my Dad could send me to the neighborhood package store with a ten spot and I could pick up whatever he wanted. He was friends with the owner, and the age laws weren't enforced like they are these days. I was drinking beer and smoking weed on a regular basis now, and I would go into Doug's Liquor and grab a 40oz and wink at the proprietor. "It's for my Dad" I would say, both of us knowing damn well my dad didn't drink forty ounce beer. Mr. Doug would knowingly glance at me and say, "Be careful Son", as I took off in the opposite direction of my house with two or three of my "Homies".

While my parents thought I was at the court shooting baskets, I was actually hanging out with the fellas getting high off weed and beer before hitting the basketball courts. My basketball game was probably improving naturally, but I had convinced myself that smoking weed improved my game. I began to believe that it made me a smooth talker with the girls and even made me a smarter student!

I noticed that my confidence level was also up while I was high, and quickly began to develop a reputation as a hot-head that didn't take any shit and would fight at the drop of a dime. I didn't win all of my fights, sometimes my mouth would write checks that my behind couldn't cash, but that didn't stop me from "mixin it up" with anyone who wanted a piece of me. Dudes on the block knew that if you fucked with me, I would fight back relentlessly even if I were losing! Surrender wasn't in my vocabulary, no matter how much pain was being inflicted upon me

I would continue to fight . . . a trait that almost proved fatal in my later years' I no longer wanted to be known as the kid with the bad ass big brother, I wanted to be known as the kid who could hold his own. I stopped telling Chris every time I got into a fight and was getting better and better at defending myself. I didn't know it then, but being beaten up so many times was beginning to affect my personality. I was changing from the carefree kid, who was always smiling, into a kid with a "chip" on his shoulder who was quick to fight at the drop of a hat. I sometimes wonder if I would have made it through my teen years had I been growing up in the 80's and 90's because back then hardly no one carried a gun, but these days a gun seems to be an essential fashion accessory for young boys growing up in the hood !

I was in public school now; my parents could no longer afford private school tuition. Attending St Martins gave me a head start on the public school students. When I arrived at Troop Middle School, I was light years ahead of the other students. I made good grades with minimal effort and the girls were impressed with the new kid who was so smart yet wasn't a "nerd". Most of the jocks were C students at best, but here I was a good looking ball player, "ladies man" *and* I got good grades! I remember the feeling of superiority I felt when I would complete a test or other assignment ten or fifteen minutes before the other kids. What they struggled with, I did with ease, and it wasn't long before I started bringing comic books to school to occupy all the free time I had. I believe that my first "drug of choice" was fantasy. Long before my first drug, I would escape reality by reading.

When it came to reading, I had a voracious appetite. My brother Chris and I would eat chocolate chip cookies and milk on our bunk beds for hours reading comic books with the likes of the Silver Surfer, Prince Namor the Submariner and a host of other underdogs who would rip shit up when provoked by the bad guys. My favorite was the Incredible Hulk because I could identify with the scrawny little white guy who didn't bother anyone, but could wreak havoc when the "evil doers" made him angry!

I was also a big fan of science fiction . . . Asimov, Vonnegut and Robert Heinlein were my favorites. Anything that took me away from reality was fine with me. It was nothing for me to read two paperback books in one summer's day while lying on my back in my dad's hammock with my dog Ishmael curled up beneath me. He would doze lazily with me until the sound of a squirrel scurrying across the fence brought him to "full alert".

I would read magazines, newspapers, encyclopedias and even the dictionary! I was an information junkie! Thank God the Internet wasn't around when I was growing up or I may have never left the house! During class, I would place my comic or paperback inside a textbook and act like I was studying when actually; I was in outer space battling Galactus for the preservation of the universe, as we knew it!

I continued to get good grades with minimal effort and took delight in stumping my history teachers with questions like, "If Columbus discovered America, how come the story says his crew saw the Indians torches on the shore? Wouldn't that make the Indians the ones who discovered America?" My favorite one was, "How come when white folks killed each other over slavery they call it a noble "civil" war, but when blacks killed white people over slavery (like Nat Turner) they call it a "savage" insurrection?" I would use information I had learned from Chris to discredit what was being taught in the history books. My true motives were not to enlighten others; they were my way of rebelling against the establishment. Eventually, my history teacher stopped calling on me when I raised my hand but he would say sarcastic shit like," Isn't that correct Professor Walcott?" after making a point, which was pleasing to me because he knew that I was quickly becoming a Black History scholar who wouldn't just sit there and take what he said as gospel!

Eventually, I began to skip class out of boredom and the thrill I got from doing something without getting caught. I learned at an early age that breaking the rules gave me an adrenalin rush that was out of this world! Whether it was stealing from the neighborhood store or groping under the skirt of a cute girl during a game of "Hide & Go Get" (Our version of Hide & Go seek where we would pair off with a girl and find somewhere to hide and fondle each other till we were discovered) Anything I could do where there was a possibility of getting caught caused a lightheaded rush in me that was just as good as any drug.

One day I was skipping class and ventured into the sub-basement of the school where the boilers and steam pipes were located, to smoke a half a joint before returning to our next class. In the sub-basement there was a long, narrow corridor that was just wide enough for one person at a time to walk through. Some teacher I had never seen before caught me and began to chase me down the narrow corridor. After a brief chase he caught me and grabbed me by the back of my collar so hard that I gagged out loud. As I struggled to get away from him I felt the necklace that my brother had given me begun to cut into the flesh of my neck. It was a black power fist on a black leather bootlace that symbolized the Black Power movement. My captor was pulling on that leather lace the way you would yank a hard headed dog, and I felt myself go from scared to angry in the blink of an eye.

I whirled around and smashed my fist into the teachers face. He let go of my necklace and looked incredulously at me as he realized his nose was bleeding. He grabbed his face and I got in a few more punches until another teacher came running towards us. At that point I took off down the long corridor and up the stairs. I burst through the hallway door just as the bell rang and students filled the hallway. I blended right in with the rest of the students changing class and made a clean getaway.

Halfway through my next class, the principle, a security guard and the teacher I had just fought walked into my class and began looking up and down the rows of students. As soon as the teachers eyes came to me he shouted, "That's him!" As I was escorted from the class, I tried to plea my case that he was basically strangling me, as I secretly enjoyed the sight of someone who had tried to hurt me all bloodied up and in pain.

My parents were told to pick me up from school or I would be turned over to the police. The disappointed look on my Moms face and the stern, angry look on my Dads made me feel like such a loser. Here was their privately schooled kid with the good grades being expelled from school for assaulting a teacher . . . I tried to justify my behavior by claiming self-defense but my dad wasn't trying to hear it.

I was sent to AMS which was the acronym for Alternate Middle School. It was, as you have probably already guessed, a school for bad ass kids who couldn't cut it in regular public school. In retrospect, this school had kids with not only behavior problems but learning disabilities and mental and emotional problems too! Back then, "problem" kids were just "warehoused" away from the general population in special-Ed classes until they were either arrested or dropped out.

Although I had punched out a teacher, I didn't consider myself as having a problem. I told my lie so often and so convincingly that even I began to believe that being held in this school for "bad kids" was unjustly punishment! I tried to downplay the fact that I shouldn't have been skipping class in the first place. I was convinced that if the teacher had not pulled that leather shoelace so hard that I gagged, I would have never punched him.

If I thought I was ahead of the other kids in regular public school, I was a genius at AMS. The majority of the students here came from broken homes and drug and alcohol addicted parents. Some had learning disabilities or mental and emotional problems. I fit right in with them and was quickly accepted once word got out that I had beat up a teacher. Some of the toughest kids from all over New Haven attended A.M.S. These were the kids that the system had given up on and society hadn't had a chance to incarcerate yet. Thank God my Dad had a car and some compassion for his wayward son because AMS was on the other side of town and my only other alternative to getting to school was to ride that fucking "half a bus" that would have permanently labeled me as a "retard"; the horrible word people used for kids with special needs.

I became well-liked by the students here because I would let them copy off my papers and I even got extra credit for tutoring some of the kids.

While at AMS, I joined their Chess Club only to have an excuse to get out of class and quickly became known as the best chess player on the team. I could even beat some of the teachers! The members of the Chess Club would practice after lunch for the City Wide Chess Tournament that was coming up in a couple of months. My dad brought me a chess book for my birthday the previous summer and I spent hours outside in the hammock solving chess problems. My game was tight and even the chess coach had to try really hard to beat me!

CHAPTER 6

Checkmate!

After weeks of anticipation, the City Wide Chess Tournament was here! I easily defeated my opponents in the first three rounds but felt intimidated by this Asian kid who was the smartest kid in the very school I was kicked out of! It finally came down to the two of us in the championship round and my low self-esteem was in full force. "*You can't beat him*" the dark, malicious voice in my head said. "*You're not good enough*".

"You don't seriously think you are going to win do you?" The Asian kid taunted as I sat at the table to begin our match. He talked to me with this arrogant tone that didn't intimidate me in the least. In fact, it had the opposite effect on me. Instead of feeling less than or insecure, I took it as a challenge. Just like when we trash talked on the basketball court. "No way am I gonna let this snooty motherfucker beat me, and if he does, I'm punching him right in the face when the game is over" I told myself! When I was in regular school, the chess club was the last place you would find me because it was only for "Geeks" & "Nerds". No wonder I hadn't recognized the teacher I punched out . . . he was the coach for my alma maters chess club! When he saw me, he looked at me in disgust as the left side of his lip curled up into an almost imperceptible sneer that told me he recognized me as the kid who kicked his ass that day in the sub-basement. "This should be easy", he said confidently to his young Asian protégé as he patted him on the head as if to say," Please beat this motherfucker that punched me in the face!" The quiet voice in my head told me to focus on the game.

Our match began and I played more intense than I had ever played before. I could see that each move he made took longer than the one before. His face was in a constant frown and I could see that he was becoming more and more frustrated with my unorthodox strategy. He would roll his eyes at my moves and shake his head like I didn't know what the fuck I was doing. But I played chess like I fought . . . distract them with a weak blow from the left and then smash them with a hay maker from the right! We were both down to like three or four men apiece and it looked like he had me, when a move that my brother Chris had taught me came to mind. I don't remember the exact move but the kid fell for it and I won the tournament!

"Yeah Boyeeee!" I yelled at the top of my lungs as I stood up with my fist balled up, over my head in a victory stance. The room fell silent as I realized that this sort of behavior wasn't appropriate for the refined students that hailed from the likes of Hopkins and other private schools in the city. I didn't care though, and continued to walk around our table doing my little cabbage patch dance! Here I was the misfit from the school for "dumb", troubled black kids and I kicked ass! I reveled in the looks on the smug white-boys faces that weren't upset because they lost, but because they lost to the cocky black kid!

I received a hero's welcome back at AMS! The trophy I won was placed in the empty trophy case in the front foyer for all to see! It was a personal victory for all of us because we knew that we were looked down upon by the other students. Not because of the color of our skin, but because we were viewed as the "bad" or "dumb" kids. I had single-handedly proved that we were just as good as the other more affluent kids!

I did a few months more at AMS, and then, at the urging of my parents and the fact that I had never been in any trouble before, it was decided that I had learned my lesson and I was admitted back to Troop Middle School to finish the 7th grade. When I returned to Troop, I knew that I was under a microscope. I was known as the kid who beat up the teacher, which was a mixed blessing because the students respected me as someone who didn't take any shit, but the teachers looked at me with disdain and were waiting for me to fuck up again so I could be expelled from school.

I would never forget the look of embarrassment on my mother's face when I was placed in AMS and I vowed to never put her through that again. My mother's adoration was very important to my fragile self-esteem. I worked diligently at my studies, and got good grades, but as soon as the bell rang, I was off to the projects where I could cop a nickel bag of weed and drink a forty ounce of malt liquor with the older guys at the basketball court.

I was living a double life as I played the reformed student at school and home, but played the "thugged out" junior hustler when I was on the streets. It was as if I had a deep seated need to prove to everyone that I could be whoever they wanted me to be; super student, athlete, ladies' man or street thug. Whatever you needed me to be, I was happy to oblige, as long as I didn't have to be myself.

I couldn't wait for summer vacation because my parents agreed to let me spend 2 weeks at my uncle's house in Upstate New York. Uncle Chester was actually a friend of my dad's since they were in high school, but out of respect we called him "Uncle" because Mr. Chester was too informal of a moniker for someone as close as he was. He was a dark-skinned man who looked like the typical anti-establishment radical from the 60's and 70's. Uncle Chester was at least 6' tall and wore his hair in a huge, unkempt afro that always had one of those afro picks with the black power fist sticking out of the back of his 'Fro. Sort of like a young Cornell West!

He graduated from Harvard University and besides his afro and the multi-colored Dashikis that he wore; he represented everything that I wanted to be. He had a successful law practice and traveled extensively across the country to represent high profile drug dealers and murder cases. During his visits to our house, I would eavesdrop on him describing to my father how he gotten guilty drug dealers and murderers off the hook on technicalities, while they poured expensive scotch from my dad's crystal decanter in the living room after us kids were thought to be asleep. His lack of morals was ignored because they looked at his success as giving it to the "Man".

His wife Sonya was at least six feet tall. She was school teacher at some fancy, private boarding school. To me, they represented the epitome of success. Nice home, cars and money! Whenever they visited, they always arrived with really cool, expensive gifts for my siblings and me, such as the junior chemistry set he brought me one Christmas; complete with petri dishes and a microscope.

Because my uncle was an attorney, my ambition was to become a professional like him. I even let my own hair grow into an afro complete with a Black Power afro pick to emulate him! It had become apparent to me that if I wanted to become successful I would have to continue to excel in school, go to college and earn a degree.

CHAPTER 7

Uncle Chester

Summer vacation had finally arrived and I couldn't wait to go to Uncle Chester's house in upstate New York. Ma took me to The Chapel Square Mall and hooked me up with new summer clothes; afterwards, we drove to the sneaker factory in Naugatuck to buy two pairs of Pro-Keds for $20.00.

My folks decided that I was mature enough to take the train by myself, and I was excited about traveling such a long way on my own. Dad gave me a bus ticket, four crisp ten dollar bills and instructed me to keep my wallet in my front pocket to avoid pick pockets! To this day, I frequently pat my pocket when in crowded places to make sure I haven't been robbed.

When I arrived in Buffalo, New York, my uncle picked me up in his Volkswagen Beetle. He was accompanied by a woman I had never seen before and I couldn't help but notice her ample cleavage and the fact that the outline of her nipples was damn near visible through her skimpy silk halter top. Uncle Chester introduced us and she kissed me on the cheek. "He's a cutie!" she said as I inhaled the aroma of her perfume. As I sat in the back seat of my uncle's car, I couldn't keep my horny little thirteen-year-old eyes off of her breasts as they jiggled each time my uncle shifted gears. "I just have to drop Monica off, Miles, then we can go grab a bite to eat, ok?" he said as I sat in the back seat hoping that one of her boobs would accidentally pop out! "Ok". I replied as I waited for my next glimpse of Monica's boobs. When he dropped her off, she gave me a kiss full on the mouth and I didn't mind one bit! "Bye sweetie, nice to meetcha!" she said as she turned to my uncle. "Nice to meet you too", I said as I tried to hide my arousal under my thin summer shorts. "Bye-Bye Baby", she said to my uncle. She threw her arms around my uncle and they French kissed at least ten seconds before she dabbed her lipstick off his lips with a hanky. "Oh shit", I said to myself, "Uncle Chester is cheating on his wife!"

As we ate the most amazing burger I ever had in my life at a place called Fuddruckers, my uncle explained to me how he and my aunt Sonya had an "open" marriage, which meant they were allowed to have sexual relationships outside of their marriage. "Cool", I said casually, as if I was used to that sort of stuff. I had actually *never* heard of such a thing, but as I wrapped my young mind around it, I had to admit . . . getting "outside sex" without having to sneak did sound pretty cool!

When we arrived at his condo, Uncle Chester showed me to my room and I began to unpack. "I'm gonna take a shower", he said as he passed my room. I had been in plenty of locker rooms at school and the YMCA so it didn't even faze me that he was butt ass naked! "Aunt Sonya's out by the pool", he said," Why don't you go out and say hi". "Ok", I said as I finished putting my clothes away.

I quickly changed into my swimming trunks and made my way through the house, anticipating a nice cool dip in the pool. As I passed through the living room, I noticed issues of Playboy *and* Playgirl on the coffee table. I couldn't resist taking a look. I had never seen the inside of a Playgirl magazine before and out of curiosity took a look. I immediately felt inadequate at the sight of penises twice the size of mine.

This was the first home I had been in where adult magazines and books adorned the coffee table! I was used to seeing Essence, Ebony and Jet magazines, not the playmate of the month! In addition to the porn magazines, I noticed various erotic pictures and phallic symbols throughout the house. "I'll see you tonight, Miss November", I said to myself, anticipating a private "viewing" session later on that night.

I stepped out onto the deck looking for my Aunt. "Aunt Sonya!" I shouted when I didn't see anyone. The deck was furnished with high-end lawn furniture, not the cheap, plastic stuff that I was used to. There was a gas grill on the deck that was bigger than the stove in our kitchen back home, and a fridge next to a wet bar that ran along one side of the oak stained deck. "Over here" came her voice from behind a high backed lounge chair. As I rounded the chair, prepared to give my Auntie a big hug, I was startled to see that she was lying there wearing nothing but a pair of Jackie Onassis type sunglasses and her birthday suit! Her light skin glistened in the sunlight and I quickly took in the sight of her naked body in all its glory! Her long legs were shapely but unshaven, and her private area was covered in razor stubble where she had apparently shaved a little too close. As my eyes made their way up to her breast, I was in awe at the most perfect pair that my young eyes had ever seen in person! Her dark nipples and aureoles' were in sharp contrast with her light skin and I was taken aback at the fact that she made no attempt to cover herself with the large beach towel that lay on the ground beside her. "Hey big guy!" she said as she rose to greet me. "Hey Auntie" I said as I attempted to tear my eyes away from her naked body. She reached for me and hugged me as if we were fully clothed. Due to her height, her breast came in direct contact with my cheek, but I didn't mind at all! I hadn't been in Buffalo for two hours yet and I had already kissed a freaking model and had a big pair of boobs mashed into my face! "*I'm going to love this vacation!*" I said to myself as she spun me around to look at me. "You have really grown into a handsome young man", my aunt said as she devoured me with her eyes. No need for those", she said, looking at my trunks," It's just me, you and your uncle here!"

A six-foot fence along with shrubs and trees made it difficult to see in or out of the yard. I might have taken my trunks off right then and there but my 12 year old genitalia had become harder than Chinese arithmetic at this point, and no way was I going to let her see me erect after just seeing the nine and ten inchers in that Playgirl magazine! I jumped into the pool just as my twelve year old woody threatened to breach the material of my swimming trunks. The cold water caused it to subside, so I slid my trunks off while I was submerged in the pool and tossed them onto the deck.

Uncle Chester came outside totally nude and said, "I guess by now you've figured out that we don't like to hide our bodies around here!" All I could muster was a weak "cool", as I continued do laps back and forth across the pool. I couldn't help but notice that my uncle had a huge package compared to my adolescent one and I immediately became embarrassed, not because we were naked but because my penis was nowhere close to the size of his. *I'll take penis envy for a thousand, Alex*!

After some small talk and getting reacquainted, I became more and more comfortable with our nudity even though this was the first time I was ever butt assed naked in a social situation. In spite of my nakedness, I made sure that I sat in a manner that at least partially hid my genitals. Even in junior high, I was extremely embarrassed to be naked around other boys my age when we showered after gym class.

Uncle Chester went into the house and returned with a bong shaped like a pair of breasts. The carburetor hole was in the "nipple" so you had to "fondle" the bong in order to get a good hit. We sat on the deck smoking weed as the sun set and I was feeling pretty nice. Not only was I high from the weed and glass of white wine that my aunt had offered me, I was high off the fact that I was smoking weed naked, with two adults that I damn near worshipped as gods due to their affluent status!

One night, my uncle was going out on a date with his friend so he suggested that my aunt and I go take in a movie. "The Omen" was playing, and because I wanted to appear more mature than I really was, I answered "No", when my aunt asked if I was afraid of horror movies. Well, The Omen scared the ever-loving crap out of me. Various scenes from the movie such as when the priest was impaled by the long spike at the top of the falling steeple played over and over in my mind as I lay in bed that night having a nightmare. The scene where the vicious Rottweiler's chased someone through a graveyard morphed into the dogs chasing *me* and as I awoke from my nightmare, I let out a frightened scream. Aunt Sonya came rushing into the room to see what was wrong and I explained to her that I was having a bad dream. She sat on the edge of the bed and held me in her arms as she rubbed my head and neck to comfort me. I quickly forgot about my dream as I became aware of her nudity.

Suddenly, I heard the front door close and I became nervous due to her nudity. Aunt Sonya reassured me that everything was ok and gently pushed me onto my back. Uncle Chester poked his head inside the bedroom door and with a stupid grin on his face, asked if he could watch. As things escalated, I found myself giving in to the intense carnal desire that was devouring my inhibitions and good common sense.

CHAPTER 8

Shame and Guilt

The moment the deed was complete, a deep wave of shame and guilt enveloped me. I felt dirty because I had knowingly crossed the line into forbidden territory. Although we weren't related by blood, I felt that I had committed a horrible sin. If I wasn't all ready condemned to hell, this would definitely seal the deal. After watching The Omen, visions of me being killed by the devil flitted in and out of my mind as I imagined what kind of demise was in store for me as punishment for the grave sin I had just committed.

The next day, I was sullen and withdrawn. When my aunt asked if I was all right, I just said, "Yeah" and tried to avoid her as much as possible. "Your uncle will be here soon", she said. "He went to grab some coffee" She prepared herself for work, and when she tried to kiss me goodbye, I shrunk away from her, disgusted at what I had let her and my uncle manipulate me into doing.

As soon as she left, I got on the phone and called my Mom. I wasn't supposed to come home for another few days but I pleaded to my mother to let me come home immediately. "What's wrong sweetheart?" she pleaded with me." Nothing, I just wanna come home", I said between tears. I was distraught at what I had done willingly. It wasn't like I was raped or forced to have sex with them. I did so willingly and therefore I figured that I owned all the responsibility and would surely burn in hell for my actions.

When my uncle got back home, the first thing he said to me with a mischievous twinkle in his eye was, "Did you have fun last night?" "Fuck you, you fucking pervert" I screamed at him through angry tears. Although I was a willing participant in the incestuous encounter the night before, I was angry at my uncle because if it wasn't for him and his pedophile wife, I would have never initiated such a sinful ménage a trois. Sure, we weren't related by blood but I had known him since I was a little kid. In my mind he was my uncle and his wife was my aunt.

I learned later on in life that I was a child and wasn't emotionally capable of making an adult decision. I also learned that I was manipulated by two adults who took advantage of a naïve kid with raging hormones, but at that time, all I knew was that I had did something that caused me to feel an almost unbearable amount of shame. I was confused and wanted these awful feeling to go away. Every inch of my body craved something, anything to take away this horrible feeling that gnawed at the very depths of my soul!

I grabbed a bottle of vodka from their liquor cabinet and went out to the pool. The sun was shining and it was warm out on the deck. It was a peaceful summer's day in spite of the turmoil inside of me. The high pitched buzz of the cicadas was like background music to a tragic screenplay as my mind processed the events of the past few days. I was so disappointed that the two people who represented success to me had just caused me to feel so bad. Where once I wanted to emulate them, I now wanted to be nothing like them. I swigged the vodka like it was Kool Aid and before I knew it I was passed out in the lounge chair.

My uncle awakened me later on that afternoon. My head was spinning and I felt like I was going to throw up, but I was able to keep a lid on it. I had actually rolled off the lounge chair and was lying precariously close to the pool. He told me that he brought me a ticket to Philly and that my parents would meet me there because they were planning on visiting with my grandmother in a few days anyways. He pressed a hundred dollar bill into my hand and said that he hoped I would keep this incident to myself. He was so nonchalant about the whole thing and that made me even angrier. Here I was in deep emotional pain and he was acting like he and his wife had done nothing wrong. I wanted to stab him or bash him in the head with something but I knew it would just hurt my Mom. I did, however, take the money! I wasn't *that* distraught!

My train was leaving the next morning so I began packing my things. I spoke to my mom later on that evening and gave her some bullshit line about a girl from New Haven breaking my heart because I knew that if I told her this, it would crush her. Protecting my mom's feelings was top priority after seeing how she felt after I got kicked out of school the year before.

CHAPTER 9

Grandma Grant

I arrived in Philly a day ahead of my parents and took advantage of the time to bond with my grandmother. She was a sweet old West Indian woman who stood about 4'9". She had a thick West Indian accent and wasn't afraid to cuss you out in "Jamaican" if you crossed her! Although she was actually from Barbados, we would call anyone with a West Indian accent "Jamaican". Her hair was white as the driven snow, but she was by no means a fragile old lady. She was short like my dad, but had the presence of a much larger person. When she walked her dog "Falla" down the street while carrying her wooden, mini baseball bat, the neighborhood kids gave her a wide berth. Grandma Grant had a reputation for not taking any guff from anyone, and if you or any of the stray dogs in the area got in her way, the bat would surely find its mark! We called her Grandma Grant to differentiate between her and my mom's mother who was known to us as Grandma Wilmore. Grandma Grant would make rice and beans that were so moist and tasty, and her baked chicken was the best I have ever tasted to this very day!

Her daily routine consisted of taking her dog for a walk first, then off to the grocer to shop for the evening meal. My grandmother was old school and didn't believe in shopping for the week or the month. "When you freeze meat, it loses its taste", she would say to me as she waited for the butcher to cut her meat. By 1pm, Grandma Grant was cooking dinner while Bob Barker hosted the Price Is Right on her floor model, black and white television. This was my time to go hang out with the neighborhood kids.

There was a park around the corner from my grandmothers where the other kids and I would go to play basketball. As we passed by the Trolley Barn on the way to the park, I was fascinated by the electric trains that showered sparks as they left on their routes. The Trolley Barn was this humongous building where the trolley cars were kept at night. The other neighborhood kids and I would peek through the windows of the trolley barn on our way to the park and watch the mechanics working on the trolley cars, fascinated by the loud noises and sparks flying as wheels were grinded and bolts and rivets were pounded into place. Coming from New Haven, I was only used to Ct. Transit busses for mass transit, so the Trolley Barn truly amazed me.

Philly was known for its trolley cars and it was always a special treat for me to take the bumpy ride downtown with my Grandma to go shopping at the department store and then share a Philly cheese-steak grinder on a park bench afterwards.

At the park, we played a few games of basketball and when we were done, we sat on the bleachers drinking forty once bottles of malt liquor and passing joints of weed amongst ourselves. I had totally forgot that my folks were arriving that day and was completely surprised when I looked up with a joint in my mouth and saw my mom and little sister Lizan walking along the fence that was adjacent to the basketball courts. She was anxious to see her son and figured she would come see me at the park instead of waiting for me to return to Grandma Grants house. I attempted to 'cuff" the joint but it was too late; she had already seen me. As I looked into her eyes, I could see the same hurt look that I saw when I got expelled from school. Ma kept walking as I greeted my little sister and nervously told the fellas that I had to go.

As we walked back to my grandmother's house, Ma didn't say a word, but I could tell by the look on her face that she was hurt by what she had seen. I had been living a double life and as far as my mom knew, I was a good kid who had gotten into a lil trouble before, but had his shit together now. Every time I let my Mom down, I actually disappointed myself and chipped away a little more of my broken personality.

I wasn't aware of it then but I used this as a perfect opportunity to rationalize and justify my behavior. I told her that the reason I was smoking "herb" was because Uncle Chester got me started and I was mad because he "made" me have sex with his wife.

"What the hell did you just say?" my mom asked. I very rarely heard her curse and I knew that what I was about to reveal to her would cause her pain, but I needed to get the heat off of me for getting caught smoking weed. I told her all about the nudity and drugs. I told her how my aunt seduced me, but I said the reason I didn't stop her was because I was drunk . . . which was a lie.

When we got to my Grandmas' house, my dad could tell by the look on mom's face that something was wrong. "Ok", my dad said, "What the hell is going on?" "Tell your father what you told me" my mom instructed. After I told the story again, my mom was in tears, my dad was fuming and my grandmother said something that totally blew me away! "Me never like dot blood clot cock sucker from the first day me lay eyes on him" my grandmother said as my jaw dropped to the ground. I had never heard my grandmother use profanity and I was shocked to hear her talk like that. I must admit though, I got a perverted sense of amusement at hearing my sweet old grandmother curse like the Jamaican Rasta from the weed spot!

My father was pacing the floor grumbling about going to Buffalo and blowing my uncles, "Gott damn brains out", while my mother pleaded with him not to. As I watched the painful and angry emotions race through my mother, father and grandmother, I began to feel responsible for their pain. I had planned on sticking to my story about having my heart broken by a girl, and the only reason I even said anything was because of my own self-centered fear. I didn't want my folks to think I was on drugs and needed the perfect excuse to justify my drug use. At the time, I didn't know anything about self-centeredness or how addicts rationalize and justify the most outrageous sort of nonsense. All I knew was that I had to cover my ass, even at the expense of my parents' feelings.

That night, while lying in bed, I could still hear my mom pleading with my father not to go do anything to his old friend. "If you go to prison where does that leave me and the kids?" my mom pleaded. "They gotta pay for this shit" my dad replied," They fucking molested our SON!" As I lay there listening, I convinced myself that this was my entire fault. This was the beginning of years and years of taking the blame for all of life's ills and internalizing other peoples pain whether I was the cause of it or not.

I kind of hoped my dad would kill my uncle but I didn't want to see my dad go to prison either. The more I thought about the situation, the more I wanted to get high off weed or have a drink. I was beginning to realize that when I got high, it deadened any bad feelings that I had inside. I hadn't experienced many negative consequences from getting high yet, and I was beginning to believe that weed and beer were a "cure all" for all of my problems.

CHAPTER 10

Self-Hatred

Eventually, things settled down . . . my Dad never went to Upstate New York to retaliate, and my life was back to being relatively normal. I was able to stay out of trouble in school and finished out the 8th grade without incident. The summer after 8th grade was bittersweet. On the one hand, I was excited about going to high school but on the other, I felt dirty and ashamed because I had willingly had sex with my aunt. Now, I was only attracted to the "nasty" girls, girls who were easy and didn't offer much resistance to my advances. The easier, the better! The "good" girls, girls who didn't "give it up" easy were off limits to me. I had convinced myself that I wasn't worthy of a good girl because of the horrible sin I had committed with my aunt.

I was on a mission to have as much sex as I could with as many girls as I could. In my mind, if a girl had sex with me, then I must be ok. I began to equate sex with love and my self-esteem became based on how much sex I was having. Sex became my next "drug of choice"! I would tell a girl anything she wanted to hear in order to convince her to sleep with me. As a result of my lies and deceit, I hurt many girls' feelings. I have always had a conscience and that only added to my feelings of shame guilt and embarrassment. Once I began my descent down the slippery slope of total self-centeredness, I needed more and more things to take my mind off of the fact that I was slowly becoming a selfish monster who only cared about his feelings and no one else's. Whether it was focusing on getting laid, smoking and drinking with the fellas or getting lost in a book, I was constantly on a mission to keep my mind off of what I was really feeling.

A strip bar opened around the corner from me on Winchester Avenue and I became a regular fixture. It was called "Disco Lady" and on Friday and Saturday nights you could find me there ogling the strippers and letting them shake their behinds so close to my face that I could smell that familiar "scent of a woman". One night, after smoking weed and drinking a few beers, this lady who had to be old enough to be my mother sat at the bar getting drunk. As she left, I offered to walk her home and she agreed.

She lived in one of the high-rise apartment buildings in the Elm Haven projects and was pleased that a "Strong young man like you" was offering to walk her home. As we rode the urine-scented elevator to the sixth floor, she turned to me and gave me a sloppy, drunken kiss. She hiked her dress up and the hideous odor that emanated from her loins didn't stop me from having unprotected sex with her like a dog in heat. "*This is all pieces of shit like you deserve*" said the familiar voice from within my wounded psyche.

My personality had been severely fractured as a result of many past traumatic experiences and I had no idea at the time why I was attracted to loose women and seedy bars where only the dregs of society hung out. At this point in my life, I just wanted to party hearty and have a good old time. Little did I know, I was beginning the journey down a long and winding road called Addiction Avenue!

My anti-social behavior began taking many forms; from shoplifting things that I didn't need to over compensating violently at the slightest provocation from teenagers and adults alike. I remember how powerful I felt when I had gotten into a fight with some kid and when his father came to break it up, I socked him in the face a couple of times too!

When I got to that point, I really didn't care too much about consequences, only in venting my rage. The ass whippings I had endured as a kid from my father and guys from the block were taking a toll on my personality. Although I was maturing physically, my emotional growth was being stunted by my drug use, so when I felt like you were bothering me, "Big Miles" was always close by to protect "Lil Miles". It was like I had a split personality . . . one minute I was cool calm and collected, and the next minute a stark raving lunatic! There was this angry monster inside of me that would take over whenever I felt threatened. This was years before folks were diagnosed with intermittent explosive disorder and PTSD!

After a summer of drinking and drugging, I was finally about to enter High School. It was here that my double life began to catch up with me. I was a fairly good basketball player on the one hand, but my smoking and drinking had a negative effect on my lung capacity and I would tire quickly when I played. My drug use also affected my schoolwork and homework and as a result my grades suffered badly throughout high school.

My dad constantly put me on punishment because of my bad grades and when I rebelled, I got the Big Black belt on my ass! I wasn't big or strong enough to challenge my dad yet so guys on the street would catch hell whenever I got my ass whipped at home. If my dad smacked me or whipped me that day, you best believe some one out in the street was going to feel the wrath of my misdirected anger!

I was beginning to win more fights than I lost and I quickly became addicted to the thrill and adrenalin rush that I got from fighting. I was always angry and although I didn't know why at the time, I used my anger as a way of keeping folks away from me. I walked around with a sullen, angry look on my face and was quick to challenge anyone who so much as looked at me the wrong way. "The fuck you lookin at nigga?" became my favorite phrase whether you were black or white.

By the time I reached my senior year, I was a full-fledged pot head and I spent the majority of my school days at East Rock Park drinking forty ounces of malt liquor and smoking weed with the other "stoners". Eventually, I dropped out of high school in the middle of the year when it became apparent to me that I would never be able to bring my grades up without repeating the 12th grade; an option that was out of the question as far as I was concerned. I was working at St Raphael's hospital as a dietary aide and dropped out of high school so I could pick up more hours. This was 1980 BC (before crack) so hustling crack on street corners to make money hadn't become in vogue yet.

My hopes and dreams of becoming a pro ball player or a teacher had dwindled away to nothing, so joining the Army became an attractive alternative. My father had told me that once I turned 18 I was on my own, so I needed to do something that would provide me with three "hots" and a cot! I considered joining the Army, not out of a sense of duty to serve my country, but as a way to get paid while traveling the world. Going to college was out of the question due to my drug use and grades and I knew I didn't want to run the dishwasher for the rest of my life.

The High School year was halfway over and I was becoming more and more rebellious towards my parents rules and expectations. I had dropped out of school and had no intentions on going back. My buddy B-Lo and I had discussed how much "punanny" we could get if we had our own place and started discussing renting a room. Back then, you could rent a room for 45-50 bucks a week!

B-Lo was short for Barri Lobo, a child hood friend of mine who, along with me, shared a healthy appetite for chicks and partying! He was from the Cape Verdean Islands and had this mop of curly black hair and a quick smile that had all the girls swooning! He always had a friend who had a friend and I was more than happy to pick up his slack. We both had jobs so rent wasn't an issue, and the very next time I had a disagreement with my Dad was the perfect excuse for me to haul ass. I just waited for him to go to work one day and came back home after acting like I went to school. I packed my things and left, not even thinking that my Mom would be worried sick about me.

My impulsive behavior patterns were beginning where I would act now and worry about the consequences later. Barri and I rented a room over Reeds Barber Shop and that's when the real partying began! We had all night parties and it felt pretty cool to sleep all day then get up at noon, hit my part time job and then back home to party hardy again! I worked in the kitchen and would steal boxes of Hummels foot long franks and burgers which we would devour once the munchies set in. I thought I was grown now, no one to answer to, no curfew . . . this was the life!

One night my buddy B—Lo invited me to a party somewhere across town. They had an open bar and I drank like Prohibition was going into effect the next day! Between the weed and liquor and the unbearable heat inside the hall we were at, I wound up passing out in the middle of the floor. When I came to, the most beautiful girl I had ever seen was kneeling over me, wiping my forehead with a wet paper towel. Her hair went all the way to her mid back and was black as the night. As she bent over me while I lay there on my back, her hair cascaded down blocking out everything except her gorgeous face. She had a mole on each cheek and a smile that melted me. Her name was Jasmine Rosario and I decided right then and there that I was going to fall in love and live happily ever after with her!

We hit it off immediately and couldn't see enough of each other. She didn't fit the profile of a "bad" girl. "Jazz" made good grades in school and didn't mess around with a lot of guys. B-Lo even teased me that I would *never* get to "hit" that! Jasmine became my new drug. I craved her day and night. Because she didn't get high, I never smoked weed around her. It wasn't necessary; being with her intoxicated me more than enough. Back then, I could stop smoking weed for days, even months without any difficulty, which was actually a curse, because later on in life I would try to just "stop", thinking it would be just as easy and wind up being totally unable to stop.

Jasmine and I became inseparable! I would meet her at school at 2pm and we would go hang out in the park or walk hand in hand downtown in the mall. I felt like the king of the world! Nice job, pretty girlfriend and my own place; what more could a guy ask for? B-Lo lived at his parent's house so he used the room primarily after school and early evenings so Jasmine and I would have the place to ourselves at night. Since I had met her, I had no desire for any other girl. She was a "good" girl and I felt great because someone as pretty and smart as her was attracted to me. Although I was only 17, I knew the difference between having sex and making love and I would spend hours making my 17 year old version of love to her and holding her close to me afterwards.

We weren't using any protection at all and it wasn't long before she became pregnant. I was ecstatic that we were going to have a baby and we would lay in bed for hours planning our future. I decided that I would join the Army and we would get married and live happily ever after! I had it all figured out, or at least I thought I did until I found out that Jasmines mom had made her get an abortion and forbid her from seeing me again. Her mom wasn't crazy about the black kid who was taking up all her daughters' time and made it very clear that she didn't approve of me. She wasn't upset that her daughter was pregnant; she was upset because the father wasn't Puerto Rican! I went to her house after she had her abortion and her mother and two of her brothers made it clear to me that if I continued to see her that there was "gonna be problems". Jasmine followed her mother's instructions and wouldn't see me anymore, much to my dismay. I was devastated! The girl who I wanted to spend my life with had dropped me like a hot potato and once again I was feeling less than, and unworthy of happiness. The pain of losing her was excruciating and I returned to smoking weed and drinking with a vengeance!

I went on a three week binge where all I did was get high day and night. I had met a guy named Big Mike who worked in the housekeeping department at the same hospital I worked and we would take our breaks together and go to the top level of the parking garage and smoke weed on our breaks. After work, I would smoke a joint on my way to my room and continue after I hit the package store for some malt liquor. I told myself that I would never fall in love again after Jasmine broke my heart. I started picking "easy" girls and bringing them to my room for the sole purpose of having sex. I soon tired of this because deep down, I wanted to have a girlfriend who I was exclusive with. I used to dream of growing old with my High School sweetheart but that dream was also beginning to fade away. I felt hopeless and depressed and it seemed like all my hopes and dreams were crashing down around me. The drugs were not erasing the pain and eventually, I went home crying my eyes out and begging my parents to let me come back home.

My parents welcomed me back with strict stipulations, one of which was to get my GED and make plans for my future. I decided that I would join the Army that fall and spent my summer vacation playing basketball and running in order to get into shape for the grueling physical activity that came along with Army life. My recruiter suggested that I begin running now so when I got to basic training I would be ready. I was in pretty good shape from playing basketball. My body was young and strong and my partying hadn't yet begun to take a major toll on my health. I was beginning to feel hopeful about joining the Army and I was looking forward to a change. I wanted to become an air traffic controller but my aptitude test results were too low for that so I settled for radio teletype operator.

After I took and passed my GED test I stopped smoking weed until I took the piss test at the Army recruiting station. I passed the physical with flying colors and was scheduled to leave for Ft Dix, New Jersey on 6 Oct 81.

My parents were proud of me, especially my Dad who served in the Army during the Korean War. He spent time with me explaining the ins and outs of Army life and for the first time in years, we were able to enjoy each other's company without butting heads. My Mom couldn't have been more pleased to see the two of us watching a basketball game together or just talking in the den. By now my parents had moved up the ranks at the Post Office and were able to splurge more regularly and take us out for dinner at Pepe's Apizza or order seafood from Kevin's Seafood on Dixwell Ave. These were happy times in the Walcott household in contrast to the last tumultuous six months. When we weren't eating out, Mom was hooking up one her signature dishes like baked pork chops and sauerkraut or her spaghetti recipe that always made me wonder if we had some Italian in our lineage! She would start her sauce in the early afternoon and it would simmer for hours, filling the house with an aroma that had you expecting to hear the old lady in the Prince Spaghetti commercial yelling, "AN-TONY !!!" at the top of her voice !

I spent the final dog days of that summer chilling with my family and enjoying their company. I had signed up to be stationed in Germany and was anxiously awaiting my chance to meet a fine German "Fro-Line"! I had passed the Army's drug test so I wasn't afraid to "puff-puff pass" with my homies! They took me out for at least five farewell parties and I got thoroughly smashed at each one!

A couple of weeks before I was to leave, my parents took me to The Chart House, a fancy restaurant situated on the New Haven harbor. My Dad said," Order a beer if you want to, you're a grown man now!" Up until this point, it was unheard of for me to drink or even appear intoxicated in front of my Dad, so for him to offer me a drink was a special occasion. We enjoyed dinner together and afterwards sat and ate dessert and talked for what seemed like hours. We were laughing and joking and my mother's eyes twinkled with glee as she congratulated me on becoming a man! I believed they were really proud that I was going to "do something" with my life, and this was their way of showing me.

CHAPTER 11

You're In the Army Now!

As October 6th approached, I began to feel anxious about not being able "cop" any weed. I would be on an Army base and under the watchful eyes of drill sergeants and the like, and my addiction told me that I had to become creative. I didn't know it at the time but I was already in a different kind of Army where the Commander-In-Chief was my addiction, and my orders were to get high at all costs! I came up with the brilliant idea of wrapping joints in plastic and foil and then sticking them into my tooth paste tube. No way was I gonna be stuck hundreds of miles away from home without my precious weed!

When I arrived at the new recruit processing center, there was a barrel against a wall called the amnesty barrel. We were instructed to place any drugs, weapons, pornography or any other contraband into it without suffering any repercussions or consequences. There were M.P.'s (Military Police) walking around with German Sheppard's that were supposed to be able to smell drugs. Anxiety consumed me as I worried about getting caught with my marijuana laced toothpaste. "Last chance", a tall drill sergeant yelled out as he stood over the barrel. It seemed like he was eight feet tall with his Canadian Mountie style drill sergeant hat. A small lanky white kid from a southern state asked, "Are you sure we won't get into any trouble?". The sergeant reassured him that there would be no repercussions and the skinny kid walked over to the barrel and dropped in the biggest plastic bag of weed I had ever seen! He turned around and returned to his seat as the rest of the new recruits stood in awe at his courage . . . or stupidity, we couldn't tell which one he was! A black kid walked over and placed a knife in the barrel and a couple more guys got up and placed playboy magazines and assorted contraband into the barrel. I was beginning to think that it would be wise to dump my drugs into the barrel when I saw that no one got in trouble for placing their contraband into the Amnesty Barrel.

"I wish you would get up, nigga!" that dark angry voice inside me said harshly. I hadn't heard "The Voice" in a while, but it was there . . . patiently waiting. "*You better not even think about it*!" the voice said again. A part of me wanted to place my tube of toothpaste into the barrel but I was so terrified of being without my drugs that I listened to that dark voice within that told me to take my chances.

After about 30 more agonizing minutes of wondering if I would be busted, a sergeant came into the room and ordered us all to gather our belongings and walk through a door where 2 German Sheppard's sniffed each bag as it went through. I hadn't even yet begun my Army career yet and I was jeopardizing it by trying to sneak 10 joints into Basic Training! My heart was beating so hard that I could feel it in my head. On the outside I was trying to appear cool calm and collected but on the inside I was a nervous wreck! *"What's Ma going to think if I come home in disgrace?" "Dads gonna be so disappointed in me". "Everyone was so proud of you when you enlisted".* These thoughts raced through my head as I made my way through the door. *"Just act calm and stop acting like a bitch"*, said The Voice.

I didn't audibly "hear" the voice, but it was just as strong as if I heard it. This was the side of me who used to just whisper insulting, condescending things into my psyche, but lately the voice had begun to get more and more aggressive. As the line got closer and closer to the drug sniffing dogs and stern looking M.P.'s I began to listen to the dark voice that didn't care about my career, just getting high. I slowed my heartbeat and remained calm and began to believe I would get through without detection.

Suddenly, one of the dogs became agitated. He began whining and pacing in front of the short, fat, white kid in front of me. The kid, who must have been from south of the mason Dixon Line by the sound of his accent, began to look very nervous, His eyes darted back and forth and he began to sweat "bullets". By now, the dogs were barking and shaking his shaving bag back and forth. One of the M.P.'s seized the small bag and opened it. He pulled out three plastic bags that were neatly rolled into tubes from the pouch and asked "Olpie", "What do you call this? The black guys from the city called all white guys "Olpie, after the character from the Andy Griffith Show. We thought all white boys were chumps until we watched one beat the tar out of a big black dude from New York for calling him "Olpie" one day! After that, I made it my business to ask people their name instead of using slurs. "Olpie" might sound innocent enough, but what we really meant by it was, "country assed white boy". Knowing he was cold busted, "Olpie" said," I don't know what *you* call it Sergeant, but where I'm from we call it sensimilla!" We all started to laugh nervously until the Military Police handcuffed him and placed him under arrest. "All right ladies!" The tall Sargeant said. "Last chance! Any drugs weapons or other contraband will be put it in the Amnesty Barrel right now or you can join "John Boy" in the stockade waitin' for the next train smokin' to whatever shit-hole you crawled out of!" At least six more new recruits walked over to the barrel and placed everything from weed, pills and knives to a freaking dildo into the Amnesty Barrel! I didn't even want to know why a dude would have a dildo in his bag, but one thing I knew was if I was going down, they would have to catch me;I wasn't giving up that easily!

When my turn came to go through the door and pass the drug-sniffing dogs, they were none the wiser. I passed through without being detected, which immediately made me feel superior to everyone in the room. *"I told you we were gonna be ok nigga, just listen to me and you will be all right"* said that familiar dark voice. As my anxiety subsided, arrogance set in as I began to believe I was a just a little bit smarter than the guys who got caught. I learned later on in life that anytime I begin to feel superior or inferior to others, I am heading for trouble.

Basic training was just what I needed! The strict regimen, coupled with drill sergeants screaming at everyone was a little bit unsettling at first, but once I realized that the cadres were strictly forbidden from putting their hands on you, I was able to relax and put up with whatever threats and intimidation they dished out. I watched other guys break down in tears and go A.W.O.L. from the stress of having a drill sergeant screaming at them for one thing or another, but it was actually comical to me when one would get in my face and scream obscenity laced orders at me. "You think I'm fucking funny Private?" a drill sergeant would yell at me. "NO SARGEANT" I'd reply with a smile on my face. "You better wipe that smirk off your face before I wipe it off for you" the sergeant would retort. I would try my best to keep a straight face, but knowing that it was some kind of psychological game meant to intimidate me or elicit a reaction from me prevented me from taking any threats seriously. My Dad had prepared me for this and told me to just say "Yes Sir/ Sergeant" and "No Sir/Sergeant" and I would be fine.

Once they realized that I wasn't fazed by their intimidation, they would move on to the next guy. Once in a while, I would go too far and roll my eyes or give them a hard look back and they would make me drop and "Give me twenty" pushups, but all that did was give me a chance to show them and the other soldiers around me how tough I was.

Once I got used to the routine, I began to enjoy Army life. Growing up as the son of an Army Vet, I was used to order and cleanliness and following orders to a "T". I quickly developed a reputation as the guy to go to before inspection to check out your gear and make sure it was "squared away". My uniforms were impeccably pressed and starched, boots shined and the rest of my gear was in tiptop condition. I prided myself on having the most squared away A.O. (area of operation) I even made a few dollars on the side "spit shining" boots for guys who weren't good at it or too lazy to do it themselves. I didn't actually use spit to shine the boots; I put tap water in the metal lid of a Kiwi shoe polish tin, and alternated a dab of black polish with a drop or two of water on a cotton ball one thin layer at a time until I built up a shine that you could literally see your reflection in! A task that I hated performing when my Dad used to make me shine my church shoes as a teen, but once I realized I could make money at it I became immensely grateful for this valuable skill.

I charged five bucks to shine each pair of boots and some nights I would have five or six pairs lined up next to my bunk waiting to be shined! We jogged every day in our boots, through rain, snow or slush, so there was always an abundance of dirty boots to shine!

I already had an angry edge to my personality and a need to be in control, and it wasn't long before I was promoted to squad leader; a role that I took *way* too seriously. In retrospect, there were areas of my personality and events that had occurred in my life that had fractured my personality, so controlling others while simultaneously presenting this façade of the "perfect" soldier was my way of keeping people distracted from seeing the scared, hurt, emotionally damaged person who was hiding inside me.

Controlling people and situations gave me a sense of power that allowed me to feel superior to the very people I feared! I was acutely aware at this tender young age of 19 that I had some emotional issues going on that needed to be controlled to prevent me from being found out as the scared insecure little kid trapped inside this young man's body. Not only was I constantly harassed by this inner voice that told me I was a piece of shit for sleeping with my aunt, but this voice also told me that I was going to fuck up somehow and get kicked out of Basic Training and return home in shame. Being successful in the Army was very important to me because I knew that I had always sabotaged anything that was important to me.

When my parents sent me to summer camp in the 6th grade, I got kicked out for cussing out the director of the camp when he chastised me for fighting with another kid. I got kicked out of junior high for fighting a teacher. Even when my father spent his hard earned money to send me to Calvin Murphy's basketball camp when I was in the 8th grade, I fucked that up by getting caught smoking weed with one of the counselors' daughters! Then, of course, I had just dropped out of high school, once again not finishing something that I started. That inner voice of mine was having a field day reminding me of that shit over and over again. My earlier dream was to go on to college and become a teacher in spite of being informed that teachers didn't make a lot of money. Teaching others was something I realized I loved when I used to tutor the other kids at AMS. Once I screwed that up by dropping out of high school, joining the Army was intended to be my vindication! I would become a career soldier, make my mom and dad proud and ride off into the sunset . . . End of story!

Here I was, doing something that I loved, something to be proud of, I was serving my country and doing a damn good job at, but I was jeopardizing it by sneaking off with the other stoners (we can seek each out with impeccable accuracy no matter where we are!), to smoke the joints I had stashed in my toothpaste weeks ago! Once again, I was living a double life; impressing the drill sergeants with my exceptional soldiering skills on the one hand, but doing reckless irresponsible shit behind their backs that would surely get me kicked out on the other.

I was an expert marksman, shooting a perfect score every time we went to the firing range. In the Army, the rifle badge indicates your score on the rifle range. You wore it on your chest when you wore your "dress greens" at inspections or special functions. If your score fluctuated, you would have to change your badge accordingly, but I always wore the highest badge, expert, due to my exceptional shooting skills. There were seasoned drill instructors that couldn't shoot as well as I could, and it gave me great pride at inspections when the sergeant or officer conducting the inspection had a lower rifle badge than me!

During the day, I was this "super soldier" but in the evening, while at the barracks, I was this sullen, "tough guy" who would over compensate at the slightest provocation by smacking the crap out of anyone who got in my face or puffing up my chest and intimidating guys with tough talk and threats if I thought they were getting it "twisted". This behavior protected my insecurities and allowed me to protect the scared little boy inside of me who used to get his ass kicked as a kid. I became my own protector now that my brother Chris wasn't around and God help anyone who messed with "Lil Miles"!

When recruits caused my squad to suffer extra duties such as extra exercise or K.P. (Kitchen Police was where a squad of soldiers were used to clean the Mess Hall spotless and do mundane tasks such as peeling potatoes or cutting up veggies under the stern eye of the Mess Sergeant), my way of dealing with them was too corner them in the latrine, jab my finger in their face and threaten bodily harm if they didn't" get their shit together"!

Intimidation became another one of my favorite "drugs" I loved the adrenalin rush that came from emasculating someone and causing them to back down in front of others because not only was I controlling my adversary, I was simultaneously letting others know that I wasn't one to be messed with. Although I wasn't a tough guy at heart, I played the role convincingly enough that the other recruits feared and respected me. The drill sergeants loved me because I made their job easier by helping to keep the troops in line and before long; I was even leading the platoon as the "cadence caller".

The cadence caller was the person who ran beside the formation with the drill sergeant and led off with a song or phrase and the rest of the platoon would repeat it: "I don't know, but I been told!" "Eskimo pussy is mighty cold!" "Two old ladies were lying in bed, one rolled over to the other and said . . . "I wanna be an airborne Ranger . . . Live the life of sex and danger!" We had countless cadences that we sang in order to keep everyone in step and on the same rhythm, while we jogged in unison through the streets of Fort Dix New Jersey! It was the early eighties and I even added a little hip hop twist to the cadences as we ran using Dougie Fresh' Ladi Dadi as if I wrote the words myself." Ladi Dadi, we like to party . . . don't cause trouble don't botha nobody ! Woke up round 6 o'clock in da mornin . . . Gave myself a stretch and a mornin' yawnin !" It may not look good in print, but when 35-40 young men ran by your barracks singing that, you *felt* it!

I embraced being a soldier, and my whole persona became Army oriented. I ate slept and shit ARMY! I had found something that I was good at, and I ran with it! My self-esteem was growing exponentially, and that dark voice that always used to berate me was silent, but I had no idea how patient it was!

CHAPTER 12

Love Connection

There were female recruits also, and although we ate at the same Mess Hall, they were housed in separate barracks. In spite of the fact that we were forbidden from fraternizing with the female recruits, we came up with creative ways to communicate. A note dropped on the floor as you passed by their table, or a phone number strategically placed on a napkin so that they could call a family member and have a "three way" conversation later were some of the imaginative ways guys and gals would get their "Mack" on ! Mind you, this was way before cell phones and beepers!

I used to volunteer to work the serving line with the Mess Sergeant just so that I could be on the serving line when the women came through for chow. This one gal in particular caught my eye and I couldn't wait for the chance to say something to her! She had dark curly hair and an amazing smile that melted me every time she came through the chow line. She was one of the few women on the base who completely filled out the back of those baggy camouflage pants, if you know what I mean! I was instantly attracted to her and was not shy about letting her know. The other guys on the serving line would chuckle as they noticed that I would place extra dessert on her tray as we exchanged flirtatious glances in the chow line.

After a few weeks, we were allowed 2 and 4 hour passes and Louise and I would go to the PX (Post Exchange Store) or hang out at the

"Snack Bar" which was a small concession stand that sold beer and chips. It was here that we would meet and hold hands while talking and sneak an occasional kiss on the cheek. Although physical contact was forbidden, they couldn't watch every one at all times!

Her middle name was Louise so I playfully nicknamed her "Weezy" after George Jefferson's wife on the hit sit com "The Jeffersons". We spent every pass together at the snack bar and when our pass was up, we were on the pay phone talking! Back then, you could make calls and bill it to your house phone and I ran my Moms bill up to like $200.00! I would send my mother the money when we got paid every two weeks and she would tease me about the girl who was "taking all my money".

Weezy and I grew closer and it wasn't long before I proposed to her! Even though I didn't even have a ring yet, I knew this was the woman I wanted to grow old with. My mom said it was too soon to be proposing but I explained to her that I knew Weezy for two months and that was more than enough time to get to know someone! I knew I was being impulsive but it felt so right to want to marry this beautiful girl who stayed on my mind! She accepted, and we planned on getting married when I finished Advanced Individual Training at Ft. Gordon Ga.

She was a National Guardsman and went back home to Greenville, South Carolina after basic training. When we finished AIT, we were allowed 30 days paid leave before being deployed to our permanent duty station and I couldn't wait to spend my leave/honeymoon with the Southern Belle who had stolen my heart!

I finished basic training and couldn't wait for the less restrictive atmosphere of AIT. We were told that it was just like being in college except you had to live in a barracks and run 5 miles every morning at 6am! Completing basic training gave an immense boost to my self-esteem. I was beginning to believe that I could become a successful career soldier like the seasoned soldiers that I tried so hard to emulate. The inner voice that told me I would fuck up and get kicked out of Basic Training was silent . . . for now.

CHAPTER 13

A.I.T.

I looked out of the window of the Greyhound bus that was taking me to Ft. Gordon Ga, and took in the familiar sights of 95 South. The furthest south I had ever been was Washington DC when Ma & Dad took us to see my sister Kandi's new baby Kianti. When I saw the giant sombrero at "South of the Border" I realized I wasn't in "Kansas" anymore! I had never been this far south before and it suddenly dawned on me that I had never traveled this far from home either. I was mesmerized as the landscape transformed from urban sprawl to rural countryside. As I dozed in and out of sleep, I would awake to see miles and miles of open land dotted with farms and stately mansions that reminded me of the slave masters houses I had seen in Alex Haley's "Roots" saga. When the bus stopped at a rest area, I was tickled at how folks who didn't even know me would say good morning or good afternoon to me as if they knew me their whole life! I was expecting rude, racist, rednecks but was surprised to find friendly easy going folks who looked you in the eye and greeted you as you passed!

For the first time in years, I was at peace. It was as if the farther the bus drove south, the farther I got away from my past. The incest, the fights, dropping out of school . . . all my troubles seemed so far away now, and once I finished AIT,I could get married, become a career soldier, and prove to the world that I wasn't a "fuck up".

When I first enlisted in the Army, I wanted to become an air traffic controller. Working at an airport directing planes seemed like a pretty cool job to do and I was confident that my entrance test scores would be high enough to qualify me to attend ATC School. When my Army recruiter told me I didn't score high enough, I was deeply disappointed. Once again, I felt less than and not good enough. I really didn't know what other job I wanted to do so I chose radio teletype operator instead. Sending encrypted communications and coordinates to headquarters from a RATT Rig during battle sounded pretty cool to me, (and safe too!) so I settled for the communications field.

When I arrived at Ft Gordon Ga., the atmosphere was much more laid back than I expected. The sergeant who met us at the front gate was wearing wrinkled fatigues and his boots looked like they hadn't been shined in months. He directed us towards a huge "deuce and a half" truck and told us to stow our duffle bags and other gear in the back and get in formation when we were done. A "deuce and a half" is a 2 ½ ton diesel truck used for troop and equipment transport. It was one of the loudest trucks I ever heard before but I was thankful we didn't have to carry our gear to the barracks. After me and the other troops created a formation, the sergeant half assed marched us the half a mile to our barracks. He didn't call cadence the way I was used to in Basic training, he just repeated," Left, left, left right left" every few steps as we looked at each other incredulously at the lackadaisical manner in which we were being marched.

As we marched past the modern looking three story buildings that were ten times better looking than the barracks at Ft Dix, I began to get excited about the "college dorms" I was going to be housed in. I was amazed to see male and female troops walking hand in hand or sitting on benches chatting and I realized that we were no longer under the same restrictions we were in Basic training. I couldn't help but stare at the young women who were walking around in shorts and tee-shirts, a sight we hadn't seen in the last 8 weeks! Although I was in love with Weezy, my teenaged libido couldn't wait to stow my gear in my cool air conditioned room and get out and fraternize with what seemed like and endless supply of fine young ladies! Little did I know I was in for a big surprise!

Apparently, the base renovations had not yet reached the barracks I was to be housed in. The barracks at Echo Company were straight out of a World War II movie. The one story, white clapboard buildings on the outskirts of the main base sat on top of cinder blocks and were in need of a paint job. When we arrived, I thought it was some kind of cruel prank that they played on the "newbies". The ancient, decrepit barracks were nothing like the modern looking barracks we had just marched by. "Welcome to Echo Company, ladies!" said the sergeant as he told us to "fall out" and retrieve our bags from the deuce and a half. Again, I found myself feeling unworthy and "less than" and that familiar voice inside my head told me that these raggedy assed barracks are just what a piece of shit like me deserved! As the sergeant ordered us to pick a bunk and a locker, it became apparent to me that this was where I was going to spend my next 12 weeks.

Once I got settled in, my buddy Reggie, who had the same MOS (Military Occupational Specialty) as I did, threw on some jeans and tee shirts and headed to the PX to check out the "chicks" and shop for some new gear with our first full paychecks from our dear old Uncle Sam! Reggie was from Augusta Ga. and we had become friends since Basic Training. He was one of the guys I shared my weed with, and one of the first things on our agenda was to find a weed connection. It was a Friday afternoon and communications classes didn't start till Monday. We had a pocket full of money and three days of free time on our hands, we couldn't wait to get this party started!

After picking up a couple of new shirts and jeans and a new pair of Nike sneakers from the PX, Reggie and I made our way back to the barracks to shit, shower and shave before we caught a cab "off post" to one of the local strip bars my homey had been telling me about.

We had already grabbed a bottle of Tanqueray Gin from the post liquor store and were swigging heavily during the 20-minute cab ride into town. "Let's go fuck wit deez hoes", said Reggie, as we puffed a joint of the blazing weed our Haitian cabby sold us. Reggie was telling me about the strip bar we were headed to and I could barely contain my excitement. I told him I went to strip bars all the time back in Ct, when in fact; I had only gone to the half assed strip bar that was opened on Winchester Ave back in the day.

When we arrived at "The Boom Boom Room", Reggie was given VIP status from the door. The bouncers all knew him and once they realized I was with him they treated me like I was one of the fellas. I had a nice buzz going but I was playing it cool with a tough look on my face.

My radar was on high alert because I was in unfamiliar surroundings and coming from "The Hood" I knew that when you were out partying, other people would watch you till you "slipped" and make you a "Vick" (victim). I scanned the room checking out the players and "playettes" and I was amazed at the gorgeous women prancing around in thongs and see through tops or no tops at all! When I was sober, "The Voice" was relatively silent, only chiming in when things got tough . . . but when I was drunk; it tended to automatically assume that I needed its "sound" advice. "Watch ya back nigga," it warned me. "Try not to get your ass kicked tonight" it said sarcastically.

Reggie said "C'mon playa" and I followed him to the VIP room, not knowing what to expect. The VIP "room" was actually a curtained off area of the strip club where you could get a lap dance from one of the dancers in relative privacy. You could get more if you wanted to spend some extra money. There was a bench that ran the length of the wall and it was sectioned off into individual "stalls" by thin strips of curtains, sort of like a men's bathroom. Reggie picked a cute white girl with Dolly Parton sized boobs and was leading her to a stall by her hand, so I scanned the room and picked out a cute, brown skinned number who was standing by herself on the other side of the room.

She looked no older than my 18 years but she was built like a Playboy Bunny. I walked up to her, gave her light hug and a peck on the cheek and introduced myself. "Hey baby, my name is Miles. How ya doin", I said as smoothly as I could. I was thinking that charm was necessary to get close to a gorgeous woman like this, but I was wrong, charm didn't carry half as much weight as dead presidents! Ignoring my introduction, she just grabbed my hand and began walking me towards a stall as she quoted a price list of various sexual favors as if we were at the Flea Market discussing the price of Nikes!

We entered a stall and she gestured me to sit down as she straddled me and began to seductively gyrate her hips to the beat of the fast music that was blaring from the DJ booth. Her hard, choppy movements were actually uncomfortable as she slammed her crotch up and down on me! "Slow down baby", I said. "Take it easy". She ignored my protests and continued her "dance", looking off into space like I wasn't even there. After a few more minutes, the song stopped, and she stopped "dancing" and looked me in the eye. "So, what do you want to do?"

By now, I was harder than Chinese arithmetic and pretty high from the gin and weed, so I said," Sure, let's go around the world". I hadn't had sex in months so it didn't take her long to earn the fifty bucks! At the precise moment of my release, a huge wave of shame and guilt enveloped me as I immediately thought of my sweetheart Weezy in SC. I had broken the promise I had made to myself to remain faithful and I felt like shit!

I pushed the stripper off of me and paid her as I rushed out of the stall. "*Look at you, you piece of shit!* The Voice was in full effect! "*You have a sweet loving girl waiting on you to marry her and you're out here whoring around!"* Internally, I hung my head in shame as my inner voice reminded me that whores were all I deserved and once Weezy *really* got to know me, she would drop me like a hot potato!

I had made a conscious decision to compromise my own set of morals and values to satisfy my need for instant gratification. My low self-esteem, which allowed me to cavort with a stripper in the first place, immediately kicked in and I began to berate myself for my dirty behavior. Having sex with loose chicks as a young teen was one thing, but I was an adult now and I should know right from wrong, right? I decided right then and there that this was the last time I would trick with anyone else, no matter how fine they were! The Voice just "rolled" its eyes and said, "*Whatever*"

When I got back to the main club area, I saw Reggie stuffing dollar bills into a stripper's g string with one hand while copping a feel of her ample boobs with the other. She just stood there with a lost look in her eyes as if she wasn't even there. Why anyone would let them self be abused and disrespected like that was beyond me and I found myself actually feeling sorry for these misguided souls who let men have their way with them for money.

Suddenly, I didn't want to, "fuck deez hoes" anymore. I was totally disgusted with myself and everyone else at the strip club and I wanted out immediately. I told Reggie I was leaving and he was like, "What da fuck man, the party just gittin started!" I told him I was catching a cab back on post and he said he would check me later. As I quickly made my exit, one of the bouncers jokingly said," What's the matter, son? You don't like pussy?" I just shook my head and bolted out of the door.

Once I got outside, I sparked up one of the joints I had rolled earlier and puffed on it till a cab pulled up. As soon as I entered the cab, the driver asked me where I was going and if I needed any weed. I told him I was "good" and told him to take me back on post. Apparently, the cabbies here also moonlighted as pot salesmen!

During the ride back to the barracks I felt the same dirty, shameful feeling that I felt after I allowed my aunt and uncle to molested me. I had finally found a "good" girl, a woman with self-respect and honor. A woman who cared about me and was willing to marry me, and the first chance I get, I have unsafe sex with a hooker! I didn't realize it at the time, but I had terribly low self-esteem and each time I compromised my morals and values, I caused it to drop even lower.

As the cab passed by the modern air conditioned barracks that were on the way to my World War II style "Tuskegee Airmen" barracks, I was reminded of how I felt as a child passing those beautiful homes on the way to the projects in Brookside. All my life, I had feelings of low self-worth, and shit like this only reinforced the negative feelings I had of myself.

As I vigorously scrubbed myself in the barracks shower, I prayed that I didn't catch the "Clap" or that AIDS shit I had been hearing about lately. When we first arrived on base, one of the sergeants warned us against unprotected sex and told us that there was shit out there that would have us "pissing fire" if we weren't careful.

"*Way to go dumb ass, now you will probably catch AIDS and die before you are 25*", said that all too familiar voice in my head. Over the next few days, I checked myself every time I took a leak or showered, expecting to find puss or some kind of rash, but after about a week or two, I figured I had dodged the "bullet".

By now, I was used to being a "double agent". All through High School, I played both sides of the fence. I could be this thoughtful, intelligent student one minute, then hell raising, bad boy the next. Even in the Army, I was a super soldier by day and a party animal by night. My tough guy persona was only an attempt to hide my fear and anxiety. I had perfected hiding my emotions and how I really felt, down to a science, so when I called Weezy that night, she was none the wiser that I felt like a piece of shit for cheating on her with the stripper. We talked for a while until I told her that I was tired from the long trip and I would call her the next day. She said," Goodnight baby", in the sweetest southern accent you could imagine, and I fell asleep with conflicting thoughts of how much of a piece of shit I was and about how nice it was going to be when we got married and lived happily ever after.

The next morning at ten o'clock, I was awakened by the sound of the squad leader clanging this annoying assed metal bell. He rang it until every "swingin dick" had his feet on the floor and told us to check the duty roster for our cleaning assignments. Even though things were a little more laid back in AIT, we were still required to clean the barracks every day. Some of the platoon had been there for a few days already so of course we "newbies" had latrine detail!

After lunch, Reggie a few other guys, and myself decided to head to the gym to play basketball. Reggie had been quiet and sullen all morning but I just chalked it up to him having a hangover from the night before. When we got to the gym, he and another guy were choosing teams and I was confident that my homey would pick me to be on his team. When he didn't, I felt "some kind of way", but brushed it off. The other guy picked me and we began playing. I resented not being picked by Reggie so I made it my business to make him wish he did by playing hard. I was a damn good ball player, and I was dominating the game with sweet jump shots and quick lay-ups to the hoop. On one particular play, I was making my move to the hoop when suddenly; Reggie stuck out his foot and tripped me. I went flying and got a nasty friction burn on my knee from the fall.

"What the fuck you do that for man?" I said as I picked myself up off the gym floor. "Stop actin' like a bitch and play ball nigga", was my so-called friends reply. So now I'm angry *and* confused. Where I came from, you always pick your home-boy whether he is good or not, and you damn sure don't intentionally trip him as he makes his way to the basket. The other guys were laughing their asses off at me and my inner voice, who never took a day off, chimed right in. "*You gonna just let this mother fucker get away with that shit?*" asked the voice. I valued Reggie's friendship and was willing to give him a free pass for tripping me, but he walked up to me, got in my face with an attitude and said," That was for leaving me for dead last night nigga". I was like," What da fuck you mean leave you for dead? I was ready to leave and you said you would check me later!" "Well, now I'm checking you" he said. And with that, he sucker punched me in the face.

As his fist made contact with my face, everything around me came into sharp focus. I could see the other guy's faces, but couldn't hear their voices. It was as if everything was moving in slow motion and a feeling of fear immediately took over me. Not so much as fear from being hurt, but fear of losing a friend and fear of being embarrassed in front of the other guys. I could taste the blood in my mouth as my anger reached an intensity that I hadn't felt in a long time.

It was as if I was above the scene watching as my best friend and I commenced to whipping each other's asses! Reggie couldn't keep up with my hands, as I popped him a couple of times in the face. He was on the wrestling team in high school though and kept trying to "lock me up" with his legs and arms. We had wrestled a couple of times in basic training so I knew better than to let him get me in one of those "death grips" with his legs. When it became obvious that I was winning the fight, other guys tried to break it up and I turned my wrath on them too, swinging at anyone who came within arm's reach. All I was able to say was," Get da fuck OFF me, get da fuck OFF me!" as I swung at anyone who came near. Although I was at Ft Gordon Georgia, my mind was on Whalley Ave getting beat up by the angry white kids or on Mansfield St getting punched in the face by Big Al. Once my "switch" was turned on, it was hard to turn it back off and I believe that to this day, at least five of those guys can still remember the crazy dude from Ct who went off at the gym that day.

Someone shouted," AT EASE" and that snapped me back into reality as I saw a short stubby guy in sergeant stripes running towards us." What da hell is going on here?" he yelled, out of breath. "Nothing sergeant" we both replied. "Damn right nothing's happening, now all a yooze git the HELL outta my gym before I call the M.P's!" We all knew better than to talk back to a sergeant, so we grabbed our shirts and keys as we hurried out of the gym.

Reggie and the other guys from Echo Co. walked back to the barracks together as I walked about a block behind them. I felt alone and rejected, as I walked with tears in my eyes." Real friends don't treat each other like that!" I told myself, not trying to understand that Reggie must have felt the same way when I left him at the strip club the night before. "*How could you be such a sucker*?" The Voice berated me as I tried to figure out how I could be so naïve and let someone "In", past my emotional defenses like that. Fighting was nothing new to me but fighting a good friend hurt like hell.

Reggie was a popular guy because he was a local and knew where all the weed, hookers and nightclubs were. He had a smooth way of talking and his "swag" drew chicks to him like moths to a flame. The other guys in our platoon including myself damn near worshiped him, and his celebrity status went straight to his head. I was an expendable friend because he had an abundance of yes men who were eager to be "down" with the coolest guy on post. Apparently, our friendship wasn't that important to him, and that hurt the little boy trapped inside my grown man's body. I was so hurt at the fact that someone I trusted fought me over something so trivial. Although I found out later that he had gotten drunk and passed out and lost his whole paycheck in town the night before, which was still no reason to fight your home boy! I had liked Reggie and my feelings were hurt now that we were no longer friends. I was an all or nothing type of guy and you were either with me, or against me. Sucker punching me in the face most assuredly guaranteed you a place on the "Against me" list! I decided that for now on, I wouldn't let anyone "in" anymore. It was me, myself and I. "Who needs friends anyway", I said to myself. From now on, I decided that I was going to focus on learning my MOS and graduating so I could get the hell out of these God forsaken barracks, marry my fiancé Weezy and get on with my life.

To become a Radio Teletype Operator, you needed a top-secret security clearance. Some of my fellow soldiers had to get reclassified into another field or even discharged from the Army halfway through their training because they lied about their criminal history. It took a while for your background check to come back because the Internet wasn't in full swing yet. When the sheet went up on the barracks bulletin board with the names of the soldiers who passed the background check, I breathed a sigh of relief when I saw my name. I was worried because I had been arrested once back in high school for punching a bus driver in the face when he closed the door on me while I was talking to this girl I knew. I would have gotten away with it but I was so angry after I hit him that I ran around the corner to meet him at his next stop and finish the job. Little did I know, the bus driver had picked up a cop and when I got to the bus, I was surprised to see one of New Havens finest waiting for me as I attempted to board the bus again! I was arrested, once again disappointing my Mom and Dad, but since it was my first offence, I was given Youthful Offender status, which meant that as long as I didn't get arrested again; my record was to remain sealed.

Reggie's last name was Williamson, and I couldn't help but notice that his name wasn't on the list as I scanned the "W's". Apparently, he had done something in the past to get his security clearance declined. His status was put on hold and he didn't even get a chance to begin classes. He was discharged a week or two later, but in the meantime he managed to get caught with a bag of weed and was restricted to the barracks for the remainder of his time. I got a big kick out of seeing him doing the 'shit" details like cleaning the latrine by his self or raking the dirt around the barracks as the rest of the platoon prepared to march to class. What comes around goes around mother fucker", I'd say to myself as I secretly reveled in his downfall. I was an expert at holding grudges and resentments, and got a twisted sort of pleasure from watching him fail. One day he came up to me and apologized for the fight and I could see the sincerity in his eyes. In spite of his sincerity, I just nodded my head and walked away with a nonchalant look on my face. Along with sincerity, I saw the dejected look on his face as he transformed from BMOC to Beetle Bailey. Now that his Army career was over, Reggie stopped caring about his appearance. He stopped shining his boots and his uniform was always wrinkled. The platoon sergeants would use him as an example when anyone got out of line and threaten us with "shit" detail like "Sad Sack" over there was doing. When the day came for him to leave, I shook his hand with a tear in my eye and said," Take care, man" then quickly walked away lest I be seen crying by the other men in our platoon. I still had that macho image to protect! Although he had disrespected our friendship, it was still sad to see the hopeless look on his face as his dreams of being all he could be were dashed away. I may have held resentment towards him, but I still had a heart, and seeing him this way tugged at my heartstrings.

I decided that I wouldn't smoke weed or drink for the remainder of my time in AIT because I was afraid to wind up like my former friend. I didn't think I had a drug problem or anything, but I knew drinking and smoking all night was not going to help me when it came time for class in the mornings. When the weekends came, I spent time in the gym trying to bulk up my skinny frame by lifting weights and using the exercise machines. All it took was a mental decision and I stopped drinking and smoking weed with no trouble at all.

I excelled in communications training, impressing my instructors with the speed in which I mastered the skill of installing and operating the RATT equipment, and learning the protocol for sending and receiving encrypted communications.

At the end of the day, we could get out of class early as long as every last soldier had finished their assignment. Once you were done, you could leave class and go outside to smoke a cigarette or shoot the shit with the other guys who finished first. When everyone was done, we would "fall in" to formation and march back to the barracks.

Every evening, after class, I would shit shower and shave after chow and get in line to use one of the pay phones so I could talk to my darling Weezy and tell her how much I loved her as we planned our future. I would rush other guys off the phone and sometimes, if I thought I could get away with it, just hang up the receiver while a dude was still talking, so I could use the phone. I needed my "fix" and no one was going to stand in the way of it! Weezy and I would literally talk for hours as I fell deeper and deeper in love with my sweet Southern Belle. She became my new drug and I found myself obsessing about her all day until I could get my evening "fix" of talking to her on the phone.

This went on for the duration of my training and every two weeks on payday, I would send my parents between one and two hundred dollars to cover the cost of our nightly talks. Where were free nights and weekends when I really needed them?

I became focused on what I wanted to accomplish and my self-esteem enjoyed a boost as I completed each block of training with ease. If I wasn't on the phone with Weezy, I was at the gym running full court basketball with the fellas or jogging around post on my own with my headphones over my ears as Dougie Fresh or Public Enemy blasted from my Sony Walkman. For the first time in my life, I was practicing self-discipline and the more I succeeded, the quieter that malicious voice inside my head became. I didn't realize it at the time, but that voice was one patient motherfucker!

Although I excelled at RATT training over the next few weeks, there was one aspect of the course that I struggled with. We were required to be able to type 60 wpm in order to complete the course, but I was only able to hover around 50 wpm. No matter how hard I tried, I couldn't get my speed up to the required 60wpm. Ever since I had joined the Army, I was able to master every task that came before me. Personal combat, firing range, drill & ceremony, communications protocol and installation of equipment all came easy to me, but I couldn't master typing for the life of me. I was beginning to get discouraged because not being able to pass the typing test was grounds for me to get reclassified into whatever field the Army needed me in. I realized how fragile my self-esteem was as I began to feel sorry for myself again. "*I knew you couldn't do it you sorry piece of shit*". "*Whatcha gonna do now? Become a supply clerk like ya girlfriend?*" My inner voice taunted me as my confidence dwindled. I walked the streets of Ft Gordon Ga. with tears in my eyes as I realized that I was about to fail the course.

There was this short skinny, nerdy guy from Tennessee named George Thompson who I also knew from basic training. He wore these thick assed coke bottle glasses like Elvis Costello and most of the time he could be found reading by himself, not bothering anyone. George and I didn't hang out together, but he was a cool dude. I played chess with him a few times, but quickly lost interest because he had this horrible case of halitosis. I had bailed him out of a few situations where other guys were bullying him by threatening to "bust their ass" if they didn't leave him alone! George could type his ass off, and when he noticed I was struggling he offered to practice with me after class and help me build my speed up. He taught me a few tricks and before long, I was right up there with the rest of the class typing 60-80 wpm! He still had halitosis, but it's amazing what we can endure when our ass is on the line!

Now, people who type for a living know that 80wpm is no big deal, but in our field, we didn't need to type long messages. Accuracy under pressure however, was essential so Uncle Sam wanted to make sure you could type in the dark, under battlefield conditions.

When it came time for the final testing module that determined whether or not you advanced to your permanent duty assignment, I passed with flying colors! "Germany here I come!" I shouted as the scores were posted on the barracks wall.

I remember vividly, the feelings of confidence, accomplishment and pride I felt after finally, for the first time in my life, completing something I started. The Voice inside me was silent as my whole being enjoyed a level of self-esteem never before experienced. I felt as though I could conquer the world. I couldn't wait to get married and travel the world with my gorgeous bride! I felt invincible as I enjoyed my newly found self-esteem.

Once I completed my RATT training, I had about a week to go before my 30 days of leave began. I was headed to Germany, so there were all kinds of paperwork to fill out. We also had to get shots and endure lectures on the dangers of un-safe sex or what to do if solicited by spies . . . yada yada yada. I had to make a will at 18 years old which amused me because other than my clothes and a few things back home, I had nothing of value to leave anyone. I did however, have substantial insurance policies that I left to my parents. ". . . And my comic book collection goes to . . ."

I decided to celebrate and treat myself to a night on the town beginning with a T-bone steak! I was so proud of myself for completing my training and now it was time to celebrate! I dined on a well-done steak that melted in my mouth and ordered a beer to wash it down. I hadn't had any alcohol in about eight weeks and the Heinekens went straight to my head. I ordered another and before I knew it, I was walking around town trying to find a bag of weed. After not smoking anything but Newport's for 12 weeks, and proving to myself that I could do anything that I put my mind to, here I was about to jeopardize everything I had accomplished!

I noticed a slim black guy standing outside of a little hole in the wall bar and asked him if he knew where I could find some weed. He motioned me to the side of the building, out of plain sight, mentioning something about watching out for the cops, and pulled out a few bags of what looked and smelled like the real thing. He told me they were $10 bags, so I reached for my wallet. Suddenly, he had a knife to my chest and was nervously ordering me to turn around. I knew that if I turned around, he could stab me and leave me for dead in the alley so I made a split decision to defend myself. If he had a gun, I might have complied with his orders, but I'll be damned if I was about to get robbed with a pocketknife! As I began to turn around, I stopped halfway and quickly swung my elbow back into his face. As my elbow smashed into his temple, he dropped his knife and grabbed his face with both hands. Seizing the opportunity, I swung as hard as I could at his head, knocking him to the ground.

As he lay there, bleeding from his face, I could have run out of the alley to safety, but my anger was taking over and "Big Miles" was pissed that this dude was trying to rob "us"! "You wanna rob me, motha fucka?" I said through clenched teeth him as I kicked him with all my might in his stomach. As I raised my foot to stomp him in the head, I remembered how my big brother Chris had stomped that guy's head when I was a kid. This dude was about to catch hell for all the ass whippings I had ever endured as a kid and I felt justified in punishing him, because he started it. As I brought my foot down, his head made that same sickening crunch I heard when Chris stomped that guy in the driveway many years ago. After I stomped him two or three more times he lay motionless and defenseless in the alley. Getting arrested and getting kicked out of the Army meant nothing to me at this point as I allowed my anger to consume me. The poor guy had definitely learned his lesson, but I kept kicking and stomping him until two teen-aged girls, who happened to be walking by, started making a commotion. I reached into his pockets, took his bankroll and his weed, and then calmly walked away as if nothing had happened. I didn't need the money, but it felt like the right thing to do!

The two girls stood there speechless and afraid, as if I was the aggressor and I let them think so as I walked by them with a blank look on my face, eyes darting back and forth, looking for a cab to jump into. My hands were shaking and my heart was beating a mile a minute, not because I was scared from the attempted robbery, but because I knew that if those two girls hadn't started screaming I may have very well committed murder that night. It frightened me that I was capable of inflicting such a beating on someone. Not only had I never felt such rage in my life, but I enjoyed it. After the first kick to his stomach, my assailant was immobilized; all blows after those were overkill. The rage that had been building up inside of me since childhood was becoming harder to control. Talk about emotional luggage, I was walking around with every resentment I ever had since childhood and every fight I got into was fueled by residual anger from years past.

The next five days were filled with anxiety as I expected the M.P.'s to pull up and arrest me any minute for murder or assault. I was beginning to become disgusted at this person inside me who was willing to throw everything we were trying to achieve away over a bag of weed. It was as if a part of me wanted to fail. There was a big part of my personality that wanted to be successful, but there was also a big part of me that wanted to party hearty, damn the consequences!

I was still riding high on my newly found self-confidence, which made it easy to convince myself that I was a victim and was only trying to protect myself. I was getting better and better at rationalizing and justifying the most outrageous sort of nonsense! Never mind the fact that I was off post, engaging in illegal activity. I kept a low profile till it was time for me to leave and luckily, I was never arrested for "damn near killing the guy in the alley.

Chapter 14

Let's Get Married!

Weezy and I were deeply in love and I couldn't wait to take the Greyhound bus to Greenville, SC. and see my bride to be. I went to the PX to shop for a wedding ring and although I couldn't afford the ring I knew she deserved, I settled for a "Princess Solitaire" engagement ring and a matching wedding set. As I placed the rings in my pocket, I closed my eyes and imagined what it would be like to make love to Weezy for the first time. Would I satisfy her? Was I good enough for her? My insecurity and low self-esteem was rearing its ugly head again and The Voice, which needed only a small opening, was interrupting my thoughts again and telling me that no woman in her right mind would marry a loser like me. I shook the negative thoughts off and continued to think of the lovely woman I was on my way to marry!

Weezy was an amazing, gorgeous young woman. She had a "Colgate" smile and eyes the color of hazelnuts that seemed to shimmer when I looked into them. Her brown curly hair perfectly framed her exotic, caramel features and high cheekbones. Not only was Weezy drop dead gorgeous, she also had the sweetest personality and could make me feel like a king with one glance or the slightest touch. She saw something in me that I didn't even see in myself and she chose me out of all those other guys to be her man! I admired her maturity and the way she carried herself like a lady, almost in a regal way, like royalty. The fact that she had a cool job with the Environmental Protection Agency was appealing also. She drove a blue Ford Fairmont and I couldn't wait for her to pick me up at the bus station.

When my bus pulled into the hot, dusty Greyhound bus station in Greenville, I felt as if I had been transported back in time to the early 1950's! The part of town where the bus station was came right out of an episode of Mayberry RFD! I almost expected Andy Griffith and his son Olpie to stroll by, fishing poles in hand, on their way to the local pond!

The first thing I noticed when I got off the bus was the intense heat. It was unlike anything I had ever felt before. It enveloped your body and you could actually see it 20 feet away, rising from the pavement in hazy waves. I couldn't believe people really lived in this kind of heat.

A woman who resembled Weezy walked over to me and introduced herself as Iris, Weezy's cousin. She explained to me that Weezy would be along soon and that I would be hanging out at her house until Weezy got off work. Iris was very friendly and hospitable and treated me as if I was a member of the family member for years! She grabbed one of my bags and said, "Come on Army Man, my house is a few blocks over".

My body adjusted to the heat as Iris and I walked the four or five blocks to her place. As we passed the small clapboard houses that were in close proximity to the bus station, Irene explained to me that this section of town was known as Porters Quarters because back in the day, the porters who serviced the trains and carried the luggage of passengers from the nearby train station lived in this area of town, hence the name.

As we approached Iris' neighborhood, I was immediately attracted to the down-home, country atmosphere. Everyone seemed friendly and they actually spoke to you when they passed you in the street. I saw magnolia trees bigger than anything I had ever seen in my life and folk's yards were well kept with flowers and palms. Up ahead, a rooster casually strutted across the street and I knew that I was officially "Down Souf" (as we say it "Up Nawf")

A well-built woman in shorts that were WAY too far up her butt, and high heels, sashayed over to Irene and I, and looked me up and down like I was fresh meat. "Who is *THIS* fine young man, Irene?" she said flirtatiously as she popped her gum. Irene sucked her teeth and said, "Good *BYE* Lucretia" He's already spoken for, and if you know what's good for you, you will back up off him!" The neighborhood hoe gave me one more flirtatious glance and then continued on her way, heeding Iris' stern warning.

When we arrived at Iris' house, she gestured for me to have a seat on her porch and offered me a mayonnaise jar filled with the sweetest home brewed ice tea I had ever tasted! She said it was called "Sun Tea" because it was brewed by placing it in the sun, as opposed to boiling the water.

As we sat and chit-chatted, I had no idea of the sight I was about to behold. I had fallen in love with Weezy without ever seeing her in civilian clothes. Her pretty face and sweet personality had already sealed the deal, but when my darling Weezy stepped out of that car, I knew I had stumbled upon the complete package. I had never seen her in anything other than Army fatigues and the sight of my beloved in those form fitting slacks and blouse, totally blew my mind! She was everything I could ever want in a woman; mentally, physically and emotionally, and I was about to marry her in five days!

I hopped down off the porch and walked over to her with a big smile on my face. "Hey baby", I said, grinning like a little kid on Christmas morning. "Hey", said my darling Weezy as we embraced and shared our first, intimate kiss. I was in ecstasy as the rest of the world ceased to exist. As we kissed, a warm feeling that I never felt before washed over my body and it felt like our bodies were charged with electricity as I melted into her embrace. I was aroused from my trance by the sound of little kids giggling at us as Irene playfully shouted, "Geez, git a room!" As my gorgeous fiancé dabbed at my face with her soft bare hands, I realized that tears of joy were rolling down my cheeks! Weezy held my face in her hands and looked me in my eyes with a look I'll never forget and said," You're not dreaming baby, I'm for real!"

After we put my bags in her car, Weezy and I took the 30-minute ride to her mom's house in the "Woods". The "Woods" was a rural area unlike anything I had ever seen before! After traveling about five miles past the city limits, we took a left down a potholed dirt road that was lined on both sides by huge moss covered trees. There were majestic Magnolias, Weeping Willows, Pines and a host of other trees, vines and bushes. "*So this is what they mean by "Deep South*", I wondered to myself as we made our way down the dirt road. After a few hundred yards, I noticed a house coming into view on the right side of the road, but Weezy continue to drive past it. We passed by maybe three or four more houses along the dirt road and I was amazed at the fact that although we were in the middle of the woods a mile away from paved roads, I was seeing lovely homes with yards and driveways! A few days later, Weezy took me for a tour and showed me a network of miles and miles of dirt roads that stretched across the county. There was everything from stately Plantation homes complete with majestic pillars, to run down old shacks that looked like actual slaves lived in them at one time. There was even a "Juke Joint" where folks hung out and played cards or shot pool just like in the Color Purple! You almost expected to hear Shug Avery singing the blues at any moment!

Just as I began to wonder just how far into the woods she lived, we approached a clearing up ahead where I noticed two lovely homes and a beautiful doublewide trailer nestled on a five-acre lot. We turned into the driveway and the gravel crunched under her car's tires alerting everyone that someone was arriving. I noticed folks hanging out in the shade that the massive trees provided. Some were seated at a round wooden table playing cards, while others were gathered around a horseshoe pit watching two older men playfully argue over the score. It was a happy, peaceful scene and I couldn't wait to meet her family.

The first person to turn towards us was a massive man who looked like he could break me in half with no problem. He stood at least 6'4" and must have weighed at least 300 lbs.! He wore a pair of denim overalls with a white tee shirt and had a bald head that reminded me of John Coffey in "The Green Mile". He had a stern look on his face as he approached the passenger side of the car where I sat and I was beginning to become apprehensive. "Don't mind him" Weezy reassured me," That's Uncle Junior, he wouldn't harm a fly!" Uncle Junior took the last few strides to the car and snatched open my car door. "Well, git on out and let us have a look atcha!" he said, with a great big, gold toothed smile.

As Weezy and I got out of the car, a small crowd of her family began to gather around us. A beautiful, middle-aged woman wearing a flowered sundress stood before us with an expectant look on her face. She had curly black hair and was a spitting image of Weezy. "This is my mom, Emma", Weezy said, gesturing towards an older version of herself. "Pleased to meet you, ma'am", I said, in my "polite army guy" voice. I extended my hand to her but she ignored it and gave me a big hug as she said, "Welcome to the family, Miles!" with a great big smile on her face.

Weezy began to introduce me to the rest of the family and I felt right at home! There was Aunt Bertha, who was sitting in a chair snapping peas by her husband, Uncle Wally, who was manning the barbecue pit. I met her three brothers, "Rusty", Mike and Doug who were a few years older than Weezy and I met her teenaged sister Dee-Dee and at least 5 or 6 more cousins, aunts and assorted family members.

As a small crowd of female family members surrounded Weezy, I could hear bits and pieces of conversation. "He sure is fine, girl", one of her cousins said. "You done found yaself a keeper" said another.

Weezy grabbed my hand and walked me over to a pick-up truck that had a pair of overall covered legs sticking out from under it with a pair of well-worn work boots at the end of them. As we approached, a middle-aged man with a Florida Gators baseball cap slid out from under the truck. "This is my step-father, Gino, said Weezy. Gino was built like a small army tank. He was at least a foot shorter than me, but what he didn't have in height, he made up for with muscle. The battle scars on his leathery brown face, hinted that he had been in his fair share of fights in his day. His massive hands looked like two baseball mitts at the end of his muscular arms.

Once he was standing, Gino wiped his oil stained hands on his clothes, and said "How ya doin there, young fella?" I shook his hand firmly, just like my father taught me, looked him in the eye, and said, "Fine, sir, nice to meet you, Sir". Gene looked me over with a serious look on his face, then broke out in a great big smile and said, "You a lil skinny, but I guess you'll do. Weezy will have you fattened up in NO time!" Everyone laughed, as I was "accepted" into the family by the man of the house!

It felt wonderful to be accepted and my self-esteem enjoyed a much needed boost, as I enjoyed being the center of attention.

Weezy, her mom, Gino and I went into the house and we all sat at the kitchen table. Her mom fixed us four glasses of sun tea, and then sat down to join us. After a few minutes of small talk, Gino got straight to the point. "So what are your intentions with Weezy?" he said with a serious look on his face. "Well Sir, I would like to marry her, if that's all right with you", I said confidently. "Well, what da hell ya askin' ME for?" he playfully asked; "You need to be askin Weezy!"

With that, I rose from the table, got down on one knee in front of my beloved and asked, "Weezy, will you marry me?" as I pulled the Princess Solitaire ring from my pocket and held it up to her. Although I had already asked her to marry me weeks before over the phone, Weezy's eyes got all watery as she stood up and said, "I sure will!" Seeing the sparkle in her eyes and the smile on her face as she accepted my proposal gave me a feeling of joy that I had never felt before. As I placed the ring on her finger and hugged the girl of my dreams, I could see Gene and her mom smiling from ear to ear.

We spent the next few minutes discussing our upcoming wedding. It was just four days away, but Weezy and her mom had everything all set up; all I had to do was show up! "No sense in wastin' good money on a hotel, you can sleep here" But no hanky panky till after the wedding" cautioned her mom.

After stowing my gear in Weezy's room, I took a shit, shower and shave and put on my "civies". When I walked outside, her cousin Ernie motioned me over to a tree where he and a few other guys were standing around smoking weed and drinking Schlitz Malt Liquor Bull. "You smoke man?" he said as he passed me a joint. "Thought you'd never ask" I said as I accepted the jay and took a couple of tokes of some of the finest weed I had ever tasted. Ernie passed me a brown paper grocery bag that held at least a half-pound of marijuana and told me to grab a few buds for myself. "Don't be shy", he said. "We gotta whole field a dat shit growin round that bend", he said in his southern drawl, as he pointed towards the road. I politely grabbed about a dime worth of weed and placed it in the cellophane from my cigarette pack. Back home, weed smoking was done in private, away from adults and children, but down here, as long as you were a discreet distance away from non-smokers, it was cool to puff in the open. I hung out with the fellas for a few minutes, shooting the shit, until I noticed Weezy walking over with a glow on her face.

"Mind if I borrow him for a minute?" said Weezy, as she placed her hands in mines and looked into my eyes flirtatiously. "Damn! I ain't never seen Weezy this crazy bout no nigga before", said her brother Rusty. "Shut up boy!" she said playfully as she gently pulled me away from the fellas. "There's some more folks I want you to meet", said Weezy, as she led me over to a small group gathered around the barbecue pit.

The way she led me by the hand, proudly introducing me to the rest of her family members one by one, touched the core of my soul in a way that can't be described in words. This beautiful woman is in love with me! As the realization sunk in that Weezy was just as in love as I was, I entered into a state of bliss. I barely heard the rest of the introductions as I emotionally inhaled the beauty of what was happening before me. I was floating on a cloud of joy never before felt in my life, and if my beloved wasn't holding my hand, I may have floated away!

After a few more introductions, Weezy introduced me to a woman who was sitting alone, away from the rest of the family. She wore sunglasses despite the fact that it was late evening and the sun had already set. "This is my Aunt Verna", said Weezy as I reached out to shake hands. As she turned her head towards me, I could tell that she had two black eyes and a swollen lip, but I ignored it and greeted her as if nothing was out of the ordinary. "Welcome to the family, Miles" she said timidly, obviously ashamed of her appearance. Weezy sensed the awkward silence and told her aunt that she wanted me to meet the rest of the family and we walked over towards the barbecue pit where her uncle was putting the finishing touches on what looked like Brontosaurus ribs, straight outta the Flintstones! As we walked away, I asked my fiancé what happened, and she explained to me that Aunt Verna's husband was an alcoholic and he had beaten her up a couple of days ago. I had never met this woman before today, but I felt a rage building up inside of me as if my very own mother had been beaten up. "What kind of fuckin man would DO that to a woman? I asked, visibly upset. "Don't worry, that will NEVER happen again!" she reassured me.

Her family seemed genuinely happy for us and I felt accepted by them all. We spent the rest of the night eating, drinking and occasionally stepping over to the "Smoking Area" beneath the massive magnolia tree. I felt like a celebrity as folks pulled into the yard and I was introduced as Weezy's fiancé.

The next few days were spent putting the finishing touches on our upcoming wedding and I felt like an official "grown up" as Weezy let me drive her car wherever we went. When I was in high school my dad was very adamant about not letting me or anyone else drive his car, so the only time I got to drive was when my best friend Jabo let me drive his moms car after he got so drunk he couldn't drive, or when my mom would let me drive home from the grocery store.

When we went to city hall to obtain the official wedding license, Weezy's brother Doug went back to the car with me when I forgot my driver's license. "Just wanna make sure you don't run off" he said to me. "I'd hate to have to get my shotgun and hunt you down!" he added. I wasn't sure if he was joking or not, but I was deeply in love with Weezy, and running away was the last thing on my mind. Once we received our marriage license and were officially man and wife, I looked at Weezy with a playful look in my eye and asked her if we could "make it official" in the bedroom. She held her hands up and twirled around slowly and seductively, showing me her amazingly sexy body and said," Are you sure you are ready for all of this?" As I gazed upon the ample curves that I had been craving for months, I said," I am MORE than ready, baby!"

We dropped Ricky off at his place and headed back to the "Woods" to her mom's house. Her mom and Gene were at work and her sister Diane was at school, so we had the house to ourselves. Weezy gave me a towel and told me to shower "real good" with a wink in her eye as she put on some slow music on the cassette player besides her bed. It was a hot, sunny day and I could hear the crickets making that high pitched buzz as I toweled myself off in Weezy's room. I turned on the air conditioner and put on some Jovan musk cologne that my big brother Chris had given to me when I first enlisted in the Army. I lay back on the bed in my boxers, anticipating my new bride's entrance to the room. She made her entrance wearing a skimpy white negligee and her magnificent beauty amazed me! She stood before me in all her glory and I could see her gorgeous body through the sheer silk teddy that she wore. She looked at me with a coy look and asked me," So, what do ya think?" I got up off of the bed, walked over to her and held her ever so gently in my arms and kissed her deeply. "I think you are the most beautiful woman I have ever seen in my life", I said to her as I began to caress her body. Although this was our first time together, we had no inhibitions. As I made love to my wife for the first time, it did something to my soul. It was as if I was bonded to her forever, as our souls left our bodies and intertwined somewhere between fantasy and reality!

Our wedding day had finally arrived. We had the wedding ceremony and reception in a hall that we had rented and even though we were on a tight budget it was an elegant affair. The ladies of the family did a splendid job of decorating the hall. From the outside, it looked like any other rural hall with a dirt parking lot, but once I stepped inside I was amazed at the time and effort that went into making this a special affair. Paper doves hung from the ceiling by clear fishing line and the tables were decorated festively with white and red hearts. There were plenty of excellent cooks in her family, so the food spread was off the hook! We had everything from Uncle Willies barbecue chicken and ribs to my mother in law's baked macaroni and cheese. There were banana puddings, red velvet cakes and everything else in between! Cousin Ernie offered his DJ services on the "ones and two's" as a wedding gift, so although we were two young kids in love on a tight budget, our wedding affair was a night to remember,

I arrived at the hall with my brother in law Mike (who I picked to be my best man) and as we walked to our places at the front of the hall, I was the proudest man in the world because I knew I was about to marry the girl of my dreams. As my beloved Weezy walked down the aisle, my self-esteem soared exponentially! The voice inside me that told me she would never marry a bum like me, sat there with a sullen look on its "face" as I experienced a joy never before felt. I was on top of the world and felt as if nothing could steal my joy. The next thing I remember is the preacher saying, "You may kiss the bride".

We sat at the head table and enjoyed the most delicious soul food dinner I had ever tasted, while I reveled in the fact that I had just married my soul mate. It was a festive occasion and her family sure knew how to throw a party!

After the wedding ceremony my blushing bride and I were about to step outside to take a few pictures when suddenly, we heard loud voices coming from down the hallway. The Drunk, who had beaten up Weezy's aunt the week before, had the audacity to show up at our wedding, demanding to see his wife. As I turned towards the commotion, I saw him push past a humble cousin of hers who was explaining to him that this was not the place or time. "I don't give a fuck WHO is getting married" he yelled. "I want Verna's ass home NOW!" He continued to walk down the hallway towards the main hall and I could hear the men in the family coming up behind us to handle the situation.

When I turned and saw the tears running down my beautiful brides face, I saw red. The voice in my mind that had been silent recently immediately chimed in and said, *"You're not gonna let this mother fucker get away with this, are you?"* At the time, my total self-centeredness told me that this guy's intent was to ruin MY wedding and piss ME off! It would be years before I was emotionally mature enough to realize that he was battling his own demons and it wasn't even about me. I pounced on him before anyone else got to him and began punching him with everything I had, not only because I thought he was a coward for beating his wife and then ruining our wedding day, but I felt compelled to prove to Weezy and her family that I wasn't a punk. I wanted to show them that I was a "real man" who wasn't afraid to fight. Although Weezy and her family already accepted me with open arms and treated me like one of the family, my low self-esteem still needed to prove to them that I was worthy of their respect. I still needed to be accepted . . . more! My warped sense of how a real man behaved, forced me to have to continuously resort to violence whenever I felt disrespected.

By the time me and five or six of Weezy's brothers and cousins finished stomping this guys back out, he was a bloody mess. They dragged him to the door and tossed him out like a bag of garbage and we all returned to the party as if nothing had happened. I received a few pats on the back from various male family members, complimenting me on my violent exhibition, and that only reinforced my distorted view of how a real man behaves.

The way we kicked this guy's ass was easily justifiable, due to the cowardly way he beat his wife, but I was beginning to believe that this was how ALL conflict should be resolved. It was as if each fight I got into was just a continuation of the last one, and all the pent up anger just "rolled over" into the next. What intrigued me though was how easily I could turn my anger on and off. I went from happy newlywed one moment, to committing a violent assault and back again in a matter of five minutes. Once I let that part of my personality gain control, I no longer cared about consequences and took on a kill or be killed mentality, then, when I no longer sensed danger, it would shut off and let my gentler side take over. This was a defect in my character that would later prove to be near fatal. No matter how convincing I was as the polite, intelligent, lovable guy, there was a scared, insecure little child right beneath the surface who had a psycho guardian ready to protect him at all costs. Not only was I trying to convince other people that I was a nice guy . . . I was constantly trying to convince myself. Every time I behaved in a way that contradicted who I wanted to be, it caused another crack to appear in my already fractured personality.

As we walked back into the main hall, Weezy asked me if I was all right and I looked at her calmly, straightened my collar, and said, "I'm fine baby", as if nothing had ever happened. I held her hand as we walked to the center of the dance floor and enjoyed our first dance together as Mr. and Mrs. Miles P. Walcott. As Weezy and I slow danced and gazed into each other's eyes, the drama that had just unfolded melted away and we enjoyed the rest of our night in ecstasy!

CHAPTER 15

Homecoming

Weezy and I decided to spend the second half of my thirty-day leave in Ct. with my side of the family, after which I would be deployed to Germany. No one from my side of the family was able to make the long trip to Florida for the wedding, and I was eager to show off my lovely bride! Weezy owned a car and since she would have to stay with my parents for at least a month or two before I could send for her, we decided to drive to Ct. so that she would have transportation while I secured housing for us in Deutschland.

The ride up I-95 north gave Weezy and me a chance to seal our bond even tighter. We talked about everything under the sun and there was never a boring moment during the long ride to Ct. (wink, wink). We stopped at a motel during the twenty-hour ride because we just couldn't get enough of each other. I was the happiest man in the world as we embarked on this new chapter of our life and I felt as if nothing could stop me from being the successful career soldier that I endeavored to be!

As we crossed the George Washington Bridge into New York, I was delighted at the look of awe on her face as my wife saw the Empire State Building and the Manhattan skyline for the first time. I told her that this was just the beginning and that I was going to show her the world!

We finally arrived in New Haven at about 10p.m. and although it was late, my mom, dad and siblings were wide awake, awaiting our arrival. When we pulled up to my parents' house it was like I had been gone for years as my dad stepped off of the porch with the biggest smile I had ever seen! "You left as a boy, but returned as a man!" my dad said as he gave me a bear hug. "And you must be Mrs. Miles

Preston Walcott" my father said as he hugged my bride warmly. "Nice to meet you, Sir" said Weezy. "Please, call me Dad" said my proud Poppa. "After all you ARE my daughter in law!" Weezy blushed as my sister Lizan said out loud that I had finally found a "keeper". My mom hugged her, then grabbed her by the hand and walked her into the house as she asked her if she wanted to freshen up after the long ride. Grab her bags, Private! My dad half joked as they went inside.

My dad pursed his lips and nodded his head up and down with approval as my darling Weezy walked into the house with my mom. He turned to me and said with a serious look in his eye, "Ya got good taste, son!" as he playfully punched me in the shoulder. He grabbed the biggest bag from the trunk of the car and I felt a warm feeling envelope me as I realized that I had my father's blessings! I left Ct as a High school dropout, but returned as a soldier in the United States Army, with a beautiful new wife to boot! This was an important moment in my life because I desperately needed my father's approval in order to feel good about myself.

The next day was a festive occasion in the Walcott household. My dad was all smiles as he shared one Heinekens after the next with me for the first time ever! Before now, it was unheard of for me to sit in the den and have a beer with my dad, but now that I was a grown man, he treated me like I was one of his peers instead of a teenager. I felt closeness with my father that I had never before felt, and it felt great to be able to hang out with him as an adult. Mom cooked her signature dish of baked macaroni and cheese with this special Italian cheese and garlic that melted in your mouth. There were ham and collard greens and sweet potato pies. It was like Christmas or Thanksgiving! I had never seen my mom cook like this other than major holidays! Not only was my family proud that I was doing something productive with my life, they were also excited about my beautiful new wife. I was such a "player" in High school, no one expected me to fall in love and get married so soon!

Everyone loved her! My sister Lizan, who thought that no one was good enough for her big brother, became Weezy's best friend. Kandi and Tamara loved her also and I felt confident that when I went overseas, my darling wife would be in good hands.

My big brother, Chris came by and even though I had out grown him by at least 6 inches and about 50 lbs., he was still my "big" brother in my eyes. I felt on top of the world when he hugged me and told me how proud he was of me. For the first time in my life, I felt like I was a man as I basked in the light of my family's approval.

Later on that day, Chris and I were riding down Dixwell Ave. smoking a joint in his Dodge Omni, when he pointed out a guy that had given him some static a few days earlier. He told me that the guy had sold him some "garbage dope" a few days ago and when he confronted him about it, the guy pulled out a knife and threatened him.

This was my chance to repay him for watching my back as a kid and the voice inside me was urging me to show my brother how my fighting skills had improved. No matter how well things were going for me, there was this angry voice inside of me that didn't give a care about anything or anybody. When it spoke, it spoke in a loud, resounding voice that was hard to ignore. I knew by now that whenever I listened to this voice, things got ugly, but I trusted it and allowed it to take over whenever I got angry or felt threatened.

This was the same voice that told me to punch that teacher in junior high. The same voice that caused me to damn near kill a man in Georgia. The same voice that could have gotten me arrested on my wedding day! It wasn't an audible voice, like a person who suffers from schizophrenia hears, but it was a voice never the less, that emanated from inside of me. There was also a soft, quiet voice inside me that told me that it wasn't that serious, and to let it ride. "You have a beautiful wife and a promising career ahead of you. Everything you asked for" it softly whispered in my ear. I ignored what I thought was the scared little boy inside me, and went with the angry voice.

I told my big brother to pull over and instructed him to wait for me to circle the block and then ask the guy for his money again when I returned. I went around the corner and parked his car and began walking over to where my brother, who had always been MY protector, was talking to this wannabe gangster who had "beat" him for ten dollars. As I approached, I could hear the guy telling my brother that he didn't have a damn thing coming and to step off. "Tough Guy" was bigger than Chris, and spoke to him with a dismissive tone that allowed me to justify what I was about to do anyway. He had no idea that I was Chris' brother, and when I got over to where they were standing I calmly asked him if he had any dope for sale. He looked at me suspiciously and asked if I was the police, probably because of my military style haircut and muscular stature. I didn't look like your average dope customer; I looked like an undercover cop! Chris chimed in and told him that he knew me from across town and that I was "cool". "Tough Guy" pulled out his bundle of dime bags and asked me how much I wanted. I told him that I wanted five, so that he would be distracted counting out the bags.

It appeared that I was reaching into my back pocket for my wallet, but I was really "palming" the chrome plated .25 caliber automatic that I kept in my pack pocket. The guy never knew what hit him as I smashed the body of my pistol into his temple. As he lay on the ground dazed and confused, I kneeled down right into his chest and grabbed him by the collar. "If you ever fuck with this nigga again, I'll kill you" I said as calmly and quietly as if we were sitting down having a cup of coffee. I didn't identify myself as Chris' brother because I had learned in the Army that information was only disseminated on a need to know basis! I told Chris to grab the bundle of dope and as I stood back up, I kicked him in the face and asked "Tough Guy" if he thought I was fucking playing. The crazed look in my eye was convincing enough and the guy hoarsely said he didn't want any problems.

Chris took out a dime for himself and tossed the rest of his dope back on the ground next to him and we walked off. We could have taken the whole bundle but there was honor amongst thieves. A dime for a dime; nothing more, nothing less!

We didn't speak as we walked away, we were too busy watching our backs just in case "Tough Guy" had a "business partner", but I could tell by the look on my big brothers face that he was proud of the way I handled myself.

The feeling of power and superiority that I felt as we walked away was intoxicating. I was no longer the skinny little teenager who used to get his ass kicked all the time, I was a grown man who was trained to kill and I wasn't afraid to use my new found skills. I felt invincible as I walked away. I didn't even turn around to see if "Tough Guy" had a gun or knife. I didn't carry myself like a tough guy and didn't think of myself as one either, but once I allowed my dark side to take over, I turned into this angry dude who had no fear. I had a false sense of pride at the fact that now; I could dish out some punishment instead of always being the one who got his ass kicked!

After enduring countless ass whippings as a teen, and the shame and embarrassment that came with them, I became obsessed with ensuring that it never happened again. I was a happy go lucky guy who was enjoying life for the most part, but right beneath the surface was this violent, angry psychopath who would try and take your head off at the slightest provocation. I had grown physically since joining the Army and my confidence level was at an all-time high, but because my personality was already fractured, I overcompensated when I should have used restraint. I didn't have this insight at the time; I just thought I was doing what a man was supposed to do!

Unbeknownst to me, my brother was dealing with his own demons. I didn't know anything about dope and couldn't understand why my brother kept nodding off when we stopped at a light or in mid conversation. I would ask him if he was ok and he would say yes. End of conversation. I naively ignored his behavior and quite frankly didn't care what was going on. All I knew was; this was my brother, who had my back since I was a baby, and I was going to be damned if anyone on the street was going to fuck with him on my watch.

My father and I enjoyed a renewed connection now that I was doing something with myself. He and I would sit for hours in the den while he schooled me on life and people. He absolutely adored Weezy and insisted on treating when we went to Captains Galley, one of the nicer seafood restaurants in our area. One night, after my mother and father took the four of us out for dinner; my father looked at me with a tear in his eye and told me how proud he was of me. We both "teared" up but quickly regained our composure as my mom and Weezy returned from the rest room. My mom gave us both a "look" because she knew us so well, but didn't say a word as we ordered dessert. They made Weezy feel welcomed and at home and I can remember her telling me how much she loved my family as we lay in bed together in the room I spent my high school years in.

I enjoyed the rest of my vacation with Weezy and my family, but the time finally came for me to me to deploy to Germany. It was a bittersweet time because although I was excited about going to Germany, I didn't want to leave my beautiful wife; not even for a moment.

CHAPTER 16

Deutschland

My brother Chris drove Weezy, Lizan and I to McGuire AFB in New Jersey. It was a dark, rainy night and we were all stressed out due to the poor visibility on the Jersey Turnpike. We all breathed a sigh of relief as we entered the Air Force base and I felt like a big shot when the guards at the front gate waved us in after I flashed my military I.D. badge.

My family walked me to the gate, and after I said my goodbyes to Chris and Lizan, they left Weezy and I to enjoy our last few minutes together before I boarded my flight. It would be at least a month or so before I could send for her and neither of us wanted to be apart that long.

We were deeply in love and it seemed like we kissed for at least fifteen minutes straight before I heard my flight announced overhead. I kissed my beautiful bride goodbye and walked towards my gate. I didn't let the tear that I had been holding back fall until I was sure I was out of her sight. My young, immature mind thought that crying in front of my wife . . . even one tear, would be a sign of weakness.

Although I had begun to carry myself like some kind of tough guy, it was all a façade. I spent most of my time in fear of one thing or another. Would I be a good husband? Would I make it in the Army? Although my new wife adored me and we had a great sex life, I still thought of myself as sexually inadequate ever since I had sex with my aunt and compared my pre-teen genitalia to the well-hung men in my aunt and uncles porn magazines. For some reason, I always thought of myself as less than or not good enough and I found myself constantly trying to prove my manhood.

I was even terrified of the flight I was about to take. I had never been on an airplane before and here I was about to take a Trans-Atlantic flight to Europe! Thankfully, the Army chartered a civilian plane, so I was able to buy liquor during the flight. I figured if I got drunk enough, I would wake up, and be in Germany. Little did I know that the flight was so long that I would get drunk, pass out and wake up again and *still* be in mid-flight! The air pockets and turbulence terrified me, and every time the plane lurched or dipped, I became visibly upset as I nervously looked out of the window. All I could imagine was my plane going down over the Atlantic in a ball of fire. The other soldiers on the flight, male and female, got a good chuckle out of the nervous, young soldier who held on to the side of his seat from New Jersey to England! Even the badass voice inside me was quiet as a fucking mouse as we prayed for the moment when we would touch dry land again!

We finally landed at a British air base where we refueled and then completed the final leg of our flight to Frankfurt, West Germany.

All incoming troops were billeted at a central processing facility that serviced all branches of the American Forces in Europe. There were Marines, Air Force guys and even a few British soldiers awaiting their respective units to retrieve them. It usually took a day or two before you got to your actual unit.

We were all assigned bunks in four man/woman dorms, and were strictly forbidden from going into downtown Frankfurt. We weren't properly processed into the country yet and they didn't want anyone going downtown and getting drunk. In spite of the fact that we could have gotten arrested, the first thing me and two other Army guys that I met on the flight over did after our showers was . . . go downtown Frankfurt and get drunk!

I was amazed at the sights and sounds of Frankfurt! It seemed like there was a Bier Haus or nightclub on every corner and the city just seemed so alive. I was tickled to death that all the yellow cabs were late model Mercedes Benz's as I realized that in Germany, a Mercedes Benz is not an expensive import!

Prostitution is legal in Germany and scantily clad ladies of the evening beckoned from the doorways and windowsills as we walked down the street. The idea of having sex with a woman who just got finished doing God knows what with someone else, just didn't appeal to me anymore. Ever since my experience with the stripper in Georgia, I believed no one did that kind of work unless they were absolutely hopeless and desperate. Besides that, my love for Weezy prevented me from disrespecting my marriage. This was the lie that I told myself, but the bottom line was, I didn't want to feel the pain that came along with that behavior. It had nothing to do with love, honor or integrity. My reasons for remaining faithful were totally self-centered!

My three new buddies and I walked around for a while checking out the sights and then stopped at a bar. I had heard a lot about German beer and couldn't wait to try one. I ordered a dark beer and downed it in a few swallows. It was heavier and stronger than the crappy malt liquor I was used to stateside, but it went down smooth. My buddies, who were on their second tours, warned me that German beer snuck up on you if you drank too much, too fast! The atmosphere inside the pub was unlike any bar I had ever been in. Folks greeted you when you entered and although there were blacks, whites, Turks, Germans and everything else under the sun, people were laughing, drinking and having a good old time and everyone got along fine. We had a few beers and then one of the guys, who happened to be a sergeant, recommended we get our asses back on post before we got arrested. The Army M.P.'s were on patrol and if you got caught on the streets without the proper I.D. it could mean trouble.

We gave the gate guard twenty bucks for not reporting us, and returned to the barracks. Because of the time difference, it was either too early or too late to call Weezy, so I crashed out on my bunk from the effects of jet lag and three Stuttgarter Hofbraus!

The next day, after I was finished being processed into the country, I was informed that someone from my unit in Nuremberg would be along shortly to pick me up. I gathered my gear and went to the parking lot area where soldiers were picked up and dropped off. I was assigned to the 3/5 Field Artillery Unit so all I had to do was identify my ride by the markings on the vehicles bumper.

As I walked across the parking lot, someone yelled out, "Private WOWcott!" in a thick southern accent. A tall Staff Sergeant in extra starched fatigues and impeccably shined jump boots waved me over from across the lot. He and another equally spit shined and starched soldier were helping an overweight, middle-aged Warrant Officer unload his gear from the black Volkswagen minivan they were driving. He must have known it was me because my plain uniform stuck out like a sore thumb. Soldiers stationed in Europe had a shiny unit insignia on their soft caps, a unit patch sewed on one shoulder and an American flag on the other, so it wasn't hard to figure out who the new guy was. "Whussup Newbie" said the staff sergeant as I began to throw my gear into the back of the van. "Good afternoon, SARGEANT!" I said in a loud, clear voice. "What the fuck are you yelling for?" he said half seriously. "I'm right the fuck here! My name is Staff Sergeant Jackson, but don't call me that unless we are around other motherfuckers! My friends call me Reggie! And NO I don't play for the Yankees! Now get the rest of your shit so we can get back on the road! "Yes sir . . . uhh . . . Sgt. Uhh . . .Reggie", I stammered, confused at the lack of formality.

Back in basic training and AIT, proper military courtesy was strictly enforced. PFC Chilton introduced himself next. "What's up man? Just call me Chill," he said as he helped me with the rest of my bags. "Relax dude, you aint in A.I.T. anymore." Chill was about my size but I could tell by the way his camouflage shirt hugged his arms that he worked out regularly. He spoke with a smooth mid-western accent and wore his soft cap ever so slightly tilted to the side. After we stowed my gear in the back of the van, Sgt. Jackson said, "Chill, hit the "Bahnhoff" before we head back to Nuremberg". Chill smiled, and said," Yes Sir, Sergeant, sir!" in a loud voice meant to mock the formal greeting I had just given SSgt Jackson a few minutes ago. We all had a laugh as Chill cranked up the volume on the cassette player and blasted Dougie Fresh's "La Di Da Di"

When I was in communications school at Ft Gordon, enlisted men never fraternized with Non Commissioned Officers like Sgt Jackson, but over here, things were different. You still had to respect a guy's rank, but when we were amongst ourselves, we were brothers. We all had each other's back no matter what, and regardless of your color, if you wore Army green; you were part of close knit group of men and women who were aware of the possibility that at any given moment, we could be at war. You never knew who you might need to save your life, so most soldiers got along well with each other.

Once we got on the highway, Chill opened up the minivan to 100 kph which was only about 70 mph but seeing the needle on the odometer go to 100 really freaked me out. BMW's and Porsches zipped by us like we were standing still as I experienced my first ride on the Autobahn. As I sat in the back seat enjoying the scenery, I noticed SSgt. Jackson pull out an empty Coca Cola can. He began to form it into a bowl shape and took his metal SSgt stripes off his hat and used the pointed ends to poke holes in the middle of the can. "La di da di, we like to party!" he said as he crumbled up a brownish red substance and placed it over the holes in the can. He lit it and took a long pull and then passed the can to me. "You smoke?" he asked as he turned towards me with a chest full of smoke. "Hell yeah" I said, and took the can. I had heard about hashish before, but had never tried it. I knew it was derived from cannabis, and being the pothead that I was, I took the can and inhaled deeply. We passed the can around a few times before Sgt Jackson told Chill to take the next exit.

After parking the van a few blocks away, the three of us made our way to the Frankfurt Bahnhof. The bahnhof was the main train station, but you could get much more than trains there. It was a huge, ornate building that was built around WWII. It had a high, arched cathedral ceiling and a seemingly endless row of bays for the trains to pull in and out. The building was immaculately maintained and folks who weren't even catching a train would come and hang out just to experience the atmosphere and shop at the many stores inside. It was also an open-air drug market. Within five minutes of entering, you were almost certain to be offered some type of drug or sexual favor from one of the many colorful characters that hung out there. Chill knew who he was looking for and after making eye contact with his dealer; we walked casually to the bathroom where they made their transaction. Once the deal was made, we made our way back to the van and got on the Autobahn headed to Nuremberg. I hadn't been "in country" two whole days yet, and I had already broken at least three laws! Although I wanted to be a successful soldier, I had a deep seated need to be accepted and if smoking hashish with a non-commissioned officer was considered "cool" then I was all in!

When we arrived at Merrill Barracks, the Army post I was assigned to, I was impressed by the tight security at the gate and the high brick wall that surrounded the base. The guards wore flak jackets and carried loaded M-16 rifles. Flanking the entrance sat two armored personnel carriers with a soldier on top, manning the .50 caliber machine gun. The base was smack dab in the middle of Nuremberg, yet it was a separate, independent piece of the United States. All vehicles entering the base were meticulously checked by the guards who had mirrors attached to telescoping poles that they used to check the underside of vehicles for bombs. Terrorists were bombing U.S. bases all around the world, so security was tight.

Once we were on post, things were more relaxed and if you didn't know any better, you would think you were on a stateside Army base. There was a Post Exchange store (PX for short), co-ed barracks, a mess hall where the soldiers ate, a chapel and even a garage where you could sign out tools and work on your privately owned vehicle. There was an Enlisted Mans club where you could order American beer, but it was empty most of the time because the G.I.'s loved to party downtown where the real action was!

I was assigned to the headquarters unit of the 3/5 Field Artillery brigade, one of the largest artillery units in Europe. As we entered the building, large pictures of canons from the Civil War to the present, adorned the walls of the hallway. Chill showed me to my room and introduced me to my roommate, PFC Joe Duffer, one of the coolest guys I had ever met! Joe was a 6'3" Italian stallion, as he liked to call himself. He was nice on the basketball court too, and whoever said white man can't jump obviously never met Joe! This dude could dunk like Larry Bird and handle the ball like Magic! He dated a black girl named Sharon and we all became friends instantly. We weren't allowed to have women in our rooms but I turned a blind eye whenever Joe and Sharon needed the room to themselves.

I met the rest of my platoon and everyone was eager to show the "new guy" the sights around Nuremberg, so a few of us agreed to go downtown after chow. I called my darling Weezy and she could hear the excitement in my voice as I described Germany to her. I promised her that I would get her across the "water" as soon as possible and how much I missed her all ready.

After chow, I took a shit, shower and shave and headed downtown with Chill, Joe and a couple other guys. Joe said, "We should take him to "The Wall", and when I asked what that was, they all laughed and I was told that I would find out soon enough. A section of Nuremberg was called The Old City, which was surrounded by a ten-foot high wall. Along the length of one section of the wall was a row of apartments where prostitutes would beckon men inside as they stood in their windows wearing next to nothing. The guys chipped in some German Marks and told me that I was about to get the treat of my life! They told me to pick a girl that I liked so that I could get “broken in”. I told them that I wasn’t interested, but they insisted that I pick a girl and get laid. As we “cruised” the “Wall”, I felt the anxiety inside me grow as I became conflicted with respecting my wedding vows and giving in to the peer pressure of my comrades and my raging hormones. The peer pressure and hormones won, and I picked out a gorgeous African girl with a pretty face and a sexy body. She looked like someone out of a Playboy magazine and my teenaged hormones began to get excited at the prospect of having sex with a “Playboy Bunny”.

When I entered her room, she motioned for me to sit on the bed while she ran down the “price list” of her services. I was ready to tell her that I just wanted to pay her and leave after ten minutes when that familiar voice inside my head began to berate me for not being a “man”. “*What are you, gay? “Would you rather bang old ass Aunt Sonya*?” the voice said. “*Weezy is all the way back in the States you pussy, now stop bein a lil bitch and bang this chick before your boys think you are some kinda fag!*” My mind knew exactly which buttons to push and no way was I going to let my friends or this total stranger think I didn’t like girls. I had sex with her and I was done in less than three minutes! I asked her if I could use her bathroom, and after I vigorously scrubbed my genitals for like five minutes, I just sat there as that familiar wave of shame and guilt washed over me.

I sat on the toilet with my head in my hands as I began to feel Just like in Georgia when I had sex with the hooker at the strip club. I felt like a piece of shit and berated myself for violating my own code of ethics and morals. It was a sickening feeling that hurt me down to the deepest parts of my soul. I was a hypocrite. I talked about how much I loved my wife on one hand, but continued to behave like a womanizer on the other. I didn’t realize it at the time, but each time I contradicted myself, I chipped away a little bit more of my self-esteem, and the fractures in my personality spread out more and more.

When I returned to the fellas, I gave them a bullshit story about how I “wore that ass out” and received a few pats on the back from the people I so much wanted to be accepted by. I hated the way I felt, and I wanted a stiff drink or two so I didn’t have to feel the pain. We found a nightclub and while the fellas were dancing and talking to the local women, I sat at the table and got quietly drunk, staring at the lights and listening to the music with a somber look on my face. A couple of pretty women approached me, but I waved them off as I slipped deeper and deeper into a drunken stupor.

I "came to" in a taxicab as Joe was slapping me in the face trying to get me to wake up. "Dude, you are sooo wasted" said Joe as I tried to sit up straight. I didn't remember getting into a cab or even leaving the club for that matter. I looked down and saw vomit on my clothes and I felt like I would vomit again at any moment. The cab dropped us off at the main gate and Chill and Joe had to grab my arms and walk me through the gate. "Damn son, you drunk as fuck!" said Chill as I stumbled along. I was mentally aware of what was going on, but was unable to control my motor functions.

Once we got back to the barracks, Chill lit up a bowl of hash. "This shit will clear ya head newbie" he said as I took the make-shift pipe. I inhaled deeply and in a few minutes I felt the effects of the high quality hashish. It didn't clear my head; in fact it made me feel worse. I ran out of the room looking for a place to throw up but I ended up in the female latrine with my arms wrapped around a toilet!

After a few minutes, I was able to pull myself together enough to make it back to my room. As I entered, I could hear Joe and Sharon having sex on the other side of my locker, but I was too drunk to leave so I just fell out on my "rack". I miscalculated my fall and my face slammed into the metal pole on the end of the bed frame, opening up a nice cut right above my right eye.

As I lay on the floor bleeding from my wound, I began laughing as Joe tried to stop the bleeding with a towel. "What the fuck is so funny?" he said as I lay on the floor giggling away. "My eye is bleeding," I said, as if it was funny. I could feel the pain in my head and see the blood all over my shirt, but I was so intoxicated that all I could do was lay there and laugh. Sharon ran into the hallway and yelled for a medic. I could hear other soldiers in the hallway asking her what all the commotion was about. SSgt Jackson came in demanding to know," What the fuck happened to "Wow Cott?" "Sarge, we took him out on the town just like you said, and got him home safe" said Chill. "But the mother fucker fell on his rack and busted his face on the bed frame!" Spc.4 Thompson, our unit medic, came in the room and was almost as drunk as me. He took one look at my eye and said, "This guy needs stitches". They loaded me into a Jeep and took me to the Infirmary, where I received a few sutures, and was released.

The next day was a Saturday, and I awoke to loud shouts of "AT EASE" coming from the hallway. The First Sergeant was in the building, which was a rare occurrence on the weekends. The First sergeant was the highest-ranking noncommissioned officer in the unit and he didn't appreciate coming in on a Saturday to meet the new troop who busted his eye open on his first night in town. "Are you Private Walcott?" shouted the seasoned, gray haired veteran as he walked into the room. "Yes Sir" I shouted, as I snapped to attention. "Don't call me Sir, Private. I work for a living!" he said, as he got right in my face. "You will address me as First Sgt. Hilliard, you got that Private?" shouted the angry 1st Sgt., as I stood there in my white boxers. "Yes 1st Sgt., I answered quietly. "You have ten minutes to get your Sad Sack ass into my office . . . TEN MINUTES, not eleven or twelve!" he yelled, as he stormed out of the room and slammed the door so hard that it sounded like a gunshot. As I hopped around trying to get my pants and boots on, Joe told me to chill out and just say "Yes 1st Sgt." or "No 1st Sgt." and everything would be fine.

The way he came into my room and yelled at me frightened me and I instinctively let the angry voice inside me take over. "*If this motherfucker thinks he's gonna talk to us like that, he's got another thing coming*" It said. "*We're in trouble all ready, so if he gets in my face I'm just gonna deck him, just like I did that teacher in Jr. High!*" I had an all or nothing mentality and this crazy person inside of me was ready to throw it all away based on fear of the unknown! A softer, quieter voice inside me said to take it easy and don't make matters worse, and I decided to listen to that voice. I didn't want to throw it all away, so I decided to see what happened before I did anything else stupid.

As I walked down the long marble hallway, I noticed other members of my unit milling about. After hearing the 1st Sgt. yelling, they had come out of their rooms to see what was going on. I didn't want them to know how frightened I was, so I put on a "tough guy" face and walked down the hallway like I was "Billy Bad Ass".

When I arrived at his office, I timidly knocked on his door and waited for an answer. "Who the FUCK is it" was the loud reply from behind the door. "Private Walcott reporting as ordered, 1st Sgt.!" I replied. "ENTER", was the equally loud reply from behind the door

First Sgt Hosie Hilliard stood about six foot six and weighed about 250lbs. In spite of his years, he didn't have an inch of fat on him. He wore a close-cropped salt & pepper crew cut and had a jagged scar on the side of his face that I later found out had come from shrapnel during a tour in Vietnam. I could tell by the ribbons and medals on his chest that he had served in the Vietnam War and was a decorated soldier. He looked vaguely familiar, but I couldn't quite place where I knew him. He made me stand at attention in front of his desk while he looked through my file and after about five minutes, he ordered me to sit down on a small, hard, wooden chair that was in front of his desk.

I sat in the chair, still a little drunk from the night before, as my eye began to throb from my injury. My right eye had a bandage over it, and I had to squint with my left, under the bright lights in his office. "Says here that you are an Expert marksman," he said, as he looked at me over his bi-focal glasses. "Yes Sergeant", I answered proudly, as I realized he looked like a taller version of my father! "Did pretty well at "Commo" school too," he mentioned, as he continued to review my records. "How long you been married?" "Three weeks, 1st Sgt., I answered. "Plan on bringing her over?" "Yes 1st Sgt., as soon as I can get off post housing" I said confidently. "Next time you see her is gonna be when she picks your sorry ass up from the airport in good ole "Connetty-Cut" if you keep *this* shit up" he said sarcastically.

"Private Walcott, do you know that I can bring you up on charges for willfully damaging or destroying government property?" he said as he walked around the desk and towered over me. I knew I had gotten drunk the night before, but I didn't remember destroying or damaging any property. "So do you care to explain to me why this report says that you damaged government property last night?" First Sgt., I don't remember damaging any property last night," I said, trying desperately to remember what the hell I had done. "You don't *remember* Private?" he screamed. "You mean to tell me that you got so drunk that you don't fucking remember what you did?" he yelled.Tears welled up in my eyes as he yelled at me. I was afraid that I was in big trouble. How would I explain to Weezy and our family that I was getting kicked out because I went out and got drunk? I began to answer him but he told me to shut the fuck up and listen. As I sat in the chair with tears running down my cheeks, wondering what the hell was going to happen to me, 1st Sgt. Hilliard explained to me that my body was the property of the United

States Army and if I got hurt under the influence of alcohol, I was in fact willfully damaging government property! He also explained to me that drinking enough alcohol to render myself unconscious was stupid and dangerous . . . anything could have happened to me while I was passed out. He told me that I had a promising career ahead of me, but if I continued to behave like I did the night before, I would be headed back to Ct. in no time.

As he pulled up a chair in front of mine and sat down, his tone softened. "Look, son" he said quietly, "I've been in this man's Army for 23 years and I've seen 'em come, and I seen 'em go." He was no longer yelling and had a compassionate look in his eyes. "You have what it takes to go somewhere in this man's Army" he said. "If you wanna make something out of yourself, you gotta leave the drugs and the liquor alone. I know the guys you were hanging out with last night, and they are bad news. I suggest you find some better friends or you're gonna be sorry". He went on to explain to me how embarrassed and disappointed my wife would be in me if she came over to Germany and had a drunken, drug addict for a husband. You can be all you can be, son, or you can be a fuck up and go home; it's all up to you! The fatherly way he talked to me and the way he called me "son", made me receptive to what he was saying. He talked to me for about fifteen more minutes and as I sobered up, I realized that he was telling me the truth. He had a way of talking that allowed me to see my life played out before me, and if I continued down the path I was presently on, the ending wasn't pretty!

He concluded his fatherly lecture on how to succeed in his unit, the intercom buzzed, informing him that the company commander was on the way to his office. He abruptly stood up and moved his chair back to its place just as the C.O. entered. Suddenly, his tone changed back to angry. "Now get your sorry ass outta here and tell SSGT. Jackson that you won a free shine" he yelled, as he winked his eye at me.

As Captain Briley entered the office, 1st Sgt. Hilliard shouted "Ten-Hut. I snapped to attention, knocking the chair over as I got up. The captain looked me up and down, pausing at my bandaged eye, and shook his head. He walked past me towards Top and mumbled, "Why do they keep sending us these fuck ups?" Top nodded his head towards the door and shouted" DIS-missed".

After I left the 1st Sgt.'s office, I saw that SSGT. Jackson was waiting in the hallway. "Damn Wow-cott, the way you looked when you went in

Tops office, I thought we were gonna need the M.P's for yo ass!" he said, looking relieved. "He told me I won a free shine" I said as we walked down the hall. SSGT. Jackson led me to a supply closet and pointed to the large commercial buffer inside. He told me that the 100-foot, marbled hallway needed to be buffed and I wouldn't be "free" to enjoy my weekend until the hallway "shined"! I laughed to myself as I buffed the floor, "Not a bad punishment for damaging government property!

CHAPTER 17

Turning Point

Merrill Barracks is a World War II era military base located three blocks away from the Dutzendikes, the parade grounds where Hitler gave a lot of his speeches. Some of Hitler's elite SS troops were housed there during the war, and he spared no expense when he built it. It was a huge compound that covered about six city blocks. The main buildings were three story "mini fortresses" that seemed impenetrable from the outside. The outer walls were made of huge, gray slabs of granite that were polished to a shiny finish, and you could still see some of the metal hinges that used to hold iron shutters during the war. Inside, long hallways with high cathedral ceilings ran the length of the building with ornately detailed rooms and offices on each side. The floors of the hallways were made of marble, and with hundreds of black booted soldiers walking on them all day, they needed constant buffing. No one liked giving them a "free shine" so it behooved you to stay out of trouble. Even the smallest infraction, such as waking up late or not having your gear or uniform "squared away" guaranteed you the opportunity to give a "free shine".

As I maneuvered the buffer down the long hallway, I contemplated what 1st. Sgt. Hilliard had said to me in his office. I knew that I was on the wrong track and I didn't want to lose everything I had worked so hard for. I wanted to bring my wife over and explore Europe with her. I was about to blow my chances at being promoted in a few months, so

I had to get my shit together immediately. I was off to a bad start, but there was still time to redeem myself. I began by giving that hallway the best shine it had in years!

There was no internal struggle to become a better soldier. No inner conflict where I battled my "demons" in my quest for excellence. I simply made a decision to handle my business and shine like I knew I could! I knew what I needed to do, so I "Just Did It" like the Nike ads.

In the months that followed, I became the soldier that I knew I could be. My room and gear were always immaculately in order, and I passed every inspection with flying colors. My uniform was impeccable, from the starched creases in my fatigues; to my boots, which were so shiny you could literally see your reflection in them. I quickly gained a reputation as a squared away soldier and within a few months, I was promoted to Private First Class! I didn't stop drinking alcohol and smoking hash completely, but I slowed down to just partying on weekends and even then, I used moderation. Our unit had regular "piss tests" where everyone had to pee in a cup, but Sgt. Jackson assured me that they only tested people who were on some ones "shit list" for fighting, insubordination or some other behavior that drew negative attention to you. As long as you handled your business, you were safe from "burning" the urinalysis.

"Top", as we affectionately called our 1st Sgt., began to reward my behavior and expertise by giving me increasingly more responsibility. We called him "Top" because he was basically the "top" dog in the unit. Although he was outranked by the commanding officer, we all respected the fact that he had more experience than anyone of us, and his medals proved that he had dodged a few bullets in his time!

I remember how proud I felt when, because of a shortage of qualified personnel, "Top" put me in charge of my own rig with a another private to assist me. Pvt. Watson and I knew we were under a microscope, so we were meticulous in caring for, and maintaining our equipment. Pvt. Watson, or "Shorty" as we called him, was a sharp brother from Jersey. He was only about 5'8" but trust me, you wanted this guy to have your back in a firefight. He was nice with the M-16 and could wrestle the biggest guy in our platoon to the ground. He was also just as skilled as I was in our specialty, so we made a good team.

Top used our rig as the platoon's standard. He would have other soldiers with more rank and experience than we had; check out our "Ratt Rig" before an inspection. "This is how a Ratt Rig should look," Top would say proudly, as my Platoon Sergeant stood by with an envious look on his face because two privates in his platoon were receiving more accolades than he was.

A "Ratt Rig" was a secure communications hut that sat on the back of a Humvee. My squad had four rigs that the eight of us manned in two man teams. Inside was a radio teletype, a wide band radio and at least five or six other pieces of secure cryptographic communications gear that were connected by a tangled web of cables that had to be connected properly. Once connected, you had to follow certain protocol to establish secure communication with other rigs in your unit and hundreds of other units scattered all over Europe. During inspection, our rigs were dismantled, and we had to reassemble our equipment and initiate communication with another rig in a certain amount of time. We always finished first, much to the chagrin of our platoon leader SSgt. "Porker" who shared his rig with Pvt. "Whatshisname".

SSgt. Porker's real name was Parker, but we called him Porker behind his back because none of us cared for him at all. It wasn't because he was overweight and had a bad case of acne that covered his face and neck. It wasn't even because he was always sweating, even in a snowstorm. It wasn't even because his uniform and boots were never even close to the standards of the very soldiers he was supposed to be "leading". This dude was in charge of our platoon, but wasn't capable of doing the same exercises that he so generously dispensed as punishment to guys with less rank than him. If he got a wild hair up his ass, which was pretty much every day, he liked to berate lower ranking soldiers in front of the female soldiers, making them get on the ground and do twenty push-ups or getting in their face and yelling at them. It was obvious that he did it to impress the women in spite of the fact that not one woman on post would date his fat ass. Consequently, he spent plenty of time in downtown Nuremberg at the "Wall" paying for companionship. Shorty and I would watch him go from room to room like a drunken man whore, while we sold liquor and cigarettes to the prostitutes and their customers.

Shorty and I became business partners because American liquor, such as Jim Beam and Jack Daniels were expensive, imported liquors to the Germans, and so were Kools and Marlboros, but soldiers could buy it for less than half of what they paid from the PX and sell them at a huge profit on the black market. The lure of quick, easy money over rode the fact that we could be court martialed if we were caught! I never heard of anyone actually getting court martialed for boot legging on the black market, except for the dumb asses who sold to undercover Military Police. Quite frankly, I believe my good ole Uncle Sam looked the other way because he made money off of our illegal activity! We were allowed like 10 or 12 liters of liquor a month . . . much more than any one person could possibly drink. Plus, I had a female soldier who worked in administration, who shall remain nameless, sell me extra ration cards.

Needless to say, black marketing smokes and liquor was quite lucrative. I had also begun to dabble in dealing hashish on a very small level to my close circle of friends. I only sold enough so that I could smoke for free and used my profits to "re-up". All this behavior was dangerous and could get me arrested, court martialed or worse, but the voice inside that used to ridicule me, now told me in a smooth mellow tone that I was too slick to get caught.

SSgt. Porker was also a black racist. Groups of people, who hate other groups of people solely because of their ethnicity, are the most ignorant people on earth, in my opinion, but at least you know where they stand. Lard Ass, on the other hand, was always referring to whites as "Crackers" or "Honkies" behind their backs, but if you were white, and out ranked him, he behaved like the proverbial "House Nigga", shuffling his feet and "Yah Suh Bossing" as he kissed the asses of any white person that out ranked him. We called dudes like him "Brown Nosers" because the amount of ass they kissed assured them a generous portion of shit on the tips of their noses!

He also seemed to resent young soldiers of any color who were better at their job than he was. No matter how much praise we got from our superior officers, SSgt. Porker always had something negative to say, and he never gave credit where credit was due.

The thing about him that I hated the most was how he openly flirted with lower ranking guy's wives and girlfriends, and would give you a hard time if you called him on it. A guy, whose name eludes me, was actually court martialed for punching this asshole in the face, after SSgt. Porker grabbed his girlfriend's ass at the NCO Club. The poor guy was a good soldier who never bothered anyone, but when he saw the Pork Meister grab his girls butt, he just "lost it". I guess by now, dear reader, you can tell that I wasn't very fond of this guy!

One night, while Shorty and I were at "The Wall" plying our wares of liquor and cigarettes, I saw SSgt. Porker alone, staggering about, with a half bottle of liquor. He veered off into an alley where I assumed he was taking a leak, when two German dudes looked around suspiciously and went in after him. We were strongly encouraged to use the "buddy system" when we went into town for just this reason. At first, I thought he was just copping some hashish, but after I heard him yell," Help!" like a scared little kid, I knew this wasn't a "business" deal.

I looked around for Shorty, but he must have been in one of the apartments handling business. The two guys who went into the alley after Sgt. Porker didn't look too tough, so I decided to go in alone. Although I detested him as a human being, he was still a U.S. soldier, and I was bound by honor to assist him. I stepped into the alley to investigate further, and what I saw next makes me laugh to this very day when I think about it! The two teenaged thugs had his pants down around his ankles, yanking furiously to get them off, probably in an attempt to keep him from giving chase after they robbed him. It was a pitiful sight to see this fat drunk, with his underwear halfway off his ass, begging two skinny assed teenagers to refrain from relieving him of his trousers!

"Hey!" I shouted, startling his assailants. The two rag tag kids, who thought the fat, drunken G.I. was an easy mark, looked up and saw me standing at the end of the alley and nervously looked at each other. "Get the FUCK outta here," I shouted again. They had to go past me to get out of the alley, and as they passed, I feigned like I was going to hit them, causing one kid to trip and fall. I had a smirk on my face because I knew they were not a threat to me and I was barely containing my amusement at seeing big ole, badass SSgt. Porter on the ground looking a "Hot Mess" in his drawers!

As he struggled to get his pants back up, Sgt. Porker began to thank me profusely. "Anything you want man, I got you", he said. "Just please keep this under your hat". He actually looked quite pathetic during his embarrassing attempt at "damage control". As we exited the alleyway, Shorty ran up to us. "What da fuck is going on man?" he said out of breath. "I saw them two niggas running, and thought there was a problem". It didn't matter if you were black, white or purple, Shorty called everyone "Niggas". I told them that Sgt. Porker and I had just kicked their asses for talking shit to us, obviously lying to save "Lard Ass" from the embarrassing truth!

"Damn, I could sure use a drink" I said, as I looked sarcastically towards Sgt. Porker. "Drinks on you sarge?" I said with a sly look in my eye. "Uh, yeah, whatever you guys want . . . there's a bar right around the corner" Sgt. Porker said with a nervous look on his face. He was in debt to me now, but I wasn't going to push him too hard, just hard enough to keep him off my ass. From that point on, I had no trouble from Sgt. Porker and he always went out of his way to make things easier on me. Need a pass? Granted. Need someone to cover a guard duty shift? No problem. He fucked up by letting me literally catch him with his pants down and I planned on milking it for all that it was worth! I told my boy Shorty later on, but I made him promise to keep it under his hat. "Never know when we might need his fat ass" I told my buddy.

CHAPTER 18

You, and Me Baby!

After about three months, I had secured off post housing and was finally able to bring my darling Weezy over from the States. We lived in a nice apartment building that the Army had leased from its German owners. There was a checkpoint at the main entrance, but other than that, it resembled any other apartment complex in this posh, suburban area of Nuremberg.

Inside, we had shiny hardwood floors and all new appliances. I had already purchased a bedroom set, but wanted to wait for Weezy to come over so we could furnish the rest together. It felt good to be able to pick out whatever we wanted and have them deliver it to our apartment. I was into stereo equipment and made sure we had the latest Kenwood tape deck, receiver and four foot speakers that shook the windows if I decided to "crank it up".

As I drove to the airport in Frankfurt to pick my wife up, I felt giddy with anticipation. It had been three months since I left her in Ct and I couldn't wait to hold her in my arms again. She was standing in the baggage claim area when we noticed each other. As we ran towards each other, you could almost the romantic music playing in the background as the two young lovers embraced each other and kissed in the busy airport.

Weezy and I spent the first two days of her arrival in our apartment getting "reacquainted". We only came up for air when we needed to eat or shower! We both took pleasure in exploring new ways to titillate each other, and I am sure the neighbors knew *both* our names!

I had taken five days off, and we spent it strolling through downtown Nuremberg, holding hands as we browsed the shops, or riding through the German countryside in our silver BMW. I felt like I was living in some kind of James Bond movie as we explored the European landscape. Whether we were picking out fresh fruit at the market or having lunch at an outdoor café, every moment together was blissful.

We held hands as I drove along the Autobahn and more than once; we pulled over to the side of the rode and made out like a couple of horny teenagers! I wanted to surprise her by showing her by showing her something she had never seen before, so I headed towards the Black Forest. The Black Forest was a dense forest about the size of the state of Rhode Island. Imagine, if you will, how romantic it was for us newlyweds to stand atop a mountain and see majestic pine trees peeking through the mist for as far as the eye could see!

I wanted to show her my favorite sight in Germany so we headed towards Neuschwantstein. The feeling of awe we experienced when we rounded a bend in the road and saw the Neuschwanstein Castle, in all its glory, was enough to take our breathe away. I always thought the castle on the Walt Disney opening credits was imaginary, until I saw it with my very own eyes. There it sat, nestled elegantly on a mountainside, surrounded by majestic pines. "Isn't it beautiful?" I said to my wife as we beheld the awesome sight. "Yes baby, its wonderful", said my lovely bride. I felt like I was on top of the world as we shared a kiss in the Black Forest, holding each other close as the sun set over the picturesque scene. We were two young lovers on a whirlwind romance and it felt like the world was ours! The young, up and coming soldier, and his beautiful bride, having the time of their lives!

Within a month, Weezy got a job at the largest PX in the area, and our income exploded! She worked as an associate in the credit department, and between both of our salaries, and the money I made on the side bootlegging cigarettes and liquor; we were rolling in the dough!

Weezy and I were a perfect match. We never argued and our household was always happy and peaceful. We loved to entertain, and the other guy's wives would tease us at our dinner parties about how sickening it was the way we were always kissing, holding or caressing each other!

We were in heaven. I never knew life could be so good. We traveled to France and sipped wine on the terrace overlooking the Rhine River. We took pictures next to a monk, in front of a cathedral in Madrid. We gasped at the majesty of the Swiss Alps as we drove through Zurich. We partied at the largest club in Munich until six in the morning and watched the sun come up as we sipped Belgian coffee on our hotel balcony. Our life in Germany was magical, and beyond our wildest dreams!

Weezy had a co-worker at the PX named Lorraine. She and her husband Vic were from England. They invited us over for dinner one night and we all hit it off from the start. Lorraine was as thin as a rail and had a head full of curly blond hair. Vic was short and balding but was built like a tank. They were always in a pleasant mood and made us all laugh with their funny jokes and antics. One time, as we sat around the fireplace at their home opening Christmas gifts, I received a "Willy Warmer" from Lorraine, and we all got a good laugh as I opened the gift bag and pulled out the twelve inch, knitted, phallus shaped gift that was supposed to be used to keep your "Willy" warm on a cold winters night! I endured the obligatory jokes about not being able to fill it up and Vic apologized that they didn't have any "small" sizes left at the store!

I was having the time of my life and couldn't remember when I was ever happier. All of the problems I had in the past seemed so distant as I enjoyed life with the girl of my dreams.

Chapter 19

Red Alert!

After terrorist bombed the LaBelle Discotheque in Berlin, the U.S. Armed forces in Europe were on high alert. We stopped frequenting local nightclubs and were suspicious of people in the crowded markets downtown. I couldn't understand how someone could be so filled with hate that they would explode a bomb around innocent civilians who hadn't done a damn thing to them.

The bombing had us all on edge, and it was starting to have an effect on me. One night, as we partied on a yacht that sailed up the Rhine River, I heard a loud pop and something hit the window where we were sitting. I grabbed Weezy and pulled her down in the seat because it appeared to me that someone was shooting at the boat. "GET DOWN!" I shouted, as I covered her body with mine. You can imagine my embarrassment as I realized that it was just a careless reveler who pointed his champagne bottle in the wrong direction! Everyone laughed, and I played it off and laughed along with them, but I was becoming paranoid about getting blown up every time I was in public.

We felt safer partying at the EM/NCO Club on post where we knew the armed guards at the front gate had our backs. Weezy and I would come out and party occasionally, but spent most of our off time at our apartment, entertaining our friends and getting our "drink on"!

One morning at about 4am, after having a party at our spot the night before, my phone began to ring incessantly. As I fumbled around on the nightstand trying to locate the phone, I could hear cars in the parking lot starting and tires screeching as they left the complex. When I answered the phone, the "Sgt. at Arms" told me that we were "on red alert", and to get my ass on post ASAP!

As I got dressed and hopped around trying to get my boots on, Weezy asked me what was going on. "Nothing, baby, I just have to go on post and handle some business", I said, trying not to alarm her. "Be careful", she said, as I kissed her goodbye and rushed out to my car.

When I arrived on post, the place was abuzz with activity. Tanks from the armored unit that we shared the base with, were rolling out of the gate, and soldiers were scrambling to get their gear aboard the "Deuce and ½" trucks that were belching diesel exhaust as they waited in line to leave post.

As I entered my unit, I could hear "Top" barking out instructions as my fellow soldiers lined up at the arms room to draw their weapons. We were each given our M-16 just like in all alerts, but I noticed the armorers loading live ammo into their vehicles. "Fuck! This is the real thing," I said to myself as I "double timed" it to the motor pool to prepare my rig for departure. Watson and I had our gear in tiptop shape; so it didn't take us long to get our rig out of the motor pool and on line with the rest of our unit. We lived in off post housing, but still had our RATT rig ready before the guys who lived right here on post!

SSgt. Porker hadn't made it in yet, and a few of the guys were dragging ass. I immediately assumed control of my squad and began to direct a few wayward soldiers to where they needed to be. One private in particular, named Bailey, was drunk and wouldn't get out of bed. Top told me to "Get his ass out here RIGHT NOW!" so I immediately went into his room, walked over to his bed and kicked the metal frame so hard that the bed moved a few inches. "Let's go, Beetle Bailey," I shouted at the top of my lungs. He rolled over in his bed and looked surprised to see me standing there. "Leave me alone, you aint in charge of me" was his response. I yanked the blanket off of him and told him if he didn't get his ass up right now, I would lose all my rank for kicking his ass! He looked up at me, saw the serious look in my eyes, jumped out of bed, and began to get dressed.

As I left his room, I told him he had five minutes to get to the motor pool . . . or else! I instinctively filled the vacuum created by SSgt. Porkers absence, and got the rest of my platoon "squared away" and ready to "roll out". As I assisted Top in directing the last of our vehicles out of the motor pool, SSgt. Porker finally arrived. He asked me if I had the crypto gear that was stored in the safe, and the codes for authentication. He also asked if all of our squad was present and accounted for. I answered, "YES Sgt." to each question, aware that I had done everything that HE was supposed to have done. As we stood outside of our vehicles, waiting for the order to roll out, Top walked up to SSgt Porter and I, patted me on the back and said, "Good job Walcott!" He looked at my half-drunk platoon Sgt., rolled his eyes, and walked away, shaking his head.

The commanding officer's jeep drove to the front of the convoy and my unit rolled out of the gates of Merrill Barracks in full battle gear . . . We were only a few kilometers from the East German and Czech borders, and with all the talk by President Reagan about tearing down the Berlin Wall; we knew that things could escalate quickly.

"I don't give a FUCK" said Shorty, as we drove down the autobahn. "I'm bustin' caps at any mother fucker who busts at me." As I locked and loaded my M-16, I exchanged macho; tough talk with my friend, but inside I was becoming acutely aware that in a few minutes I might have to actually use deadly force against some Russian or East German soldier who wanted to kill me. We were strictly forbidden from having live ammo, but Shorty and I would steal a round or two each time we went to the firing range until we had enough to fill a magazine.

"Whussup Walcott?" said Shorty, as I sat in the passenger seat, smoking a cigarette. "You kinda quiet over there". "Nothin, man" I said, as I suspiciously eye balled each car we passed. Any one of them could be a potential terrorist and I wasn't taking any chances. I didn't want to kill anyone, but if I were forced to, I wouldn't hesitate. I used to look at Germany as a friendly environment, but ever since the La Belle discothèque bombing, I had become increasingly paranoid.

We pulled off the autobahn and drove through the Black Forest for a few miles until we reached the staging area. Shorty and I had our rig "online" and were draping camouflage over our area to conceal us from aerial surveillance. The commanding officer, 1st Sgt. and Sgt Porker came by to inspect us and we were commended on our area of operation. After a brief Q & A by the C.O. that we passed with flying colors, we were instructed to join the rest of the unit in formation. Once we were all present and accounted for, we all breathed a sigh of relief as the commanding officer informed us that it was all just a drill.

As we broke down our rig and prepared to head back to base, Top came over and asked me to walk with him. "I'm proud of you son," he said as we walked around the perimeter. "You had me worried when you first got here, but you've turned out to be a damn fine soldier". "Thanks Top", I replied. "You showed true leadership skills this morning during the alert, son. Your orders are on my desk," he said as he removed my PFC stripes and replaced them with "Specialist 4th Class" insignia. Specialist was a rank equivalent to corporal and I was so overjoyed that I couldn't contain myself. "YES" I exclaimed, as I made a fist and jerked my elbow back and forth. "Thanx Top" I said as I attempted to hug him. "Whoa" said my 1st Sgt. as he held his hands up. "I don't hug anyone but my momma, son, and even then she better have a damn good reason!" he said with a playful smile.

In the weeks that followed, my self-esteem and confidence grew tremendously. I was proving to myself that I was worthy of happiness and success. I no longer felt like I was destined to be a "fuck up" and I enjoyed my new status as a potential candidate for sergeant stripes. When I told Weezy, she was elated! She was so proud of me. Her face beamed as we celebrated over a bottle of white zinfandel at a cozy little jazz club on the outskirts of town. We sat at our table excitedly making plans for our future, because we both knew that my promotion meant above all things, more money! When we got home, she playfully referred to me as "Specialist Walcott" as we incorporated my new rank into a little game we liked to call "Soldier Boy"!

CHAPTER 20

Movin' on Up!

I enjoyed being a soldier immensely, and it showed in the way I did my job and how I carried myself. Whether I was in uniform or in "civies", I walked with a confident stride and my gear was always "squared away". To this day, I still tuck my laces down the insides of my shoes and keep my gig line straight. I used Top as my role model and emulated his military style. 1st Sgt. Hilliard had a certain swagger about him that exuded confidence, and as my confidence grew, the easier it was for me to walk tall and proud. I had his style down to every detail. From the way he creased his hat, to the "T" crease that was starched into the back of his uniform shirt.

When I was addressing my subordinates, I addressed them with authority, but always in a respectful way; just like Top. Other than a few minor verbal altercations, I got along great with all the soldiers in my unit, even my superiors. I developed a reputation as a "squared away" soldier and earned the respect of my chain of command. Others soldiers throughout the ranks only hung out with guys and gals of their rank, but I enjoyed the best of both worlds. I could hang out with the lower ranking soldiers and party like a rock star till the break of dawn, but I could also be the poised, well-mannered gentleman when my wife and I were invited to the Command Sergeant Major's home for dinner. Weezy and I were quite the social butterflies and frequently got invited to the social events of the higher-ranking cadre. It was almost unheard of for a lower ranking soldier such as myself to be invited to an officers home, so you can imagine the pride I felt as I watched my wife have cocktails with the Sergeant Majors wife as I drank 30 year old scotch with the elite members of my unit.

The same commanding officer who had asked my 1st Sgt. months ago, "Why they keep sending us these fuck ups", had become impressed with my soldiering skills also. He pulled me to the side one day after inspection and suggested that I enter the soldier of the month competition. I accepted his nomination gracefully and couldn't wait to tell my buddies. Most of my peers dismissed the competition as bullshit because it meant putting extra time and effort into your appearance and how well you did your job. To even be nominated meant that you were displaying exemplary military skills and had caught the eye of your chain of command. If a soldier planned on making a career and moving up the ranks during peacetime, this wasn't a bad award to have in your file. I accepted the challenge with enthusiasm and immediately called Weezy with the good news.

In the weeks before the competition, Weezy helped me study basic military knowledge and gave me mock interviews to prepare me. I ate drank and shit Army as I became obsessed with the challenge before me. My peers even playfully began to refer to me as "Sarge" because although I was just a Spec 4, I carried myself like I was already a sergeant!

Up until this point in my life, I had thought of myself as a loser. A High School drop out that joined the Army only as a last resort when his hopes of becoming a teacher went down the drain. I had finally found something that I not only was good at, but also enjoyed immensely. No longer was I just Miles Walcott from the block, I had become Specialist 4th Class Miles P. Walcott of the United States Army and nothing was going to stop me from becoming "All That I Could Be !"

Some of the fifteen or so competitors in the running had more rank and experience than me, but I wasn't fazed in the least. I knew deep inside that I would have to compete at least three or four more times before I actually won, but I was determined to give them a run for their money! As we sat in the lobby of the command suite waiting for our interviews, I watched the more seasoned and decorated soldiers make final adjustments to their uniforms in front of the floor to ceiling mirror that adorned the lavish suite of offices that the company commander, the executive officer and 1st Sgt occupied. Some stood alone by themselves and you could see the intensity in their eyes as they spoke to themselves in low tones, practicing answers to the anticipated questions. I sat calmly in a chair, confident that if I didn't know it now, I never would. When my turn came, I walked confidently into the Sgt major's office and won the competition . . . hands down!

I enjoyed somewhat of a celebrity status as I walked around on post and people whom I didn't even know came up to me and congratulated me. I was brimming with self-confidence. Okay, honestly? I became and arrogant SOB and I felt as if I was untouchable. Instead of taking my honor with humility and grace, I began thinking that I was "The Shit". The fact that I was selling and smoking hash, bootlegging liquor and cigarettes on the black market and STILL won soldier of the month made my ego swell to huge proportions. Every time my unit had a piss test, my urine was never tested because I was cool with the 1st Sgt and I never gave him any reason to think that I was doing any illegal drugs.

I thought I was being slick, but what I was really doing was perpetrating a fraud on myself. I was violating the very morals and ethics that I was trying to embrace. I was "super soldier" by day, practicing honesty and integrity, but after the final formation of the day when Top handed out mail and made special announcements, I became the opposite of what I was representing all day long. I would go home to shit, shower and shave before I put on my street clothes and head to downtown Nuremberg to get my "hustle" on.

At least 50% of the soldiers on post smoked hashish. For reasons unbeknownst to us, good old-fashioned marijuana was scarce in Germany. Occasionally, one of us would receive a twenty-dollar bag of weed from a friend back in the "States" and turn it into a hundred dollars easily, because marijuana went for twenty bucks a matchbox. It was much too risky to do on a regular basis because if you got caught you would surely get court marshaled.

Hashish on the other hand, was available abundantly. The Turks had the hash game on lock, and if you wanted to buy or sell hash, you needed to have a Turkish connect. On any given day, I could make 50 to a hundred dollars pocket money, but every two weeks on payday I would make no less than 500 dollars in one night, all from a one hundred dollar investment. Guys were getting busted all the time trying to go to the bars and cop hash. It was hard to tell a bearded Turk from a bearded undercover cop. If they weren't caught in a "sting", the Polizei picked them off as they left the bar with the hash in their pockets. Americans stuck out like a sore thumb. If a G.I. walked into a bar and was followed into the bathroom by one of the many Middle Eastern drug dealers, it didn't take a rocket scientist to figure out what was going on.

If you were caught "copping" by the German Police or "burned" a piss test, Uncle Sam would prosecute you to the fullest extent of the law. As much as American soldiers loved to smoke hash, there was too much risk involved in copping it. However, if someone, say me for instance, copped hashish wholesale and bought it on post, it would eliminate the risk of getting arrested! I had a pretty good relationship with a couple of Turkish drug dealers and once I found out how much money I could make buying wholesale, I was more than happy to facilitate the supply and demand process! I found out that I could make up to five hundred dollars off of a hundred dollar slab of hash and quickly became quite the "entrepreneur"!

My "connect" lived in an apartment that was off the beaten path. It was in an affluent neighborhood with locked gates at the entrances. I would go to his lavish apartment and have a drink or two and share a bowl of hash with him as we listened to the latest rap music. I would marvel at the Turkish tapestries on the walls and the fancy, bejeweled silver chalices that he insisted we drink from, years before "Pimp Cups" became fashionable for thugs. He had a hand carved marble chess set in the middle of his coffee table and it was mandatory that we played at least one game before we got down to business.

Akbar, aka "The Turk", would buy as much American liquor as I could carry and we both made a hefty profit from it. He had connects with local bar owners who paid him handsomely for the coveted Jim Beam and Jack Daniels that I sold him. He always put an obscenely large piece of hash in his "Hookah" pipe but I never took more than two or three pulls because the hash was just that good. Afterwards, I would pay him $100 and he would wrap a piece of hash about the size of a pack of cigarettes in Saran Wrap. I would then place the package between my butt cheeks and drive right past the drug-sniffing dogs that were at the front gates of the base.

Once inside, I would go to Shorty's room where I would cut it up into $10 and $20 pieces re-wrapped in cellophane for sale. After cutting off a nice slab for my buddy, I still had enough left to smoke and make a nice profit.

Chapter 21

Head Nigga in Charge

Winning soldier of the month made me eligible to compete in the soldier of the year competition. To become soldier of the year, I had to compete against over 400 other soldiers from different units from all over Germany, in a series of semifinals. It was so cool being driven to different Army posts, escorted by my company commander and winning the competition each time. We were judged on how well we did on a written test, drill and ceremony skills, firing range scores and an interview with the Brigade Commander, who was a general. During the interview, we were judged on our appearance, overall job performance and how well we answered his questions. The Voice, made a pathetic attempt to discourage me, but I quickly dismissed it due to my newfound confidence and self-esteem. All the contestants waited anxiously in the courtyard as our scores were tabulated. I was competing against more experienced soldiers than myself, most of which outranked me, so you can imagine my surprise when it was announced that Specialist 4th Class Miles P. Walcott had won soldier of the year!

My ego was swollen with pride and arrogance now, and no one could tell me a thing. Sgt. Porker tried to discipline me during formation and I openly defied his authority in front of the rest of the platoon. He pointed out that I had missed a loop with my belt and to fix it "Right now". As I fixed my belt, I muttered words to the effect that my belt was still tight enough that two skinny German kids couldn't pull my pants off, much to the amusement of the rest of the platoon. By now, everyone knew secretly about the incident in the alley, and when the whole platoon burst out in laughter, I enjoyed watching the look of embarrassment on his face. I had become a thorn in his side as I took advantage of the fact that I was the H.N.I.C. I felt untouchable and abused my celebrity status instead of remaining humble.

He "called me on the carpet" in front of Top and accused me of undermining his authority. I acted all innocent and pointed out that maybe he was giving me a hard time because he didn't win Soldier of the Year. Top told him that I was about to become a sergeant soon, and if he had something to say to me, Sgt Porker should do it away from the other troops. This further inflated my ego and infuriated Sgt Porker. After that, I strutted around post like I was the H.N.I.C. From that point forward, I would always look at Sgt. Porker with a defiant "I wish you would . . ." look on my face. He backed off me but I knew he was waiting for me to slip up because he would make little slick comments about people selling hash on post and then look at me when he was done talking.

They say, "You can take the boy out of the 'hood, but you can't take the 'hood out of the boy" and that was certainly true in my case. Instead of using my intelligence to become a better soldier, I began to use it to become a better hustler. I began to purchase larger quantities of hashish from Akbar because the more you brought the more money you could make.

I became quite creative at the ways in which I would complete my drug transactions because CID was becoming increasingly more aggressive in cracking down on dealers and buyers. C.I.D. was the Criminal Investigative Department of the Military Police. I had a system where I would stash $20 pieces of hash around the barracks and when someone wanted to buy, I would have them place the money in a desk drawer, and then instruct them where to retrieve their drugs so that no one ever actually saw me make a transaction. Guys I didn't know that well would come up to me with a total stranger and ask for hash and I would angrily tell them that I didn't sell hash and to never ask me again or I would turn them in. I knew that the undercover M.P.'s would try and trap dealers that way, so I only dealt with people I knew.

There was a soft, quiet voice inside that told me that I was better than this . . . that I had too much to lose, but there was also a much louder voice that told me that there was too much money to be made. I chose to listen to the latter. That Voice that used to ridicule me when I fucked up, was no longer just my antagonist, it became my biggest fan! "*You are making a KILLING man*!" it would say. *"You are too slick for these mother fuckers, Miles. Just be careful, and you can make a mint!"* I was rolling in the dough, and my arrogance spilled over into my marriage.

The "woman of my dreams" was no longer "enough" for me, and I justified my philandering ways by listening to the Voice inside that told me that I was much too young to be devoted to just one woman. I began to get into arguments with my wife because I would come home late, and sometimes not come home at all till the next day. "*How dare she question you?"* The Voice would ask. "*Doesn't she realize who you are?" "You are Soldier of the mother fucking YEAR! And you can do whatever the fuck you wanna do!"* The voice inside was trying to convince me that my behavior was perfectly acceptable, and I liked what it was saying. I had become totally self-centered, and her needs were no longer important to me. It was all about me and what I wanted.

I had become well known down at "The Wall" as the "go to" guy for hash and American liquor. Instead of hanging out on the street to ply my wares, I would set up shop in one of the prostitutes "flats" and have her ask the "johns" if they needed hash or liquor as they passed by. Most of the time, they would give me one sort of sexual favor or another for a twenty dollar piece of hash or a $12.99 bottle of Jim Beam. I justified sleeping with hookers because I didn't actually pay cash for ass like most guys did. Never mind that it was morally reprehensible. Never mind that these women slept with men all day every day for a living. All I knew was that when I was "in the house" I got treated like a king. Once I opened up a bottle of American liquor and fired up some hash it was "on and poppin"!

One chick in particular would let me "set up shop" in her apartment for a few hours a night and call her friends and associates, who would come buy hash, liquor and cigarettes from me at a discounted price. It was always party time, and I got a twisted sense of pride when my buddies would come by and see me on the couch with no less than two sexy hookers dressed in next to nothing, rubbing on my chest and crotch, as I tossed a piece of hash on the table and told them to "spark dat shit up".

Deep down inside, I was dying. All that "Gangsta" shit I was doing was just a façade to impress my peers. Winning Soldier of the Year wasn't even enough to fill the void within me. I was living a double life, and it was beginning to catch up with me. I started coming to work late and my uniform wasn't as sharp as it used to be. My job performance was suffering and my relationships with my superiors and subordinates began to suffer. I was downright insubordinate to Sgt Porker and came close to punching him in the face one day if it wasn't for my man Shorty pulling me away from him.

Life at home was beginning to suffer also. We were no longer the happy couple that we had been in the past, now all we did was argue and fight. I resented my wife for calling me on my unacceptable behavior and even got into a fight with her one night when I came home drunk. I put her in a headlock during the fight and she bit me on my chest so hard that I still have the scar to this day. Needless to say, that was the last time I put my hands on her!

I was spending more and more time out partying and whoring around at The Wall and didn't care about anything but the next drink or hit of hash. I had gone from smoking just on the weekends, to smoking every day. As soon as I got up in the morning, I took a couple hits of hash before I even got out of the bed.

Eventually, my wild ways began to catch up with me and I "burned" a piss test. Top was deeply disappointed that his star soldier tested positive for THC and he made it a point to use me as the example for the rest of the unit. I felt ashamed and embarrassed, not because I was remorseful, but because I got caught! I was busted down a rank to Private First Class and my ego was crushed, as I was restricted to the barracks and given latrine duty. I also had to endure the smart assed remarks from other soldiers as I gave the hallway a "Free Shine". The worst part of my punishment was not being able to go home after the day was over. Because of all the dirt I had done behind my wife's back, I imagined her doing the same to me while I was restricted to the barracks, in spite of the fact that she was a virtuous and loyal woman.

Being "Top Dog" had become my identity, and now that I had lost that title, I felt like a failure. I began to feel hopeless. I had lost all hope of ever making sergeant and the voice inside me was relentless in its antagonism of me.

"Look at you, you piece of *shit*" it would tell me. "*You had it all, and now you are just a punk-assed private again, buffing the hallways like the fuck up that you are!*" I began to lose all of the false pride that I had built myself up with. The façade came crumbling down as I lost hope. My Army career and my marriage were in a shambles and these were the two things that I relied on to show the world I was somebody. No longer was I spit shined and polished, I walked around post with dull boots and a wrinkled uniform. There is nothing wrong with being proud of yourself, but when you are filled with false pride you see how shallow it is when shit goes wrong. I began to consider suicide and was constantly thinking of the M-16 rounds that I had stashed in my apartment. "*A bullet through the brain would make all this go away,*" said the menacing voice in my head, but a softer, gentler voice insisted that I hold on and not give up.

I was forced to attend drug and alcohol "classes" where they tried to help me see the errors of my ways, but I was convinced that my only problem was letting myself get caught dirty on the piss test. Instead of trying to figure out how I was going to stop getting high, I was more concerned with how I could "beat" the next piss test! I had become so entangled in my web of self-deceit that I truly believed that it was the Army's fault things were going sour and if my life was going to get any better, I needed to get out of the Army!

I went from Soldier of the Year to Fuck Up of the Year. I would get so drunk at the Enlisted Men's Club that my buddies had to carry me back to the barracks at night. They gave me the nickname "Half Dead" from the movie Penitentiary because now, when I drank, I drank myself into a "Half Dead" stupor.

After I had been on restriction for 30 days, I was allowed to attend the company party that was held at a park called the "Dikes". I used to mingle with the upper echelons of my unit at such functions, but now I pretty much stayed to myself. I had alienated myself from both the upper and lower ranks and was now an outcast. The higher ranking soldiers looked at me with disdain and the lower ranking soldiers didn't want to be caught associating with a known "Head" which was the moniker we gave people who smoked anything stronger than cigarettes.

CHAPTER 22

The Company Party

"Damn Shorty, I'm high as fuck!" It was hot as hell outside and I'd been drinking all day at the company party, I was smoking a hash laced joint with my homeboy "Shorty" from Jersey and his cute, German girlfriend, Milla". We preferred to smoke hash out of a bong or pipe, but it was too risky. Occasionally, the Military Police would come through the barracks with drug sniffing dogs and being in possession a hash pipe was a quick way to get busted and sent to military prison, so we used rolling papers with a 50:50 mix of hash and tobacco.

"Puff, puff, pass, nigga!" Shorty scolded, prompting me to pass the jay, as I took my third long pull. Lately, I wasn't the sociable get high partner I had used to be . . . now, one of anything was too many, and a thousand was never enough! My appetite for drugs was beginning to become insatiable and my friends had begun to shun me due to my greedy habits. Getting high was no longer a social thing; it was something I HAD to do. I treated every opportunity to get high as my last, trying to gobble up every last drop, puff or whatever else I found before me, not caring if whoever I was getting high with got their fair share. People didn't really care for folks like me who would hog the whole joint, bottle or whatever else we were getting high off of.

After we finished the jay, Shorty and his girlfriend returned to the party, but I had to get home and get some sleep because I had guard duty in 6 hours. I staggered along the bike path as I struggled to keep my 6'3" tall, dark and handsome frame from veering off into the bushes! Five years of regular exercise had me in top physical condition, but I was no match for warm brandy and hash on a hot summer's day.

Suddenly, the sound of more than one dirt bike filled the air and, although I was drunk and high as hell, I figured it might be a good idea to get out the way. Three white dudes, dressed in black, raced by me on dirt bikes . . . a little too close for comfort! I quickly stumbled to the side of the path to avoid being hit. "Geez, you almost ran me da fuck OVER", I shouted as they sped past. They sported Mohawk haircuts, black eye liner and were covered in tattoos. They were wearing dusty, black leather boots with silver buckles and their long, black leather coats flapped in the wind as they raced up the path. "Fuckin' punk rockers," I said out loud, as I continued on my way. Suddenly, their bikes slowed, and they spun around to face me. I could feel my heart rate increase as they stared at me from about 50 feet away." *Look at you*", said that familiar voice in my head "*Don't just stand there like a little bitch . . . DO SOMETHING*!" I flicked my cigarette away, but held on to my bottle of liquor as they revved their engines and began to speed towards me.

"Go back to America, Nigger Boy", one of them shouted as they began their approach. I could see now that these weren't the kind of punk rockers that I used to see hanging around Toads Place when me and the fellas would go downtown New Haven to "hit" on the "Yale Chicks". These dudes had swastika tattoos and a tough look in their eyes that said," We ain't here to pass a hash joint around with you or share your bottle!" "These guys must be those skinheads I've heard about", I said to myself as I began to emerge from my drug and alcohol induced fog.

FUCK YOU, American Nigger!" another one yelled, as they continued to taunt me. "*Hmm . . . never been called an AMERICAN nigger before*" I chuckled to myself as I quickly became aware that this shit was about to get ugly.

I was full of rage at myself for screwing up my Army career and that rage took the form of me abusing drugs and alcohol. Instead of lashing out at others, I turned my rage inward and it became self-hatred. I was happy abusing myself and disrespecting all that I thought I stood for, but I was going to be damned if I was going to let these three skinheads disrespect me!

"Fuck you too, cracker!" I yelled, as one rode pass me. I was carrying a half drunken bottle of E&J brandy in my right hand and I was beginning to get nervous because with each pass, they came closer and closer to mowing me down with their dirt bikes. He and his two buddies had been harassing me for the last hundred yards or so, shouting racial slurs at me and spitting at me each time they passed.

"Is "fuck you too, cracker', the best you can come up with?". Fear and adrenalin raced through my veins as I quickly began to sober up and wonder how I was going to hold my own against these three guys. I was having flashbacks of the white guys who jumped me when I was a kid and I wasn't going to let these bastards hurt the "little boy" trapped in this grown man's body!

On their next pass, a well-placed "hock" spit found its mark smack dab in the middle of my face and that was enough to convert me in the blink of an eye from a drunk, frightened young soldier into a vicious sociopath who would stop at nothing to protect "Little Miles". It was as if a switch had been flipped in my brain and suddenly, all the rage that I felt towards myself was turned outwards towards my attackers . . . damn the consequences. It wasn't so much of an impulsive, drunken decision as it was an acutely calculated, fine-tuned choice. Now, instead of imploding, I was ready to explode . . . the likes of which I had never seen before! I didn't give a fuck anymore and had nothing to lose. I knew deep inside that I wasn't going to stop smoking hash or "hustling", so it was only a matter of time before I was going to get kicked out. Might as well go out with a bang!

Instead of flying into a rage, I stopped walking and acted like I was just standing there wiping my face with my left hand and smearing the disgusting phlegm on my pants leg, but in my mind, I was carefully planning my attack. No longer feeling the effects of the hash and alcohol, the adrenalin had taken over, my senses became fine-tuned and I began to formulate my course of attack. My Dad always said," The best defense is a damn good OFFENSE!

Images of my past suddenly came flooding through my mind. Vivid pictures of the scared, confused 12 year old boy being molested by his aunt and uncle, images of the white boys who jumped me in front of Molly, images of "Big Al" busting my lip wide open . . . the guy in the alley with a knife to my chest. All the rage from each and every time I was ever hurt came flooding into my mind adding more fuel to the raging inferno that burned within me. I decided right then and there that these sons of bitches, who thought they could spit in my face, would pay for all the times that I was ever a victim.

With my head tilted down, I continued to wipe my face but I was peeking through my fingers, carefully timing the moment that the next skinhead would come within arms reach. It was as if the sun had become brighter and my sense of hearing became acutely intense. I could hear them speaking in a foreign language, and although I didn't understand what they were saying, I knew they meant business and it was time to take action or become a victim. I could see one of them approaching as I wiped the vile smelling spit from my face, I could hear him "hock" up another load of spit and at the precise moment he reared his head back to unload another spit bomb at me . . . BLAM! I took a quick step towards him, swung the E&J bottle with all my might and caught him square in the face.

He didn't even see it coming! The impact of my blow shattered the bottle. Glass and liquor flew everywhere, as he flew off the back of the dirt bike and landed on his back, slamming his head into the pavement. The momentum of the dirt bike caused him to slide about twenty feet on his back and he came to a stop in a bloody heap. My attacker lay motionless, on the ground and the rider less dirt bike crashed into a bush with its wheels still spinning. The other two skinheads jumped off their bikes to tend to him and when they saw how badly he was injured, they cursed loudly in German. Now they turned their attention to me.

Not giving them a chance to formulate an attack, I immediately pounced on them and began wildly punching them both with my fist and the broken remains of the E&J bottle while screaming at the top of my lungs," Leave me alone! Leave me the FUCK alone!"

One of the skinheads was able to land a hard blow to my head and I felt myself losing consciousness. I was sure that if I got knocked out they would surely kill me, so I shook my head wildly, trying to regain my focus. I instantly made a conscious decision that today I would NOT get my ass kicked like in the past! The days of Miles Walcott getting his ass kicked were over, and I was willing to do whatever it took to protect myself. The "anger switch" that I used to be able to control at will was broken. For the first time in my life, I was unable to control the rage inside of me. It was a combination of rage towards myself for fucking up my marriage and my Army career coupled with rage against every aggressor that ever hurt me. It was as if all the fury that had been building up inside me since childhood suddenly came flooding out in an uncontrollable torrent.

Flashbacks of the nonchalant looks on my aunt and uncles faces as they stole my innocence, and the way the "white boys" laughed as they ran down the street after kicking my ass in the snow flickered through my mind. I could see the smug look on the chess coaches face as he grabbed my collar in that dank basement hallway back in junior high and Big Al's fist coming at me in slow motion as he scarred my face for life. I could see my buddy Reggie laughing after we fought and the guy in the dark alley's face when he thought he had found an easy mark. I also saw the sarcastic smirk on SSgt Parkers acne covered face as he supervised me buffing the floors after my fall from grace.

I had heard of people's lives flashing before their eyes just before death, but this was slightly different. In a brief instant, I saw the faces of everyone who ever hurt me flash before my eyes and each vision added fuel to my fury. It was as if I was having an out of body experience as I contemplated taking the life of my present aggressors.

As the second skinhead lay, bleeding on the ground holding the side of his face to stem the flow of blood from his gaping facial wound, I stood over the third, holding his collar with one hand and the broken bottle . . . deciding whether or not to stab him in the neck with it or just slam his head into the concrete.

The next things I knew, the German Polizei were ordering me to drop the bottle and get on the ground. As I began to return to reality, I looked at my bloody hand and the sharp remains of the E&J bottle in disbelief. Was that *my* hand holding an instrument of death? Was I about to stab someone in the neck, quite possibly killing him? As I took brief pause from my murderous mayhem, I could hear shouts in the distance.

At first, it was as if the shouts of "Halt" were coming from far away, but as the voices became more and more clear, I could see police uniforms in my peripheral vision. I felt a brief feeling of relief wash over me as I mistakenly thought that help had finally arrived. I dropped the remains of the bottle and began to rise up off the skinhead, and then suddenly I was tackled by a German police officer.

I quickly realized that the Polizei were not there to help me! I became even more enraged. I was being treated as the aggressor and felt a level of rage never before experienced rise up inside me and consume my mind. *These* guys started it. *They* were the aggressors not me, and yet I was being told to get on the ground. Now I was in a full-blown rage again and I was convinced that the Polizei were in league with the skinheads. It was me against them. "The Voice" said that they were about to kill "us" so I struggled free of the Polizei officer and went berserk, swinging wildly and screaming for everyone to leave me alone like I was a scared little child. It seemed like the German police were multiplying at an exponential rate like the "Agents" in the Matrix movie. It was as if everything began to move in slow motion as I anticipated each Polizei's blow and counter-punched with a blow of my own.

Whack! I felt the impact of the Billy club on my skull as one of the Polizei who couldn't have been much older than me, cracked me in the head. I let out an animalistic, guttural growl and caught the stick in midair as he took his second swing. The Billy club smashed into my hand, and I ignored the pain as I snatched it from him and began beating him and anyone else who came close enough. I was out of control, and it seemed like I was watching myself from above as I mentally transformed from a scared 23 year old into the Incredible Hulk! I fought like a crazed animal and I didn't think I would make it through this fight alive as I watched more Polizei pull up, tires screeching, to reinforce the 6 or 7 who were already there.

Realizing that I wasn't going to give up, one of the German Polizei stood in front of me and leveled his 9mm automatic at my chest and yelled, "HALT, you fuck, or I shoot you!" in broken English. I could see by the nervous look in his eyes that if I didn't stop immediately, he would justifiably blow my ass away! I was high as hell, but not stupid! I was in what appeared to be an uncontrollable rage, but the site of the 9mm snapped me back into reality. My Momma aint raise no fools, so I lay face down on the ground and allowed myself to be handcuffed, but they were not about to let me off that easy.

As I lay on the sidewalk handcuffed, they began to kick me full force. They kicked me in the back, the ass, the nuts, head, anywhere they could connect with their boots. When they were done whipping my ass, they dragged my bloodied body across the street and were attempting to throw me into the back of police van. Even the German citizens who had begun to gather at the scene were pleading with the Polizei to stop beating me! My clothes were in tatters and it seemed like I was bleeding to death by the amount of blood that covered my face and clothes. I observed some of the German police bleeding from their heads and faces from the melee that had just occurred as three of them tried to put me into the police van. I wouldn't comply with their orders to place my whole body into the van and they began slamming the door on my leg as I screamed at the top of my lungs for them to leave me alone. I was beyond rage by now, oblivious to the world around me.

Sounds of more sirens and the shouts of concerned German citizens and police were muffled by the pure adrenalin rush that had possessed my body; my heart was beating so hard I could feel each beat in my temples. Badly beaten and horrified that I was about to be beaten to death, I began kicking dents into the side of the van. I kicked a window out and at that point the Polizei managed to shackle my feet together. I was growling like a rabid animal by now and even tried to bite the police dog that they put in the van with me in an attempt to intimidate me. They sprayed mace in my face and that just added fuel to my rage as I began kicking wildly with both legs tied together. Although I couldn't see, I was able to kick a couple of them by following my ears. The dog was biting my sneaker and shaking my foot back and forth so I pulled my legs into the fetal position and then, with all the force I could muster, slammed the dog's head into the inside panel of the van. He let out a high-pitched whelp, and the next thing I knew a Billy club blow to my head knocked me out cold.

I don't remember anything after that until I was awakened by the sound of a billy club being banged against the bars of my cell. As I was aroused from my stupor, I noticed the floor of the cell and my clothes were splattered in brown spittle and spit. Apparently, getting medical attention for the asshole who just whipped at least six of Nuremberg's finest wasn't a priority. While I lay on the floor, shackled, beaten and unconscious, the tobacco chewing Polizei used me for target practice with their tobacco spittle! I attempted to wipe the repulsive brown goop from my face and realized that my hands and feet were still shackled. I could hear the voices of German police nearby and began to fear that they would resume my beating if I woke up, so I lay there motionless, feigning unconsciousness.

As I lay in a pathetic heap on the cold cell floor, I suddenly heard an American voice loudly demand that I be untied immediately. I looked up and was relieved to see three Army M.P's. who had come to retrieve me from the German jail. They knew I had committed some type of crime, but they also knew that one of their own was lying on a cell floor badly beaten and covered in spit! If any of them ever read this book, I want to thank them for standing up for me, even though at my court martial, the commander of the military police headquarters had nothing in his report describing the condition they found me in.

After the Army MP's untied me and stood me on my feet, I began to sob uncontrollably. I wasn't crying from the pain I was in, I was crying because I truly believed that I was going to be beaten to death that day, and I was relieved to see American faces. I had already decided that if the Germans ever untied me, I was going to punch the closest one in the face as retaliation for all the spittle that stained my tattered clothes. I knew once I did that, the beating would resume and I may not make it out alive, so the sight of American faces gave me hope in what appeared to be a hopeless situation.

As reality kicked in, I became aware that every part of my body was in agonizing pain. My face was horribly disfigured from the beating and the bites from the German Sheppard. I could barely walk due to the pain in my ankles from being hog tied, and my back and torso screamed out in pain each time I tried to move. The German police laughed and ridiculed me in German as the M.P.'s escorted my beaten, broken body through the police station, out to the waiting van.

"Auf Wiedersehn, Schotsy", said one of the German police officers, a salutation reserved only for females, as the rest of them laughed and mocked me. I just ignored them and held my head down in shame, as I was damn near carried out of the German police headquarters by the Military Police.

CHAPTER 23

Auf Weidersehn Deutchland!

At my court martial, I found out that the skinhead who hock spit in my face was actually an off duty German cop. That explained why the police report mentioned nothing of them attacking me. They portrayed me as a drunken animal that attacked a police officer and his friends for no apparent reason. I acknowledged the drunken part, but tried to explain that I didn't become aggressive until I was spat upon.

Sgt. Porker was called to testify, and when asked by the prosecutor whether I should be given leniency, of course he testified that I was an "incorrigible" who should be sent to prison. He actually looked happy that I was being prosecuted as he finally got to see the thorn in his side removed. The "dirty" urines were also brought up, and that killed any credibility I had, if any.

After hearing of the injuries that I had inflicted on the German police, the judge asked me if I had ever had any martial arts training and I replied, "Only what the Army taught me". When the judge asked if the Army also taught me to assault officers of the law and innocent civilians, I knew I had lost any hope of leniency, and accepted the fact that I was going to do time in prison. The rest of the trial is a blur to me but I do remember the pained look on Tops face as his star troop was led away in shackles. The look on his face gave me such a strong feeling of guilt and embarrassment that I broke down in tears. Sgt. Parker leaned in and said, "Not so tough now, are you? He thought I was crying because I was going to jail, but my tears were from letting myself and everyone else who believed in me down.

The prosecutor wanted to give me the maximum sentence, but my lawyer kept bringing up my exemplary military service and the fact that I had won soldier of the month, quarter and year. I was sentenced to one year of hard labor in prison, suspended after six months, busted down in rank to private and given a bad conduct discharge. I no longer needed the voice to tell me how much of a loser I was . . . I believed it myself.

I plead my case to my congressman and senator back in Connecticut and they both sent me letters that basically said, "You're on your own kid!" I became so enraged that not even my own elected officials wanted to help me that I never voted again until Barak Obama ran for president! I knew that I did a lot of dirt in my time, but in this particular instance I was a victim who was being treated as the aggressor.

If I was embarrassed before, I was now embarrassed times ten! As I was transported to the Mannheim prison under armed escort I thought of Weezy, who was left to fend for herself. While I was doing my time, she was left to bare the shame of being the wife of the fuck up. The Army provided airfare for her to get back to the States and also shipped our personal belongings home, but this was one of the most shameful and embarrassing times of both our lives. The voice inside me reminded me of this twenty-four hours a day.

Thank God for my parents who opened their home up to her until I got back home. They had a vacant apartment in the house they owned an offered it to us rent free until I got back home and was back on my feet again.

Chapter 24

Hard Labor

While awaiting transport to the U.S. at the Army prison in Mannheim, I listened to other prisoners describe Ft. Leavenworth, Kansas. Ft. Leavenworth was one of the oldest maximum-security prisons in the country where only the most hardened prisoners from the armed services went. They told me tales of chain gangs and gang rapes that scared the living shit out of a young soldier such as me. I couldn't believe that after all I had accomplished, I was on my way to the worst prison I could imagine, when all I was doing was defending myself.

I was still of the belief that my problems were the result of an unjust system and that my drinking and drugging had nothing to do with my predicament. It would be years before I was able to make the connection between my drug use and the unmanageability that wreaked so much havoc in my life.

Because I was sentenced to less than a year, I wasn't sent to Ft. Leavenworth as I expected. I was sent to a minimum-security facility at Ft. Sill Oklahoma where we weren't even referred to as inmates. We were called "Correctees" and wore regular Army uniforms instead of the black and white striped jumpsuits that they wore in the "Big House".

My "Hard Labor" consisted of picking up litter around Ft. Sill with the other "correctees" and riding around on a pick-up truck collecting garbage from the regular Army units on post. It was almost like Basic Training all over again as we were awakened at 6am and given physical exercise before being allowed to eat our breakfast. The food there was actually delicious. We dined on fried chicken and steak regularly and even had rabbit stew a few times, which I thoroughly enjoyed!

Although I deeply resented being locked up, I did my "hard labor" with no problems and even got time off for good behavior. None of us "correctees" bothered each other because we all were sentenced to less than a year, and no one wanted time added on to their sentence for fighting. I kept to myself and spent most of my time either doing push-ups next to my bunk or reading. I had taken a sort of "vow of silence" and only spoke when the correctional officers addressed me or if I wanted to ask for seconds in the mess hall.

At first, some of the other "correctees" would try and make small talk or ask if I wanted to play cards or something, but I would just give them an angry scowl and say," Get da fuck out my face". After about a week, no one bothered to say anything to me, which was perfectly fine by me. I was miserable and disgusted with myself, and didn't want anything to do with anyone. All I wanted was to do my time and be free of this place so I could return home to my family and resume my life.

I thought I was better than the "common criminals" that I was locked up with because they deserved to be locked up! I, on the other hand was being "unjustly" persecuted for defending myself. Never mind that I had broken more than a few laws by selling hash, black marketing liquor and cigarettes, smoking hash etc., I truly believed that I was being wrongly prosecuted in spite of the fact that I was under the influence of illegal drugs when the incident with the skin-heads happened.

Reading became my new "drug of choice". Since I couldn't get high anymore, I was able to escape reality in the many books that the facility's library had to offer. My appetite for reading became insatiable as I devoured whole books in a day or two. I read everything from Stephan King novels to the Bible. Sometimes, I would do so many push-ups that I could barely hold the books as I read them.

One day, after I had been locked up for more than a month, I was summoned to the sick bay over the intercom. I had no idea what they could possibly want, but I followed the red tape on the concrete floor to the medical unit. After sitting in the Spartan waiting room for about 15 minutes on a hard assed wooden chair without so much as a Time or Newsweek to read, a pretty, brunette captain came out, wearing a form fitting military style skirt that was just below her knees and introduced herself.

She may as well have been wearing a mini skirt and bikini top because suddenly my hormones were raging. As I assumed the position of attention and attempted to salute her, she offered her hand for me to shake. As I shook her hand, I noticed the softness of it and breathed deeply as I savored the aroma of her subtle perfume. My facial expression softened as I delighted in being in the presence of a woman for the first time in months, and gladly followed her into her office as I checked out her behind and legs as she rounded her desk and sat down.

"So, Private Walcott, how have you been sleeping lately?" she asked. "I've been sleeping fine, why do you ask?" She looked down at a paper on her desk and informed me that the other correctees had been complaining that I was disturbing them by shouting in my sleep. She told me that they reported me yelling, "Get the fuck off me" and "Leave me alone" while I was sleeping. I knew in my mind that I had been having nightmares of my aunt and uncle molesting me and also dreams of being beaten by the German police, but I had no idea that I was shouting in my sleep. She prescribed a sleep medication that apparently worked because there were no more reports of me yelling in my sleep. The nightmares however, persisted.

While I was incarcerated at Ft. Sill, I took a small engine repair class in spite of the fact that I had no interest in mechanics at all. The only reason I took the class was because they gave you time off of your sentence for completing the class. Although I was not mechanically inclined in the least, I passed the class with no problems. It's amazing what a person can accomplish when their freedom is at stake.

Eventually, the day came for me to be released and I was put on a bus to the Oklahoma City airport. I was forced to wear my dress uniform when I was released and it was obvious that my Specialist insignia had been removed, leaving a bare spot where it was previously sewn on. Imagine if you will, a former soldier of the year walking through the airport past other service members who couldn't help but glance at the bare spot on my uniform. As our eyes made brief contact as we passed each other, I felt embarrassed and ashamed of the predicament that I found myself in. Once I was checked in and waiting for my flight, I removed my jacket and carried it over my shoulder in an attempt to hide my disgrace.

Now that I was out of the Army, I had no one else to direct my anger towards except myself! Rage turned inwards becomes depression and little did I know that it would be a very long time before I was able to shake that depression. Hell, I didn't even know I was angry with myself at the time; I still blamed the Army for my misfortune.

CHAPTER 25

The Prodigal Son Returns

My father was a decorated veteran of the Korean War. When I was a kid, I marveled at the pictures of him and his fellow soldiers that were kept in our family album. One picture in particular captivated my attention more than the others. It was a picture of my father and another soldier holding a full-grown eagle by its wings. The eagle had to be at least three feet in height and its wings were spread open to at least four feet. As my father stood holding this eagle with a serious look on his face, it made me feel like he was invincible! When I joined the Army, I felt like the character Kronk in the Disney animated movie, desperately needing my dad's approval. "*Way to go, loser*" said the voice sarcastically. "*Your father will NEVER forgive you for this*!"

Weezy picked me up from Tweed New Haven Airport in our 1986 navy blue Toyota Celica. Although I had been court martialed, the Army was obligated to ship our entire personal belongings home, including our vehicle. As I exited the small airport and walked towards the parking lot, I saw my beautiful wife pulling in with a big smile on her face. It was a cold November evening and I was wearing just my thin dress green jacket and "cunt cap", but when she hugged and kissed me hello, I felt warm all over.

The emotional pain that I had been feeling for the last few months just melted away as I embraced the woman of my dreams once again. We stood in that cold, dark parking lot for what seemed like an eternity and hugged and kissed each other like two teenagers in love! After a while, she put both of her hands on my cheeks and said," You're freezing baby, let's get in the car". Once inside the car, I hit the play button on the cassette player and was happy to hear Public Enemy's "Fight the Power" come booming out of the speakers. On the ride back to my parent's house we spoke of fresh starts and new beginnings. I promised her that we would be fine, but in reality, I was frightened, and had no idea how I was going to support us. I was so happy that my beloved hadn't given up on me. She could have given up on us and went back to Florida, but she decided to hang in there with me. I didn't know how I was going to do it but I vowed to make her proud of me once again.

When we arrived at my parent's house, I felt safe, and at ease . . . a feeling I hadn't felt in a long time. While I was incarcerated, I always felt on edge like I had to watch my back, even in my sleep, but now that I was home I could breathe a sigh of relief. As Weezy and I walked up the stairs to the second floor of my parent's house, I could hear the voices of my parents, siblings, nieces and nephews speaking in excited tones. "He's here!" shouted my ten-year-old niece India, as she ran halfway down the stairs and jumped into my arms. My father greeted me next as I entered the living room with a big smile and a warm bear hug, and kissed me on the cheek. I had no idea how much I missed his scruffy beard gently scratch the side of my face. I couldn't remember the last time he hugged me so tight and I enjoyed every second of it! I searched his face for signs of disapproval, but all I could see was a father who was happy to see his son.

My mom gave me an equally warm embrace. When she was happy, her eyes had a certain way of twinkling! It just went on and on as each of my family gave me a hero's welcome. My niece and nephew Mike and India were amazed with my uniform and didn't give a rat's ass if my stripes were missing or not. Their uncle was home and that's all that mattered. Mike and I recited the rap we had made up when he was a child and India couldn't stop rubbing the tight waves that I had brushed into my head while incarcerated. You would have thought I returned a war hero the way my loved ones greeted me. They could care less of the circumstances of my return; all they cared about was the fact that I was HOME!

The atmosphere in my parent's home was festive. I could smell the distinct aroma of my mom's cooking in the air as I greeted my family for the first time in about three years. Ma playfully suggested to Weezy that she fix her man a plate and my wife happily prepared a plate for me that was fit for a king. As we feasted on my mom's signature dishes of baked macaroni and cheese, collard greens, candied yams and other culinary delights, I basked in the glow of my family's love.

After a few hours of laughter and lighthearted banter with my family, my father and I retired to the den where my dad and I cracked open a couple bottles of Molson Ale. Charlie Walcott only drank the best of anything when it came to alcohol. His bar was fully stocked with Johnny Walker Red Label, Cutty Sark and a wide variety of other "top shelf" liquors and when it came to beer, he only drank Molson's or Heineken's.

Dad's den was his sanctuary. My mother decided the décor of the rest of the house, but the den was dad's realm. The walls were covered with dark, mahogany wood paneling that gave it a cozy feel. Family pictures and African artwork adorned the walls along with an amazing collage that my father created using a three foot enlargement of the Angela Davis picture in which she rocks a huge afro and has her hand raised in a Black Power salute. Pasted around the perimeter of her afro were famous quotes and pictures of famous African Africans. My dad's collage was a work of art, while at the same time, a complete lesson in "Black History".

African statues were lined up on the top of the familiar bookshelf that my dad built himself. It had everything from Herman Melville's Moby Dick and Kurt Vonnegut's Slaughterhouse 5 to The Autobiography of Malcolm X and Message to the Blackman by The Honorable Elijah Muhammad. There was also a healthy serving of the poetry of Langston Hughes and Maya Angelou.

As a teen, my mother and I would spend hours reading in this very den while we waited for dad to return from his job at Harlem Hospital in New York. Sunday mornings were not complete until my father and I sat at the kitchen table reading the Sunday paper. I would start off with the comics and then read each section after my dad was done with it. If it were not for my parents instilling a desire to read in their children, I probably wouldn't be writing this book!

As my father sat down in his plush, brown leather reclining chair, he motioned for me to close the door. I closed it, returned to my seat on the couch and took a swig of my beer. My eyes scanned the room, getting reacquainted with the familiar décor. Dads face became serious and he looked me in the eye and said, "How ya doin, Chief?" using his special nickname for me. I replied that I was ok and happy to be home. He asked me again how I was doing, but this time he paused a second and punctuated the question with, "Really".

I said nothing for a moment while I sat there and pondered how I was really doing. I had just returned home from the Army in disgrace and felt incredibly ashamed and embarrassed of myself. I was full of fear, anger and resentment and had no idea what I was going to do with my life. I was unable to articulate my feelings, so all I could do was let my eyes well up with tears and tighten the muscles around my mouth. I clenched my fists as hard as I could and began shaking my head from side to side as my face contorted into the "ugly face" people make when crying from emotional pain.

My father let me experience my feelings for a few minutes, then sat beside me on the couch and put his arm around my shoulder as I sobbed on his chest. The tighter he held me, the more intense my cry became. My chest heaved as I purged myself of some of the emotional pressure that I had been carrying around for the past year. "Let it out, son" he prompted me. "Cry all you want. If you hold it inside that shit will eat you alive".

All these years, I thought a guy crying was a sign of weakness, but here was my strong, masculine father telling me to cry all I wanted. I looked up to my dad as the ultimate man, and if he said it was ok to bawl my eyes out then so be it. I don't think I had ever cried this hard in my life and the tears kept coming!

There was something cleansing and relieving about crying like that because when I was done, I felt at peace and relaxed as I enjoyed my father's strong embrace. I looked into his eyes and could tell that he was feeling my pain, but I could also see that he loved me. It was so comforting to know that my father was there for me because I had expected him to be angry with me for getting kicked out of the Army, but the exact opposite was true.

After I regained my composure, my father passed me a white linen hanky. As I wiped my face and blew my nose, he sat back down in his recliner and took a sip of his beer. My father was never a man to mince words, so he got right to the point. "You fucked up, son, he said bluntly. "But it's not the end of the world. The best thing you can do is hit the ground running and never look back". I expressed my fear that I wouldn't be able to get a decent job with my record, and he went on to explain to me that it would take at least six months before my record caught up with me, so the sooner I started applying for jobs, the better. "Instead of looking for excuses why you can't get a job" he said, "try looking for reasons why you *can*!" He reassured me that Weezy and I could stay in the first floor apartment rent-free until I was employed, which relieved a ton of stress from my mind. That evening, in my father's den, I experienced unconditional love as he gave me hope in what I thought was a hopeless situation.

After we wrapped up our conversation and shared one more hug, my dad pressed a one hundred dollar bill into my hand. "Take your wife out to dinner tomorrow" he said to me as he winked his eye. I hugged my mom goodnight after kissing her and told her that I loved her as she handed me a large Tupperware container filled with a delicious variety of leftovers from the awesome meal she had prepared.

Weezy said goodnight to my parents before we went downstairs to our apartment and I admired the way she kissed them good night and called them "Ma" and "Dad". Witnessing their affection towards each other was one of the most beautiful things I had ever witnessed.

My lovely wife did a wonderful job decorating our apartment and I complimented her on the fact that she prepared our home all by herself. It was nice to see the black leather living room set and glass coffee table that we purchased in Germany, along with our stereo equipment. My stereo system was my pride and joy. While we were overseas, Weezy worked at the Post Exchange, which entitled her to a nice discount. Over time, we acquired a complete Kenwood stereo system piece by piece; from the reel to reel and cassette deck to the receiver and four foot tall Kenwood speakers. We also had a Kenwood VCR deck and a 36" TV. All that electronic gear fit nicely in our gold trimmed, black lacquer entertainment center. I took great pride in the fact that I owned some of the best stereo equipment on the market and I was very adamant about no one other than Weezy touching it.

While Weezy was putting our food away, I couldn't keep my hands off of her and she playfully scolded me for being "fresh". "I have a nice surprise for you in a little while", she promised. I ignored her admonitions and continued to grab her from behind and try to kiss her neck. She would let me kiss her for a moment, and then squirm away as she made sure the kitchen was straight. "Take that uniform off so I can throw it away, and meet me in the bathroom" she instructed. I happily obliged her and as I made my way back through the house, I found her running a nice hot bath for me.

My beloved instructed me to get in the hot, bubbly water while she went and "got ready". As I sat soaking in a tub for the first time in over a year, she told me to relax and that she would be right back. I lay back in the hot water with a washcloth over my eyes and heard the familiar voice of DJ Vaughn Harper of radio station WBLS coming from the living room speakers, announcing that, "You are now listening to the Quiet Storm".

I heard the bathroom door open and removed the cloth from my eyes as Weezy entered wearing the red and white silk kimono that I had given her on her birthday a couple of years before. She didn't fasten the silk belt that came with it and my eyes devoured her caramel colored body. She was holding a crystal ashtray that contained a fat joint in one hand, and an ice bucket with a bottle of our favorite white wine. She went back to the kitchen and returned with two of our expensive Pfaltzgraf lead crystal glasses that she had begun to collect in Germany. She set everything down on a small table and let the kimono slowly slide off her beautiful body to the floor. My eyes devoured the sight of her smooth flawless skin and the luscious curves of her amazing body. "Mind if I join you?" she asked as I sat straight up in more ways than one. "Not at all baby, there's room for both of us in here" I said with a mischievous smile on my face.

We took a few puffs of the joint and tapped our glasses together as we toasted the fact that we were finally together again and proceeded to have one of the most memorable nights that I can remember.

CHAPTER 26

New Beginnings?

With ample encouragement from my wife, parents and siblings, I was able to dust myself off and get back into the swing of things with ease. Within a month, I landed a job at United Parcel Service delivering packages, which gave my self-esteem a tremendous boost. It made me feel good to be able to help my wife with the bills and not have to depend on her and my parents for money. I have always been a bit of a show off and it made me feel good to step out of my fancy sports car, wearing my brown U.P.S. uniform as the neighbors greeted me when I got home from work. I had just gotten kicked out of the Army and should have been struggling, but I hit the ground running and came up smelling like roses! This was years before I had any idea what a loving God was.

Weezy got a job in the administrative department of the New Haven Register, the local newspaper, so we were able to enjoy a comfortable standard of living. We went out to dinner and movies on a regular basis, enjoying seafood at Captains Galley by the West Haven beach or steaks at Chucks Steak House on the Boston Post Road. The transition from Army life to civilian life went smooth for me, but the voice inside me said that this idyllic life was boring, and I agreed. Deep down inside, I longed for the fast life that I was accustomed to.

Weezy and my cousin Lynne had become close while I was incarcerated. Lynne who was at least fifteen years older than me was my favorite cousin. When I was a kid, she would walk me around the neighborhood in a stroller or take me with her for a bus ride downtown and treat me to ice cream or a slice of pizza. She was drop dead gorgeous and at one time aspired to become a model. Even though she had three kids, she still turned heads wherever she went and she could dress her ass off!

While I was incarcerated, she would come by and scoop Weezy up and they would go out for drinks at the local clubs or meet for lunch since they both worked in close proximity to each other. Lynne and Weezy were like two peas in a pod and I was glad that they had become so close.

Lynne's boyfriend Delvin was one of the biggest coke dealers in New Haven. He was built like a grizzly bear and was as intimidating as one too. He was about 6'4" and had to weigh at least 300 lbs. His dark skin and permanent scowl, framed by a short, salt and pepper gray Afro made him look very intimidating. He carried a 9mm pistol in the back of his waistband at all times and whenever we got into his Mercedes Benz Coupe, he would pass it to me and say, "Put this under the seat for me". He always asked me if I needed any "heat", but I always declined. I didn't feel the need to carry a gun and quite frankly, with my temper, I knew it wasn't a good idea.

Our favorite night spot was a club named "Daniels" in Hamden, and he would insist on paying the tab every time, teasing me that, "They don't take food stamps here". Before we hit the club, Weezy and I would meet Delvin and Lynne at her house where Lynne would help him bag up powdered cocaine for sale. Weezy and I puffed on a jay and had a couple of drinks while the stereo played the latest hip hop and R&B. He would fill a plastic zip lock bag with $50 and $100 packages that were color coded so that he could distinguish between the two.

While we were getting our "buzz on", Delvin would empty out about a quarter of a Newport 100 cigarette and add powdered coke into it. He would then roll it between his big sausage fingers, thoroughly mixing the coke and tobacco, and then run the flame of a cigarette lighter along the length of the altered cigarette, melting the cocaine inside. Once his "Cokerette" was complete, he would light it and pull slowly on it, smoking it halfway down and then pass it to Lynne, who would always take one puff and then set it in the ashtray. The smell of the "Cokerette" was sweet and enticing but I stuck to my weed and beer. Lynne's thing was sniffing, and she would take two to four healthy sized snorts before sitting back and finishing the "Cokerette" as the effects of the coke made her eyes glaze over. They always offered, but I was adamantly against using cocaine in any form since I had seen what it did to people.

Since coming home, I saw a few girls who wouldn't give a guy the time of day in high school, walking up and down the "Hoe Stroll" propositioning men in cars for sex in order to get more coke. Dudes who used to be jocks and playboys walked around in dirty clothes begging for money or trying to sell TV's and VCR's for a fraction of what they were worth. I wanted nothing to do with a drug that would make you go out like that.

Once we got to the club, Delvin was always greeted like a celebrity as the valets thanked him profusely for the twenty-dollar tip that he always gave them. When we got inside, the manager would escort us to a VIP table and order a complimentary bottle of champagne for our table. I must say I was quite impressed with the way he carried himself and the way folks kissed his ass as we walked in the club.

He wore what I used to call a Mr. T "starter kit" which consisted of about five gold chains that started out thick around his chest but got smaller and smaller in circumference as they reached his neck. I would tease him about getting a Mohawk haircut to complete the look, but he never found my little joke funny. "This shit 'round my neck cost more than most mother fuckers make in a year" was his stern reply.

As we sat at the table partying and enjoying the music, "Big D" as I called him, and Lynne would get up and go to the bathroom every five or ten minutes to "handle business". Big D would serve the guys and Lynne would serve the gals. A customer would walk over to our table and nod their head and "Big D" or Lynne would nod towards the rest room area. On the way back to our table, women who didn't know that he was with Lynne would flirt with Big D or try to stop him to talk and inevitably, Lynne would quickly rush over and yell "Stay the fuck out my niggas face, bitch". The women always walked away sheepishly because Lynne had a way of talking that let a person know that she meant business. Big D loved to see her "spazz out" on other chicks and would let her make a scene for a minute before putting his arm around her and walking back to the table.

Big D spent a lot of cash at Daniels and the manager loved the fact that D's clientele in turn bought plenty of drinks to intensify their coke fueled partying! This was during the mid-eighties, and cocaine, at least powdered cocaine, was all the rage. Sniffing powdered coke was considered a status symbol because it was known as the "Rich Mans High".

Before I joined the Army in 1981, I had never even seen cocaine. The main drugs on the block were weed and heroin aka "dope". I never had a desire to try heroin because I grew up seeing dudes staggering around the block or nodding out on a bench, sometimes with the needle still stuck in their swollen, bloody, abscessed "Popeye" arms. There was just nothing appealing to me about a drug that dragged a person to the ground like that.

I'm sure the weed and heroin dealers of the seventies and early eighties were making money, but they weren't making it the way the coke dealers of 1986 were! Here it was, only five and a half years later after I left New Haven and 18-year-old dudes were driving around in BMW's and wearing fat ass "dooky" ropes of gold around their necks. For those of you who don't know, a dooky rope was a gold chain with the diameter of . . . well, a piece of dooky! They had cats twice their age running sales for them 24 hours a day, and the money never stopped flowing. The streets were flooded with cocaine and anyone who wanted to could open up a franchise as long as they didn't sell on the wrong corner.

By 1a.m. "Big D" would sell out, and we would all go back to Lynne's place while they "bagged up" the next package. While we sat in her living room smoking weed and having drinks, I would watch 'D" count the fat wad of cash he made that night and tease him about robbing him once he passed out drunk. "I got something for niggas that wanna rob me" he would say as he placed his 9mm on the table. "Instead of robbing me, why don't you roll with me and make some real dough"

I was making a decent living at UPS, but this dude was making twice what I made a week in one night! I would try to tell him about the money I made in Germany from selling hash and bootlegging cigarettes and liquor, but he would always shut me down and say, "Where's all that money now, nigga? You gotta pay the note on that fancy ass car of yours plus you and your wife like to dress nice. You need to get down with me and make some REAL loot!" I explained to Big D that I didn't have any connections or clientele for that matter but he said that I could make money by just riding to New York with him and watching his back when he copped and also by "serving" his customers at the club. "I'll pay you a two hunnit a night just to hang out at the club with me and serve mother fuckers!" Big D made over a thousand bucks a night selling 50 and 100 dollar packages of powdered cocaine, so two hundred dollars to pay his bodyguard/employee was a drop in the bucket to him. His offer was so attractive that I told him I was "in". He told me that he would pick me up the next day around 3pm.

He pulled up in front of my house the next day and when I jumped in his ride he handed me a .38 caliber pistol and told me to tuck it in my pants. I checked the safety and stuck it in my waistband as he pulled off. During the ride to the Bronx Big D lit up a "Cokerette" and explained to me that it was harmless. "As long as you stay away from that crack shit" he explained, "You aint gonna get hooked" "This aint nothing but a mellow high; nothing like crack"

The sweet aroma of the coke-laced cigarette in the close confines of his Benz was so enticing that I told him to "Let me hit dat shit". I took a couple of long, slow pulls of the "Cokerette" and my mouth immediately became numb. As my lungs absorbed the cocaine, I felt a very light euphoria spread through my body as we drove down I-95 south towards New York. "This shit aint bad" I said as I pulled out a joint of marijuana. Other than the tingling sensation in my mouth, I preferred the weed high to the lite high of the coke-laced cigarette.

A group of high-rise projects to our left, named Co-Op City, let me know that we had arrived in the Bronx. As we pulled off the highway onto Bruckner Blvd, Big D explained to me that once we were in the building to let him do all the talking and not to pull out my pistol no matter what. "The pistol is for the mutha fuckas in New Haven, New York niggas don't fuck with me cuz I spend "mad dough" with 'em"

We parked on a side street adjacent to a ten-story tenement building and walked back around to the front. A kid of no more than ten years old was standing on the corner and as we got closer, he looked towards the five or six tough looking guys on the stoop and shouted," Ayyy Yo". The guys on the stoop turned their attention to us and one of them ran over to us with a serious look on his face asking us what the fuck was up. As the guy was approaching us, Big D told me to "Keep your fuckin cool soldier boy", when he saw me reach for my waistband. "They got mutha fuckas in the windows too, you pull that shit out and we both dead", he said as the dude reached us. "Oh, what up Connettycut" said the guy as he recognized Big D. He looked at me suspiciously and Big D assured him that I was with him and that I was cool. "We here to see

Flocko" said Big D. "Fourth floor" said the guy, as the other "guards" on the stoop made an opening for us to enter the building.

They nodded at us as we entered and we nodded back. We entered the foyer and the first thing I noticed in the dark hallway was the strong stench of urine. The very next thing I saw was more guys scattered about with their guns out in plain view. Most of them had pistols, but a couple had sawed off shotguns. "What the FUCK am I doing here?" I said to myself as I felt fear creeping into my heart and imagined myself being gunned down in this piss stained hallway.

That familiar voice inside my head chimed right in and said, "*Don't bitch up now nigga. You wanted to be a thug, well here's your chance*" I tried to ignore the "voice" but it was relentless. "*These aint no punk ass German boys, these are some real niggas that will bust a cap in yo ass if you try and break bad! You better man the fuck up and stop acting like a bitch or Big D aint gonna fuck with you no more*" Sensing my anxiety, Big D looked at me and whispered "Relax man, everything's cool" as we headed towards the elevator. "These are the good guys"

Big D pressed the "Up" button, and when the loud elevator door opened, two people got off, but one passenger remained inside. I could see a silver handgun protruding from his waistband and the look on his face told me that he wouldn't hesitate to use it if he had to. "Where to?" said the armed "operator". Big D looked at him and said, "Flocko". The "operator" pressed the number six, and the elevator door closed and began its squeaky ascent to the sixth floor.

As we stepped out of the elevator, more armed thugs were milling about in the hallway and they instructed us to wait in line with the seven or eight people who stood along the side of the hallway. Marijuana smoke permeated the air so I pulled out the rest of my jay and sparked it up. "This is the real deal soldier boy" Big D said to me as I puffed on my joint and started to relax. As folks left the apartment at the beginning of the line and our turn came closer, I was amazed at how "normal" the whole scene was to everyone else.

At each end of the hallway, a look out peered out of the windows and dudes were talking into hand held walkie talkies and bulky cellular phones. "Three coming up" squawked the radio of a guy standing close by. "Send 'em up" was the reply. The whole operation ran like a well-oiled machine as Big D and I waited our turn.

When the time finally came for us to enter, the guard at the door motioned us in. In the vestibule of the apartment, a sexy Latina girl in tight jeans and a skimpy top that showed way too much cleavage asked us what we needed. Big D held up two fingers and she returned with two ounces of cocaine. She walked away and Big D told me to stuff the two packages down my pants. I did as he instructed but reminded him that he asked me to watch his back and that carrying his product costs extra. Big D told me not to worry and that he would take care of me.

During the ride back to Connecticut, I was nervous and anxious as hell. I knew that if we were stopped by the police, I would find myself right back in prison. On the other hand, the adrenalin rush that I had from doing something so dangerous was exhilarating. Knowing that I had just "copped" at a major drug operation with armed thugs who could have killed me and was now riding down the highway with two ounces of cocaine down my pants gave me a high that was out of this world. The fact that I had a gun tucked into my waistband only intensified that high.

When we got back to Lynne's house, Big D and I locked ourselves in her bedroom because we didn't want her kids to walk in on us while we "bagged up" the cocaine. Before we began, Big D handed me three crisp one hundred dollar bills and said, "I'll pay you the rest after we finish at the club tonight. I wasn't even expecting more money, but I told him that was cool as I lit up another joint.

Weezy and Lynne arrived a little while later and I couldn't wait to tell her about my trip to "The City". When they came into Lynne's room, Weezy had a look on her face that told me she wasn't happy. We excused ourselves and went into the living room. "I didn't know you were going to New York with D" she said in an angry whisper. "You told me you guys were just going for a ride" "Don't worry baby, I got this" I said as I put my arms around her waist and drew her closer. I explained to her that I was "down" with Big D's operation now and we were going to be making some serious money. "Baby, we are already making good money and it's *legal*" she said. I kissed her on her neck and felt her body relax as she hugged me back. "Don't worry baby, I got it all under control. A couple of trips to the city every week and handle a lil business at the club that's all. It aint like I'm gonna be standin' on the corner sellin' crack or somethin" I took out one of the hundred dollar bills and stuck it into the cleavage of her blouse and said, "Here's a lil something for you, baby"

I knew neither one of us got paid from our jobs for another few days and her eyes lit up at the fact that we had some extra dough. As Weezy hugged me, her hand touched the pistol in the back of my waistband. "What the fuck is that?" she shouted. "Just a lil protection baby, you know how it is out there. I gotta make sure no one gets it twisted," I said, feeling proud of the fact that I was carrying a pistol. I was excited about the fact that I was about to get back into the "drug game" and wasn't even thinking about the consequences of my behavior. Living the "thug life" gave me a false sense of confidence and my already low self-esteem enjoyed a false boost at the fact that I was doing what the "Ballers" and "Shot Callers" on the block were doing. Being a soldier in the Army had become my identity, and now that I lost that, I was desperately seeking a new one.

Weezy pulled away from my embrace with a hurt look on her face and shouted," You just don't get enough do you? I was confused. I thought she would be happy that I was making extra money. "What's wrong baby?" I said with a confused look on my face. "You aint been outta jail for three months and you are about to go right back! Why would you jeopardize your freedom by being a damn drug dealer? I just waited a long time for you to come home, and I'm not going through that again"

Weezy had tears in her eyes and I was becoming angry with myself because I was letting her down once again. I tried to justify my behavior and began shouting at her. "Every time I get paid, by the time I pay the bills and buy food, I aint got but a few dollars left! Don't you wanna enjoy the finer things in life like before? Don't you wanna travel and have fun like we used to? Well, we can't do all that busting our asses at a nine-to-five job! Just trust me, ok? I got this!"

"I want to go home right now" said Weezy. "Ok, just let me see if D needs anything first". She told me that she would be waiting in the car, and stormed out of the house. When I went back to Lynne's bedroom, her and Big D were just finishing a coke cigarette. I told Big D that I had to take Weezy home. "What's the problem? Lynne asked. "Man, she's trippin about me havin a pistol and makin some dough, I don't know what the fuck her problem is" Lynne said she would talk to her later, and Big D told me to meet him at the club at about ten o'clock." Leave your heat in the car, Ram-Bro" he teased. I laughed and told him I would see him later.

When I got to the car, Weezy was balling her eyes out. "What the fuck is the big deal? I yelled. "I can't believe you are getting right back into the same old shit again" Weezy screamed. "You didn't have a problem when I gave you that hundred dollars, did you?" I screamed back. With that, Weezy threw the hundred dollars in my face and said," I don't want your fucking money. I just want my husband back! We rode in silence after that as I thought about what she was saying. Of course I didn't want to go back to jail, but the lure of fast easy money was too much to resist. I figured as long as I was careful and watched my back everything would be fine.

When we got to the house I kept the car running and got out to open her door for her. "Oh, you're not coming in?" Weezy asked. "Nah, I gotta handle some business, I'll be back later". She sucked her teeth and shouted, "Here we go again" as she slammed the car door and stormed into the house.

Chapter 27

Close to the Edge

I made sure she got into the house ok and then "peeled out", making my tires squeal and almost skidding into the parked cars on our quiet little side street. I was angry at myself for upsetting my wife, but I was also upset at her for not feeding into my new "business venture".

"Man, fuck her!" said my inner voice. "We gotta do what we gotta do!" As the cassette deck in my Toyota Celica blared Public Enemy's Fight the Power, I turned my fitted Yankees cap to the side, slid down in my seat and leaned to the right with only my left hand on the steering wheel. I put an angry scowl on my face and when I pulled up to the red lights, I gave the other drivers a "What the fuck are you looking at?" stare.

I drove through the streets of New Haven for an hour debating in my mind whether or not to get out of the insanity of becoming a drug-dealing thug while I had the chance, or to dive in head first; damn the consequences. On the one hand, I had the love and support of an adoring wife and family, a great job and another chance at redeeming myself. On the other hand, I had an opportunity to make fast, easy money and enjoy the excitement of living the thug life! Although my father had instilled a strong work ethic in me, there was an angry side of me that wanted the easy way out. I felt like the world owed me something for all that I had been through in life and if it meant selling drugs with Big D then so be it! I was too spiritually immature to see the blessing in securing a job with U.P.S. and I had no idea how blessed I was to have the love and support of my wife and family. I had become addicted to "more"! More money, more women, more excitement, and even more danger!

After the adrenalin rush of riding to New York with a pistol in my waist, copping drugs from an elaborate drug operation and the possibility of being arrested with enough shit on me to send me back to prison for a long time, I was insanely drawn to the "street life".

In retrospect, working a "nine to five" actually *was* the easy way out, but my dysfunctional way of thinking along with that malevolent "voice" of mine had me convinced that dealing drugs was the quickest and easiest way I could become successful. Getting kicked out of the Army was a tremendous blow to my already fragile self-esteem and in spite of the love and support of my family, I felt like a "nobody". The money, power and respect that drug dealers got on the street seemed like the best way to feel like I was "somebody". As I drove down Dixwell Avenue that evening, I made a conscious decision that I was going to become a full time drug dealer and work at U.P.S. on the "side" to justify the obscene amount of money I was going to make.

I pulled into the parking lot of Daniels nightclub and tossed the valet my keys. This was my first time there without my wife so I let my eyes linger a little longer on the pretty ladies who were at the club. When I entered, the sound of Grand Master Flashes "The Message" was pumping from the speakers. "Don't push me cuz I'm close to the edge . . . I'm tryin' not to lose my head. It's like a jungle, sometimes it makes me wonder how I keep from goin under Ha Ha Ha Ha Ha Ha!"

I saw Big D at his usual table and was making my way over to him when this drunken dude bumped into me. It was a crowded club, so I thought nothing of it. I kept walking, and when I passed him he turned around and yelled, "Hey, you fuckin "mooly" where's your manners?" He said it so loud that the people who were close by turned to see what the commotion was. I looked at him with an innocent look on my face and said, "Excuse me, Sir. I didn't mean to bump you . . . YOU FUCKIN FAGGOT!" He looked at his friends and knew that he had to save face. I could see Big D walking over as his friends began to surround me so I knew that I had to save face also; I couldn't look like a punk in front of Big D. As he approached me with his fist balled up, I held my ground. "You wanna piece of me?" said "Drunk Guy" I said nothing as I watched his friends through my peripheral vision. I was ready to take his head off as soon as he came within arm's reach and already had the chair picked out that I was going to start swinging if his friends jumped into it when Big D walked up and put his arm around my shoulder. To everyone else, it looked like he was doing it in a friendly way, but I could tell by the tight grip he had on my shoulder that he wanted me to stay put and follow his lead. I didn't try and break free even though now I couldn't see "Drunk Guys" friends to my left.

"Gentleman, what seems to be the problem?" he said with that big smile on his face that irked the fuck out of me. "This fuckin "Mooly" needs to learn some manners is the problem" said "Drunk Guy". Big D kept the smile on his face and said, "No need for that kinda talk man, he didn't mean nothin' by it, let's get a drink on me and forget about the whole thing. What are you drinkin' man?" I couldn't believe Big D was offering to buy this asshole a drink but I kept my cool and walked over to the bar with them. "Drunk Guy" ordered a rum and coke and when the bartender brought it to him, Big D looked at me and said," I'm a little short on cash Soldier Boy, take care of this for me. Now I knew Big D always kept no less than a couple hundred dollars on him so I squinted my left eye and gave him a "what the fuck" look. He knew I was confused and said, "Don't worry man, next round is on me!" as he walked back to the table. I paid the bartender as "Drunk Guy" walked away with a smug look on his face and rejoined his friends. I was fuming as I walked back to the table, how the fuck could he make me buy a drink for this guy. Didn't he realize I was one second away from breaking this motherfucker's jaw?

My anger subsided as I noticed the two sexy ladies sitting down at the table with him. As I approached them, I put on my "Billy Dee Williams" face as I surveyed the scene. D handed me a glass of champagne and motioned for me to sit next to one of the finest women I had ever seen. "Ladies, this is my main man Miles. Miles? Meet Kitty and Trudy" he said, pointing to each one. "Whussup ladies?" I said, still attempting to keep my anger under control. As I sat down on the semicircular bench that surrounded the table, the one named Trudy scooted over close to me and whispered in my ear, "You and me are whussup, baby!

Trudy was wearing a short black dress with high-heeled black pumps. Her dress was low cut in the front, exposing 80% of the most awesome pair of breasts I had seen in a while. She spoke with a sexy Latin accent and her shiny black hair smelled sweet and clean as she leaned into me. My hand had been resting on the back of the bench at first, but now it had dropped down and was slowly rubbing Trudy's soft derriere while she gave me light kisses on my neck and blew into my ear. I looked over at Big D and he and Kitty were doing pretty much the same thing. He gave me a "What do you think" look with his eyebrows raised and a quick nod of his head towards Trudy and I gave him a thumbs up.

After a few more minutes of making out with a total stranger, Big D passed Kitty and Trudy a $50 package of "caine" and suggested that they go to the ladies room and "powder" their noses.

As soon as the ladies left, I started to ask Big D why he had me buy Drunk Guy a drink, but he leaned over with an angry look on his face and said, "Look here Soldier Boy, I need you here to watch my back and help me get this money. I don't need you in jail for kicking some drunken ass white boy's ass for calling you a name. Plus, it's bad for business. You get in a fight, the lights come on, the cops come in and nobody's buying any "caine?" do you understand me, nigga?" "Yeah, but . . ." I began. "Aint no fuckin' "buts" about it man!" he said angrily. "We here to make money and fuck bitches. Only time you play Ram-Bro is outside. When we in here you gonna have to take a little bit of shit sometimes. Most muh fukkas here know you wit me so there shouldn't be any more problems. Are we clear?" "Yeah man, we clear" I said. "But I aint gonna let motherfuckers talk to me any old kinda way. I aint no bitch ass nigga" "Call it what you want Soldier Boy, but all the tough guys are either in jail or six feet under! If you wanna git money, take it easy and learn how to let some shit go. "You didn't notice" he continued, "That four of the guys that posted up around you when that shit was going down, were bouncers who happen to be very good friends of mines! If that guy woulda took a swing at you they woulda dragged him out back and stomped his ass!"

Do as I tell you "Soldier Boy" and everything will be fine! When we at "work" there's a certain way to do things so we can keep the money flowing!" I was still pissed at the way "Drunk Guy" disrespected me, but I nodded my head in agreement at what Big D was saying. I had already made up my mind that rolling with Big D wasn't going to work out for me. Where I came from, no one came on your spot and talked shit unless they were ready to go "head up" with you.

On top of that, I was beginning to resent the way Big D talked down to me . . . First of all, I was not here to "fuck bitches". What if Weezy and Lynne walked in? It stroked my ego to have a pretty "model chick" rubbing all over me at the club, but I didn't want to lose my wife over this bullshit! I was here to do business, and to have more money at the end of the night than what I started with. I was also beginning to dislike him calling me "Soldier Boy". At first, it was cool. In spite of the fact that I had been court marshaled, I was proud that I had served in the Army. Lately, however, Big D said it in a condescending way that made me feel like he was insulting me. I was definitely against the idea of letting someone get away with disrespecting me for the sake of money, and I'd be damned if I was going to be buying drinks for people who disrespected me! "*Let's play the game for a few more days, and then get our own package*," said the malevolent voice inside me. I acquiesced to its idea even though it was the same voice that got me into this mess in the first place! Once I had my own package, I wouldn't need to hang with this fat fuck that talked to me like I was one of his kids.

All of this was going through my mind as I sat and nodded my head to the beat of the music. After I calmed down a bit and had a few more sips of my drink, I leaned over to Big D and asked over the loud music, "What's a "Mooly" anyway, man? Big D let out a deep bellowing laugh, leaned in towards me, and said, "It's an EGGPLANT! You fuckin' mooly!" he shouted as he continued laughing. I sat there with a straight look on my face, not finding any humor whatsoever in what he had just said. My face went blank as I tuned out all the people dancing and the loud music and my mind went back to the times I had been beaten by white guys who called me derogatory names and even the most recent time when the Skinheads spit on me as they called me an "American Nigger". I felt that familiar rage rising up from within again. "*You aint gonna let that mother fucker get away with this are you*?" said my angry inner voice. I wanted to get up right then and there, walk over to him and smash a barstool over "Drunk Guys" head. Fuck the money. "Fuck the cops and God help anyone who gets in the way" The inside of my head roared with angry thoughts that drowned out the sound of the loud music coming from the clubs massive speakers. I was internally visualizing myself going berserk and wiping up the club with "Drunk Guy" and Big D must have sensed something was wrong because he reached out to shake me back into reality. "You all right man?" he said as he went to shake my shoulder. As soon as I saw his hand enter my peripheral vision, I raised my left hand in a defensive posture and balled up the fist of my right, ready to strike. After a second, I snapped back to reality and began to hear the thumping music again. I saw the fearful look in Big D's eyes as he realized that a second ago, I was about to take his head off. My sudden reaction caused a few heads to turn, but as I drifted back into reality they turned back to their partying. I relaxed my defensive posture and leaned back in my seat, letting the back of my head rest against the wall. My heart was beating wildly in my chest, which was a physical manifestation of the mental and emotional rage I held within me.

"Fuck is wrong with you man? Relax. The same motherfuckers who call us "Mooly's are the same motherfuckers that spend over a "G" a night with us! They can call us anything they want, long as they bring that paper". "Fucking sellout," I said to myself. No way was I going to be disrespected for the sake of "business".

He handed me a sandwich bag with twenty small packages in it and told me to put it away. "The white ones are "fifties" and the ones that look like newspaper are "hunnits," he told me. When they tell you what they want, get the money first then go into a stall and leave the shit on top of the toilet paper dispenser. Just make sure the motherfucker who gives you the money goes into the stall after you. And we take *NO* "shorts". I tucked the bag into my jeans pocket and downed the rest of my drink, grimacing at the burning sensation of the Hennessy going down my throat. I wiped my mouth with the back of my sleeve and walked towards the bathroom so I could take a leak and throw some cold water on my face. I was still feeling out of sorts from the mini "black-out" I had just experienced.

On my way to the bathroom I passed "Drunk Guy" who gave me a defiant look as I walked by. He acted like he still had his teeth in his mouth because I was scared of him or something. "These mother fuckers don't know who you are! "It took every bit of self-control I could muster to avoid walking over and planting my foot up his ass, but I just shook my head and continued on my way, remembering the lecture on "Drug Dealing 101" Big D had just given me. As I looked at myself in the mirror in the men's room, I could see the vein in my temple throbbing, a telltale sign that I was experiencing intense anger. After splashing water on my face a few times, I was able to regain my composure and return to the table.

When I got back, the ladies were in front of our table dancing together as Big D sat there with a huge smile on his face. With the lights so low and his dark complexion, you could barely see anything besides his big assed white teeth and his Mr. T starter kit! Trudy, the one who was flirting with me a few minutes ago, was shaking her teardrop shaped ass slowly and seductively as her hips gyrated to the music. When she noticed me approach the table, she directed her attention towards me and eased over to where I was standing and started grinding her soft behind up against me as I stood there coolly, with both hands on her hips, nodding my head to the music. After a few more minutes of that, I gently pushed her away so I could sit back down. All I needed was for Weezy to come in and see some chick dressed like a hooker grinding up against her husband.

I sat down and took a swig of my drink and lit up a Newport as I slowly scanned the room. There were sexy women all over the club and when they passed our table, a few would look at me flirtatiously and I'd just smile and let them pass because I could tell by the vibe I was getting from Trudy that I already had a "bird in the hand"! Big D leaned over and asked me what I thought of his two "friends" and I turned my head slowly towards the two "models" dancing in front of us, then slowly back to Big D and nodded my head in approval. "You wanna take 'em to the motel?" he asked. I immediately gave him the "Duh" look, and said, "Hell yeah!" Even though I had a great wife at home, I totally disregarded how fucked up it would be to cheat on her. At times like this, I didn't even try and resist the sweet sound of that inner voice saying, "*Go for it*!" I had no idea at the time that behavior like this only chipped away at the personality and self-esteem of the "real Miles" trapped inside this "wanna be thugs" body.

We spent the next couple of hours drinking and watching the ladies dancing between making trips to the men's room to handle "business". When women wanted to cop, they just sat down beside me and acted like we were chatting while we discreetly made our transactions beneath the tablecloth. Around 1:45am the house lights came on and Big D told me what motel he'd be at, and to meet him there in a half hour. "Are you straight to drive?" I said acting like I really cared. "I'm good, I just gotta pick up somethin' from Lynne's house and the chicks are gonna meet us at the "Telly". I nodded my head and started to make my way to the door when "Big Booty" Trudy grabbed my arm. "You're comin' right?" she asked flirtatiously. I moved in close and gave her a light hug with a lingering kiss on the cheek and said, "Yeah baby, see you in a few"

I knew deep inside that the main reason these chicks were coming to the motel with us was because Big D had a pocketful of coke, but the combination of the alcohol; and the incessant voice in my head told me that they were also coming because of me! I knew that going to a motel with Big D and two women was wrong and I felt ashamed of myself for being willing to cheat on my wife, but that didn't stop me from going along with the plan. After all, didn't real men have lots of sex? In spite of the fact that my wife waited patiently for me at my parents' house while I did my bid at Ft Sill, in spite of the fact that she took good care of me and put up with my childish behavior and total self-centeredness. The dark, sinister influence I was under prevented me from "doing the right thing". This inner "Svengali" who so easily influenced the decisions of my fractured personality made it easy for me to give in to my selfish, animalistic desires. I made a conscious decision that I was going to violate my own morals and values and sacred wedding vows again; causing me to sink further and further into the abyss of self-hatred that, unbeknownst to me, I had been tumbling down for quite some time! I didn't have this personal insight back then; I just thought I was doing what hustlers do!

I slid my parking slip and a five dollar bill into the valet's hand and stood back under the awning smoking a cigarette, while I waited for him to retrieve my car. As I waited, "Drunk Guy" came staggering out and walked towards the parking lot. He didn't see me as he made his exit, and I watched him as he made his way to his car, like a lion watches the slowest gazelle in the herd. "You should KILL that smug motherfucker," said my angry, inner voice. I thought of the pistol stashed under the seat of my car, but quickly dismissed the thought, not because killing a man was wrong, but because I knew that I wouldn't make it out of the parking lot without being swarmed by the Hamden police if I shot him. Thank God I didn't have a silencer or I may have given the idea of shooting him more thought! The deeper I got into this insane way of life, the more I believed I could actually pull the trigger on someone who made "Lil Miles" feel threatened.

When the valet brought my car to me, instead of leaving, I circled around to the back of the parking lot where "Drunk Guy" was leaning against the side of a pickup truck vomiting. I could feel my heart begin to beat faster as that familiar adrenalin rush began to race through my veins. After checking my surroundings, everything except my "prey" faded out as I became acutely focused on what I was about to do. I threw my car into park, turned off the headlights and got out of my car; intentionally leaving it running.

I approached him from behind and asked, "Hey man, are you ok?" feigning concern. "Drunk Guy" mumbled something about having a little too much to drink and resumed heaving up his guts. When I got right behind him I said in a low, menacing voice, "So, I'm a fuckin' Moolie, huh?" He turned around and when he recognized who I was, made a feeble attempt at apologizing. Before he could complete his sentence, I smashed my fist into his face as hard as I could. The force of my blow caused him to fall back onto the side of the pickup truck. As he attempted to regain his balance I tore into him with a flurry of unanswered punches to his face and torso. It was like opening a pressure relief valve, as I beat him without mercy.

It was an unfair fight due to his inebriated state, but I didn't care. He had disrespected me in front of a club full of people and had gotten away with it. I didn't give a damn about Big D's business or the cops; all I knew was that he had to pay. Not only was he paying for calling me a "Moolie", he was paying for the skinheads who spit on me in Germany, the white guys who jumped me as a kid and every other ass whipping, physical or emotional, I had ever endured!

He fell to the ground onto his back, and lay there defenseless, moaning in pain as I towered over him. I squatted down next to him and grabbed him by the collar with both of my hands. He looked up at me and began to apologize profusely through his bloodied mouth. "I'm sorry dude!" he said as blood dripped from his mouth and nose. "I didn't mean nothin' by it". I actually enjoyed seeing the look of fear in his eyes and the feeling of control it gave me as I twisted his shirt tightly around his neck. It was like some kind of new drug that made me feel powerful and invulnerable! As he lay there, defenseless and exposed, I hocked up as much phlegm as I could muster and unleashed a violent flow of spit into his face. "Next time you wanna call somebody a fuckin' mooly, remember me, bitch" I said between my teeth as I stood up. I stomped him one last time in his stomach so hard that all he could do was let out a dry heave and ball up into the fetal position. I heard some girls giggling as they made their way to their car and my countenance changed immediately to cool, calm and collected. I left "Drunk Guy laying there between the pickup and another car and calmly walked to my still running car as if nothing had happened at all. "Goodnight ladies" I said to the gaggle of drunken party girls as I put my Toyota Celica in drive and slowly exited the parking lot.

During the ride to the hotel to meet Big D and the "ladies", I thought of Weezy sitting at home worrying about me and began feeling ashamed again at what I was about to do. There was a soft quiet voice inside of me that said to go home and patch things up with my wife, but the louder, more forceful voice was telling me that I would be a fool to pass up the opportunity to "bang" a fine ass chick like Trudy.

As I pulled into the parking lot of the hotel, I saw Kitty crying in the back seat of a police cruiser. Trudy was sitting on the ground in handcuffs as a police officer was searching through her purse. He pulled out the small package that Big D had given her earlier at the club as I made a three point turn and exited the parking lot. "Whew! That was too fuckin' close for comfort!" I said to myself. As I pulled out, Big D was pulling in, and when he saw me, I shook my head and passed my finger tips back and forth across my neck, signaling him that there was trouble. "Meet me at the Mobil" I shouted as Big D noticed the police.

Deep down inside, I really didn't want to cheat on my wife. I was just being a "follower". I thought I had done something slick by avoiding arrest because I was "dirty" as hell with a pistol and drugs in my car, and it wasn't until years later that I would even begin to understand that, quite possibly, it may have been some other power that was greater than me, doing for me what I lacked the power to do myself! Today, I don't believe in coincidences but back then, I just thought I was a smooth ass hustler!

A few minutes later, Big D pulled into the gas station and said "Yo, them bitches goin' to jail tonight, nigga!" as he laughed at their predicament. Another thing that irked me about Big D was that he was always laughing or grinning like the Cheshire Cat, even when shit wasn't funny. "We made a killing tonight," he said with a big smile on his face. "Meet me back at Lynne's so we can settle up".

When I pulled up to my cousin's house, I placed my pistol in the front pocket of my black leather Bomber jacket and held onto it as I got out of my car. If anyone tried to rob me, I wanted to be ready. I played the role of a tough guy, but I was really a scared little kid trapped in a grown man's body. I knew what it was like to have my ass kicked, and I promised myself that the next motherfuckers who tried to hurt me would regret it.

Once I was buzzed in and safe inside the hallway, I placed the safety on my pistol and placed it into the back of my waistband. When I got upstairs and knocked, Weezy opened the door with a distressed look on her face. I could tell she had been crying so I asked her what was wrong. "I was worried about you tonight baby, I'm just glad you are ok," she said as I wrapped my arms around her. "I'm just tryin' to make it happen baby," I said calmly. I was relieved that Big D's little "sex party" hadn't materialized. Although I was willing to participate, a big part of me didn't want to violate our marriage.

"You don't have to do this baby, you have a good job already", my wife pleaded. "I got this, baby," I said to her, trying to sound cocky and confident, but underneath my tough exterior, I was afraid and confused. I knew what I was doing was wrong but it seemed like I was powerless to resist the temptation of the streets. Deep down inside, I wanted to live an honest life. I wanted to work hard, enjoy my family and do the right thing. It was as if a battle between good and bad was raging within me; and the bad side was winning. I held her close and rubbed her back, trying to convince BOTH of us that everything was going to be all right. After a few minutes, she whispered into my ear that she wanted us to go home, so I told her that Big D and I had a little business to handle, and then we could leave. She looked at me with those innocent brown eyes of hers and said, "For real baby, I wanna go home and take a bath with you and then make love to my man" I looked back at her and said, "Just give me five minutes"

When I got to Lynne's room, Big D asked her if she would give us a few minutes. She sucked her teeth and mumbled, "This is *my* fuckin room, why I gotta leave?" Big D tossed her a packet of cocaine and she grabbed her straw off the table and walked pass me with a huff. When I entered the room, Big D looked at the door asked me to lock it.

"So, whatcha got? He asked. I pulled a fat wad of bills from each of the front pockets of my jeans and placed them on the bed. After he counted the money, he peeled off a bunch of bills, passed them to me and said, "That's yours, count it". I counted the money twice and realized that for a few hours "work" I "earned" three hundred dollars! When I tried to give him back the four or five "50 cent" pieces that I had left in the baggie, Big D said, "Keep 'em. Do what you want with 'em, you earned it!" I had just made over six hundred dollars in one day! It would take me a whole week to make that much at U.P.S.

When Weezy and I got home, she ran a bath for me while I got undressed. I put the cash I had earned into my wallet and placed it on top of my dresser. I stashed my pistol and the cocaine in my sock drawer, and slipped on my house shoes and a towel as I made my way to the bathroom. DJ Frankie Crocker was on WBLS tonight and he informed me that I was now listening to The Quiet Storm!

As I sat down in the cologne infused bath water that my darling Weezy had drawn to just the right temperature, I felt a stinging sensation in my knuckles as the hot soapy water enveloped my body. I looked down at my hands and realized that I had scraped the skin on my hands during my earlier "interaction" with "Drunk Guy". As I winced from the pain, Weezy asked what was wrong. "Nothing, baby. I must have scraped my hand when I gave this guy's car a jump start earlier" I said. The lie flowed easily from my lips. I asked Weezy to grab us a joint from our well-stocked mahogany humidor that I had purchased back in Germany hoping that the pain would subside by the time she got back. As I massaged and examined the backs of my hands, I noticed small abrasions on my knuckles and a general soreness from the beating that I had inflicted on "Drunk Guy". I had never even smoked a cigar at this point in my life, and had no intentions on beginning. I purchased the humidor at a sidewalk bazaar in Strasbourg, France one summer because Weezy liked the elephant carvings on the outer cover.

While Weezy was in the living room, I could hear the soft sounds of "Reasons" by Earth Wind and Fire emanating from the stereo. I asked her to turn the volume up a little bit and began to wash my face. When I went to rinse the cloth off, I was shocked at the sight of women's makeup on the white washcloth that I was using. I had forgotten about my little make out session with Trudy back at the club and frantically scrubbed my face and neck as I heard my wife making her way back to the bathroom. My face and hands were literally soiled from the decadent lifestyle I was leading and if it weren't for the police pulling the chicks from the club over, more than my face and hands would have been soiled. In spite of the love and devotion I received from my wife, my self-centeredness and low self-esteem caused me to constantly seek validation of my manhood from other women and my fractured personality required these women to be as easy and loose as possible!

Weezy had already lit the joint and passed it to me as I sat there hoping I had gotten all the make-up off of myself. After I took a few pulls of the jay she took it from me and placed it in the ashtray. She took the washcloth from my hand and pulled my shoulders forward so she could wash my back. I loved the way she vigorously scrubbed my back and let out a low moan to express how good it felt. "Feels good baby?" my devoted wife asked. I moaned again and said, "Yeah baby, that feels great" She leaned me back upright and began to wash my face and neck slowly making her way down my chest as she gave me an erotic bath.

The tender moment we were sharing was interrupted by the Voice "*You are such a piece of shit*" it said. "*This beautiful woman cares so much about you and all you wanna do is whore around*" Suddenly, a strong wave of shame and guilt washed over me and I replaced the rag over my face and lay my back against the shower wall. I was beginning to believe that I *was* a piece of shit! The way I was cavorting with Trudy at the club was dead wrong, and if they didn't get arrested, I would have definitely went through with my plans on sleeping with her. I was becoming totally self-centered and didn't worry about anyone's needs but my own. Every time I made money with Big D I spent it on new cassettes, clothes, sneakers or partying when I *should* have been helping Weezy with the bills or paying my parents back for the time we stayed there rent free!

The way I beat "Drunk Guy" in the parking lot was overkill, he didn't deserve the beating I gave him. I was punching him and kicking him like he smacked my mother or something! All my life, I couldn't understand why I felt sorry for people who had hurt me and that caused me great internal angst. I felt sorry for Big Al when I found him drunk in the park. He literally scarred me for life just for sticking up for my dog. I felt remorse after the white guy who had jumped me with his friends in front of Molly, and then begged for his life as my big brother stood over him with a sickle. I even felt sorry for the skinhead/cop who had "hock-spit" in my face that day in Germany, when I saw the jagged scars on his face at my court martial! Whether I was right or wrong, I always felt tormented on the inside whenever I hurt another person.

At first, Weezy was unaware of my tears, but when my chest started heaving up and down, she removed the rag from my face and asked what was wrong. I lied to her and said something about wishing that I were still in the Army, which was true, but the real reason I was crying was because I felt genuine remorse for the way I was behaving behind her back. She was a good woman and truly didn't deserve the things that I was doing behind her back. She could have been done with me when I got kicked out of the Army, but she hung in there and stood by her man, and here I was trying to hop into bed with a "coke whore"!

After I dried off and got in the bed, I lay on my side, with my back turned towards her. Weezy snuggled up behind me and began to rub my back. As her hands caressed my thighs and worked their way around to my groin area, I gently grabbed them and mumbled something about being too tired. I really wasn't too tired, I just felt filthy and dirty. Even though I hadn't actually had sex (this time), I had never the less cheated on her in my mind and by the way I behaved at the club. I relaxed as the effects of the marijuana soothed my mind and drifted off to sleep.

The next morning, I woke up and got ready for work quietly, careful not to wake Weezy. I left the house without even kissing her goodbye; something I had never done before. I always kissed my wife goodbye when I left for work, but I felt so ashamed of myself that I skipped that part of my morning ritual. I was beginning to believe that I really was a piece of shit that didn't deserve to be loved. As I drove to the U.P.S. terminal in North Haven, I couldn't control the steady stream of tears that flowed down my face as The Voice reminded me of my disgusting behavior.

When I arrived at work, my supervisor could tell something was wrong with me and asked what was going on. I lied and told him that a close friend had passed away, hoping for some sympathy. I hadn't been working there long enough to get paid time off, but he told me to take the day off and come back the next day.

During the ride home, I puffed on some weed as I tried to understand why I constantly tried to sabotage everything good in my life. My thirst for drugs and the street life had caused me to drop out of high school, get kicked out of the Army and was now causing trouble in my marriage. Weezy had everything I wanted in a woman so why was I jeopardizing our marriage by chasing after loose women? Why would I jeopardize my job, my freedom and the respect of my family by carrying a pistol and selling drugs with Big D? It was as if a part of me didn't want to be happy or successful. It dawned on me that I was behaving like someone who didn't love himself at all. As the effects of the weed took over my mind, I said, "Fuck it" and headed home, so I could change clothes and head towards the Ashmun St. projects and try to get rid of the cocaine I had left from the night before.

CHAPTER 28

The P J's

The Elm City Housing Projects better known as "Ashmun St." for the main street that ran through the middle of it was the biggest "project" in New Haven. It was a sprawling housing complex that consisted of about six ten story "high rise" buildings and about twenty two and three story "low rises". All the buildings were the same color as pretty much every housing project in the country; reddish brown brick. Back in the day, it was actually quite a pleasant place. The yards were kept clean and some folks even installed small white plastic fences around their yards in an effort to show pride in their living areas.

"Ashmun St." was spread out over about ten city blocks, which seemed to last forever to me when I was a child. I remember sitting in the window of my grandmother's "low rise" apartment, drinking grape Kool Aid while waiting for my mother to pick me up after she got off work. Once my mom picked me up, we would return to the "suburbs" of the Brookside housing project. LOL.

Elm Haven housing, as it was formally called, was not a bad place to live when I was a child, but by the time I returned home from the Army in 1986, it had deteriorated into a drug infested battleground. There were still some decent, hardworking families residing there, but the drug dealing "crews" who brazenly sold coke and dope out in the open, outnumbered them. Once such crew, the Green Eyed James Crew, was so bold that at any given time they had a line of ten to twenty customers standing outside of the apartment with "runners" escorting them up when it was their turn to cop. The once peaceful Ashmun St Projects had morphed into an open-air drug market.

The hallways and elevators of the "high rise" buildings reeked with an acrid urine odor that literally burned the inside of your nostrils when you entered the building. Some well-meaning residents would try and eliminate the odor with Pine Sol and bleach, but it just made it smell like Pine Sol, bleach . . . and urine!

Since I had hung out with most of the current dealers in my high school days, I felt comfortable enough to walk freely about the projects without fear of being robbed or otherwise harmed. Carrying a loaded .38 in my waistband also added to my feeling of safety.

It had snowed the night before which partially covered the garbage that was strewn about the ground. Empty beer bottles and used pampers poked their heads out of the soot covered snow, reminding me that this wasn't the pristine housing project that I remembered as a kid. I was glad that I had worn my "wheat" colored Timberland boots as I trudged through the dirty snow that covered the ground. As I walked around, discreetly asking people who obviously looked addicted if they needed any coke, an old friend of mine who used to be a starting guard on my rival high school's basketball team walked up and greeted me. "Yo, Milesey! Long time, no see," said my old buddy (who shall remain nameless). He looked about thirty pounds lighter than he did in high school and I could tell by his raggedy clothes; beat up sneakers and the wild look in his eyes that he was probably going to be my first customer. I gave him that familiar greeting where two men clasp right hands and then lean into each other giving each other a pat on the back with the left hand and asked him if he knew anyone that was looking for some "work". "Whose work you got?" my old acquaintance asked. "I got my own work, nigga. You know I always roll solo!" I said, trying to sound tough. "Yo man, if you aint down with none of these niggas out here, you better not get caught "slinging" unless you want somebody to bust a cap in yo ass!" "These muh fukkas got the projects sewed up tight and if you aint down with a crew you won't make it out of here alive slinging on your own, man!" He had such a sense of urgency in his admonishment that my instincts told me I had better take heed and reassess my business plan! Getting shot was definitely not part of my poorly thought out business model!

He then looked around suspiciously and asked if he could see my product. We dipped into an alleyway and I handed him a packet of the coke I had gotten from Big D. I watched him closely as he put his index finger to his tongue and gently touched the white powder inside the package. "Yo man, this shit is blazin!" he exclaimed. "How much you got?" I told him that I had enough and asked him if he wanted to buy some or not. The ex-basketball star said, "Hell yeah, but we gotta get away from here before you get us BOTH shot!" "Come on, let's go to Sherry's crib and cook this shit up!"

We walked a few buildings down and entered a dark piss smelling hallway and proceeded to the third floor. As I followed him up the stairs, I pulled my pistol from my waistband and held it inside my front jacket pocket because I didn't know if I was being set up or not.

As we arrived at the third floor landing, I heard a commotion outside and peered out the small, hallway window. Three young boys who couldn't be more than 17 years old were stomping the crap out of some older dude as he sobbed," I'll get you your money, man . . . I swear!" I looked on in wide-eyed amazement as one of the young boys pulled out a pistol and pointed it at the older guys face. It looked like he was about to shoot him until an older black woman poked her head out of her window and shouted, "Y'all leave that boy alone!" When they realized someone was aware of their assault, the one with the pistol smacked the older guy upside his head with the butt off the gun and said, "Have my fuckin' money by tonight or yo ass is DEAD!", as they slowly walked away, laughing as if this type of shit happened every day. When I was growing up in The Elm City, the older guys ran the streets and the young boys showed them respect . . . now it appeared as though the tables had turned!

"E" knocked on the greasy, graffiti covered door and a skinny, haggard looking, dark skinned woman opened the door wearing a dirty bathrobe, and let us in. She looked at me suspiciously and "E" introduced me. "This is my man Miles, Sherry. I knew him since high school" he said as we entered the filthy apartment. There were empty beer bottles strewn about and cockroaches crawling all over the place. A child sat on the couch staring blankly at an old black and white television set and didn't even seem to notice the two men who had just entered the apartment. "Ooh, he cute" said the woman, giving me a flirtatious smile through her rotten teeth. I gave her a half smile and nodded my head towards her, but the look in my eye made it obvious that I wasn't interested. "Y'all come on into the kitchen," she said eagerly, anticipating a free high. As she sat at the table, her robe became undone, exposing her shriveled, acne covered breasts. "So, what y'all got?" she asked as she tightened the belt on her robe and reached into her pocket to pull out a cigarette lighter and a half smoked Newport.

"E" told her that I had the "Bomb" and asked if we could cook some up. "Long as you look out for me, you can cook up whatever you want" said Sherry. She placed a greasy glass that was half filled with water on the table and went over to the sink and rinsed off a large tablespoon that was charred black on the bottom. Next, she opened up her refrigerator which contained nothing more than a plastic jug of water and a box of Arm & Hammer baking soda along with a plate with some undistinguishable food on it. She grabbed the box of baking soda and placed it on the table. She offered me a chair, but I chose to remain standing, fearful that a cockroach would run up my leg. I removed my pistol from my jacket and placed it on the counter as I counted out five "fifty cent packages and placed all but one back into my pocket.

I didn't know a damn thing about crack except that it made you look like shit if you smoked it long enough, and if you sold it, you could make a shitload of money. I was planning on the latter!

I passed "E" the "fifty cent piece" and watched as he poured it into the spoon and added baking soda and water to it. He held a lighter under the spoon until the concoction began to bubble and then added a little cool water. As he swirled the mixture around with the end of a wire hanger, a hard, white piece of crack, about the size of a Now&Later candy materialized. He removed it from the spoon and exclaimed that it had "jumped back stupid!"

"E" placed the crack on a plate and asked me if he could cut it up. I nodded my head and watched him make a bunch of M&M sized pieces. I was amazed that $50 worth of powder turned into almost $100 worth of crack cocaine and gave them each a piece to smoke as I placed the rest into a piece of aluminum foil.

Sherry had produced a pipe made from a soda can with tiny holes poked into its side and placed ashes from an ashtray on top of the holes. Next, she chipped off a piece of crack and placed it on top of the ashes and lit it with a cigarette lighter. The white rock began making a sizzling noise as it melted into the ashes. She inhaled the smoke, closed her eyes and placed the can on the table. As she slowly exhaled, her body seemed to relax and she placed her hands between her legs and said, "This some good shit! She saw that I was watching her hand work between her legs and when our eyes met she gave me a broken tooth smile, looked down at her crotch and back up to me and said, "You want some of this?" I didn't want to tell her that I wouldn't sleep with her if someone held a gun to my head, so I politely told her that I was a married man and stood in that filthy kitchen wondering what the fuck I was doing there in the first place.

"E" took a hit of crack, leaned back in his chair and said, "This shit better than anything out here. It aint gotta drop of cut on it!" I had watched Big D package his coke and he never used Inositol or any of the other cutting agents because his clientele sniffed coke and most "sniffers" could tell if cocaine has been cut. The cocaine that I had was raw and uncut and if I mixed it with the right amount of cut I could damn near triple its worth and make a mint!

Suddenly, someone was knocking loudly on the front door, so I placed my pistol in my pocket at the ready. Sherry looked at me and said, "It's cool baby, relax" and got up from the table to go answer the door. As she passed me, she looked at me and licked her lips, giving me what I guess she thought was a seductive look. I was repulsed at the thought of doing anything sexual with her and could tell by the way that she kept her house that her personal hygiene probably sucked also!

A dude I had never seen before rushed in and sat at the kitchen table. He fumbled around in his pocket and produced a small glassine envelope and proceeded to dump the small white rocks on the table. As he picked up one of the rocks and placed it in what appeared to be a broken car antenna, Sherry interrupted him and said, "Where's my house hit?" He quickly slid a couple of small pieces across the table towards her and returned to lighting his hit.

As he placed the fire to his pipe, instead of melting, the rock turned brown in the tip of his makeshift pipe and produced an acrid smoke that smelled nothing like the crack that I had just witnessed "E" and Sherry smoke. "Fuck", exclaimed the guy. "I KNEW I shouldn't a fucked with that nigga." He slammed his pipe down on the table and began digging in his pockets again. He patted a wad of bills stuffed in his sock and said, "This is my rent money, I can't fuck up again or my wife gonna put my black ass out!" He pulled a twenty-dollar bill out of his pocket and said, "Yo "E", go get me some real shit man!"

"E" nodded his head towards me and said, "My man got that good shit right here!" I sold the guy two dimes and watched as he lit piece after piece like he was in a rush. By the time he gave Sherry her obligatory "House Hit" off of each dime, he only had enough left for one or two hits. As soon as he finished his second dime he pulled out a twenty from his pocket and asked for two more dimes, which I was more than happy to supply to him with.

I had "E" cook up two more of the "fifty cent" pieces that I had in my pocket and when he was done, I cut it up into dime sized pieces and packaged them in small squares of foil that Sherry was more than happy to cut up for me.

As they continued to smoke the "cooked up" cocaine, I began to notice that each of them had different reactions to it. Sherry would put one hand in her crotch and rock back and forth in her chair and nervously look at the third floor window as if she was expecting someone or something to come through it at any moment. She kept trying to catch my eye so she could give me that "I wanna fuck you look" but I ignored her and kept my ears peeled for footsteps in the hallway as I scanned the greasy, filthy kitchen floor, hoping that a cockroach didn't climb up my leg.

"E" would take a hit and pick furiously at his fingernails after each hit with his pocket knife. I noticed that his fingernails were reduced to short stubby nubs, and the skin around them was raw and looked like it was about to begin bleeding at any moment.

The guy who was buying the crack began to sweat profusely and his hands shook so badly that he was barely getting the crack into his pipe each time he took a hit. Eventually, Sherry had to hold the lighter for him as he frantically sucked on his pipe. I wanted to tell him to slow down because it didn't look like he was enjoying himself, but I said nothing because each time he finished his dime, he immediately asked for two more. After he brought about a hundred dollars' worth of dimes from me, I noticed a paystub fall out of his pocket as he searched for money to buy more. I asked him what time he had to be at work and he just looked at me with sad eyes and waved another twenty-dollar bill at me, signaling that he wanted two more dimes. The crack was having such an adverse effect on him that he couldn't even speak anymore. He just sat there moving his lower jaw back and forth, with his eyes wide open as if he was startled, which I found quite disturbing. A few minutes ago he was very talkative; cussing and swearing about getting "beat" for twenty dollars, and now all he did was just nod his head or grunt when someone asked him a question.

It dawned on me that this dude was supposed to be at work and was blowing his whole paycheck one twenty-dollar bill at a time and that bothered me; but it didn't bother me enough to stop me from supplying him with more.

I began to look at the three of them in disgust. "E" was a high school basketball star a few years ago and now he was pretty much a down and out crack head. Sherry was letting strange men into her disgusting, roach infested home with a child sitting in the living room as she smoked crack in the kitchen. This other damn fool was spending his whole paycheck on crack and from the Yale University ID badge that hung around his neck, I could tell that by now, he probably was a "no call no show" at his job.

"What kind of sorry assed people would let a drug reduce them to this level of living?" I asked myself. I sat in judgment of these unfortunate souls, in spite of the fact that I had just been kicked out of the Army because of my own drug use! Looking down on others helped me feel good about myself and I told myself that I would NEVER let any drug control me like this!

A few more "crack heads" came by Sherry's house and by the time I ran out of crack I had made about $400.00 in about three hours. I couldn't wait to go back to the Bronx with Big D and cop my own package from Flacko! I fantasized that I was going to make a "killing" selling this shit and then get out of the game and go "legit".

As I walked to my car, which was parked about a block away, I received a hard look from a group of angry looking teens that I had never seen before and stared right back at them. "Whussup fellas" I said with a smug look on my face, knowing that I had just made a pocketful of money right under their noses.

I got into my Celica and started it up, and blasted Eric B & Rakims "Paid in Full" as loud as I could without piercing my eardrums when a late model BMW pulled up beside me, preventing me from pulling out. It just sat there and I couldn't see inside of it due to the heavy tint on the windows. I naively remained calm figuring the car would pull off in a second when I noticed the passenger side window go down and the passenger motioning me to roll down my window. I pressed my power window button and asked him what was up. I turned to my stereo to locate the volume control knob to turn the music down and when I turned back, I was staring down the barrel of a 9mm Glock. My eyes got big as big as two John F Kennedy fifty-cent pieces as my tough guy façade completely vanished. I was about to be shot in the face as I looked fearfully into the eyes of my assailant. "You think you slick motha fucka?" said the teenaged occupant. "What man? I ain't do shit!" I said sheepishly, as I imagined how painful it was going to be when the bullet smashed into my face. "If we catch you out here again it's gonna be a problem, motha fucka!" With that, the vehicle sped off, spraying rock salt and sand all over the hood of my car.

I sat there about to shit my pants for about two or three minutes before my heart stopped trying to burst through my chest. "*Stupid motherfucker, didn't you hear "E" when he told you not to sell any crack out here*? My inner voice angrily berated me for being so foolish. I was so busy trying to crank my music up and show off that I let someone get the "drop" on me! I could have had my brains blown all over my car and my only thought was that I needed to be more careful in the future! There was another voice inside of me softly urging me to depend on the money I made from UPS and leave this madness alone, but I obstinately ignored it as I succumbed to the greedy, self-centered voice that seductively told me that I could become rich if I just watched my back a little better.

I held my pistol in my right hand and drove with my left, as I nervously exited the projects and turned right onto Dixwell Ave. When I got to the stop light on the next block I realized that my hands were shaking uncontrollably and I had a giddy light headed feeling. I turned right onto Henry St and pulled over and began vomiting before I could even get the door opened! I guess a little bit of vomit on the upholstery was better than a little bit of brains!

Chapter 29

My First Time

I parked across the street from Doug's liquor store on Winchester Ave. and quickly hopped out. Leaving my car running, I walked blindly across the street, thinking only of the soothing effect a couple swigs of liquor would have on my frazzled nerves. I almost got hit by a passing car as I crossed, and as the driver blared his horn, I ignored him and just raised my middle finger in his or her direction as I made my way across the slush-covered street. When I entered the store, Mr. Doug, the owner, looked at me suspiciously and asked if I was all right. I ignored his question and placed a twenty-dollar bill on the counter and asked for a pint of vodka. "What kind, son?" he asked. "Majorska" I replied, because that was what my dad drank. He placed the pint on the counter and I grabbed it and started to walk out of the store. "Your change!" said Mr. Doug as I hurried outside. I grabbed the change and almost dropped the pint because my hands were still shaking. I was still pretty shaken at the thought of almost getting my brains blown out. "Are you sure you are all right", asked my old friend Mr. Doug, with a very concerned look on his face. I crossed the street, hopped back into my car, and took a long swig of the harsh liquor. I winced at the burning sensation as it went down my throat. I took another long swig and sat there in a daze as I decided that it probably wasn't such a good idea to sell coke in the PJ's!

Instead of realizing how dangerous my new "occupation" was, and deciding to get out of the game before I got killed, I was sitting there trying to figure out a safer way to ply my wares! "*Maybe working with Big D aint such a bad idea after all.*" said the voice.

As I sat there in my car waiting for the liquor to calm my nerves, my home boy Jay walked by. "Nice wheels, my nigga" he said as he admired my Celica. "Hey man" I said. "Long time no see!" My nerves had calmed down enough that I wasn't shaking anymore, so I got out of the car and gave him some dap. We reminisced about the old days for a few minutes and then Jay said that he had just copped some weed and invited me to his house to party. He lived a couple doors down from Doug's so I turned off my car and followed him across the street to his house. "My mom is out of town till tomorrow, and I have the house all to myself" he said as we walked up the stairs to his house.

When we got inside, I could hear a few of the "fellas" inside, talking loud and commenting on the ongoing "rap battle" between MC Shan & KRS1. Hot 98.7 a popular New York radio station was blasting and they didn't even notice me until I shouted, "Whussup my niggaz!" "Oh shit! The soldier-boy done came back from the war!" shouted my old friend Al Ski. Everyone was either rolling jays or fixing drinks, but I noticed Al at the table cooking up some "caine" in a glass test tube that was about the size of a Cuban cigar. "Nigga, you can't make no money with that little bit of shit", I shouted over the music, thinking that the only reason a friend of mine would be "cookin up" was because he was trying to get his hustle on. "Nah man, this is for us", he said. I raised one eyebrow up and incredulously asked, "You *smoke* dis shit?" "Don't worry GI Bro, said Al. "You won't get caught out and start suckin' dicks for hits. Just don't smoke it every day and you won't get hooked!"

Up until this point in my life, I had been getting high on one thing or another since I was about thirteen years old, but didn't think I was an addict or anything. I felt invincible, and the "voice" told me that I could NEVER become a "fuckin crackhead" like "E" or that chick Sherry! "*Your mind is stronger than that*" it told me. "*People like that come from weak stock*".

When Al finished cooking the crack, he drained the remaining water into a cup and dumped a marble sized crack rock on the plate before him. He took a single edge razor and cut it up into small pieces and spread them out on the plate. Jay passed him a round glass pipe with a glass stem sticking out of its side and I watched as each of my child hood friends took hits and passed the pipe to each other. I didn't notice them displaying any of the weird behaviors that I saw "E" and Sherry display earlier that day. Although I was disgusted with the way Sherry was living and the crazy way her, "E" and the other guy behaved when they smoked it, the voice inside convinced me that I would never get caught out on a little white rock. Plus, I *was* kind of curious of how it felt to smoke it, so, when the pipe was passed to me, I said "what da fuck" and took a long pull.

At first, I felt nothing. I was about to say something like," I don't see what da big deal is . . ." Then suddenly, I noticed that although no one had turned the radio down, I could no longer hear it. I could see the "fellas" lips moving as they talked but I wasn't hearing any of their voices; more like muffled echoes! I could feel my heart beating harder than it had ever beaten before as I became extremely anxious and paranoid. I thought I was about to be another Len Bias; the famous Boston Celtic who died of a heart attack at the age of 23 from a cocaine overdose! I instinctively backed up against the wall and grabbed my pistol from my waistband because I felt myself losing control. Everyone was looking at me like I was crazy, and I was about to start shooting them all because I thought they were playing a horrible joke on me. After a few more seconds, my heartbeat settled and a warm feeling originated in my loins and I began to feel all warm and fuzzy inside. At first I thought I was having an orgasm, but the feeling began to spread throughout my whole body! I was having a "bodygasm"!

Nothing else in the world mattered to me except the fact that I was experiencing an awesome tingling from my head to my toes! Slowly but surely, the music and the "Fellas" voices came back and I plopped down on the couch and enjoyed a euphoria that I had never felt before. While I sat back with my arms spread out at each side and enjoyed my high, Jay grabbed my pistol and reassured me that he was just going to put it on top of the refrigerator. I ignored him as the cocaine raced through my veins, giving me the best high I had ever felt. After about five minutes, the euphoria wore of and I immediately craved to feel that "bodygasm" again. Although this was my first time smoking crack, I knew deep down inside my soul that it definitely wasn't going to be my last.

CHAPTER 30

Insanity

I spent the next few months chasing that first intense high, but it always eluded me. No matter how much money I could get my hands on, all I could get was a subtle glimpse of that first "bodygasm". No matter how much crack I smoked the intense euphoria that I felt the very first time always seemed just out of my reach. It was as if that first hit literally burned away the brain receptors that were responsible for the feeling that I was searching for. I became obsessed with feeling it again and within a few weeks, I began spending every penny I could get my hands on to buy more crack.

Big D stopped dealing with me because after he smacked my cousin Lynne during a fight, I used that as an excuse to steal an ounce of his cocaine from the private stash he had in Lynne's closet. I totally denied it when he confronted me; I even insinuated that Lynne had probably taken it. Lying was becoming easier and easier for me to do.

My parents were beginning to get suspicious because they constantly heard Weezy and I arguing, and I always had an excuse for why I needed to borrow 20 or 40 dollars until payday. Our relationship was going downhill at a high rate of speed.

I kept buying grams and half ounces of cocaine, thinking that I could "flip" them and make my money back, but I always became my own best customer. Before I knew it, I had burned all of my "bridges" and no one would loan me money anymore.

The straw that broke the proverbial "camel's back" came when, after spending all night at a hotel smoking bag after bag of crack, I snuck back home while everyone was at work and robbed my own house! I took my prized stereo system and VHS deck to the pawn shop and went back to the roach infested hotel on Whalley. Ave to continue to my search for the elusive "bodygasm". When I finished spending all of my money, I sat there feeling ashamed and perplexed. I couldn't understand how, in a matter of weeks, I had become what I had abhorred! Instead of becoming a big time crack dealer, I had become a big time crack *smoker*!

The "Voice" inside me was relentless! "*Look at you, you sorry piece of shit! I thought you were stronger than that!*" it taunted. "*What happened to making a shitload of money? What a fucking loser!*" The same "Voice" that had convinced me that I wouldn't become addicted, was now ridiculing me because I had succumbed to the charms of my new "mistress". I was beginning to believe that I really was a piece of shit, undeserving of happiness and destined to become the very thing that I despised; a low life crack head!

As I sat there in my roach infested hotel room, I began to assess the mess I was making of my life. Court marshaled from the Army, addicted to crack and reduced to the point of burglarizing my own apartment. I began to think that if I just blew my brains out, all of my problems would disappear. I picked up my pistol from the nightstand and held it in my hands, wondering how much pain I would feel before I died. As I sat there contemplating suicide, the malicious voice from deep inside my soul said, "*Just put the barrel in your mouth and pull the trigger, you fucking pussy!*" I sat on the edge of the bed trembling, with tears running down my face, raised the gun to my face and stared down its barrel. When I switched the safety to the fire position, I lost my nerve and pointed the pistol away from myself. I didn't really want to die; I just wanted the deep emotional pain I felt inside to go away.

The soft, gentle voice that had always been there inside me said nothing, but I was aware of its presence. In spite of the emotional pain that hung around my neck like an albatross, I knew that there was a part of me that wanted to enjoy life and become successful. There was a part of me that knew I could do better. Just becoming aware of this fact was enough to make me reconsider my suicidal thoughts and deal with the consequences of my insane behavior.

After my three day crack binge, I dragged my tired ass home from the seedy hotel with my tail tucked between my legs, to face the music. My family was disappointed in me and I cried when they asked me with tears in their eyes why I would destroy my life like this. Unfortunately, at this point in my life, I didn't have an answer for them. I was beginning to sink into a bottomless pit of self-despair and self-loathing. I couldn't understand why anyone would want to have anything to do with a loser like me because I believed that I was a failure at life and didn't deserve to be loved.

We decided that what I needed was a change of atmosphere, a fresh start. My father paid for a moving van with his credit card, and gave Weezy and I five hundred dollars cash, so we loaded up the truck and we moved to Greenville. Little did I know that no matter where I went . . . there I was!

CHAPTER 31

A Fresh Start . . . Again!

My parents threw us a going away party and as we sat down and talked at the table, I tried to convince them (and myself) that I was done smoking crack and once I got to Florida I would get myself together and do the right thing. After a tearful goodbye, my wife and I drove the U Haul truck with our Toyota Celica in tow, to I-95 and began our trek to "The Promised Land", where my addiction to cocaine would just fade away into the sunset!

Weezy had no idea that I had "copped" three bags of crack before we left and at each rest stop, I would go into the men's room and take a couple of hits before we got back on the road. I had no intentions of stopping; I just had to figure out a way to *control* my crack use!

I hit the ground running, again, and landed a job as a water purification system salesman. It was a sweet job because I got to ride around in my car and dress in a shirt and tie while meeting all kinds of different people. I was doing "cold" sales which meant I would basically ring a person's door bell and convince them to let me in and listen to my spiel. I had an innocent, boyish face along with a charming personality that, when coupled with my "gift of gab" made me the perfect salesman. When I pulled up in folk's yard with my fancy Toyota Celica that still had my military plates and stepped out wearing a shirt and tie along with a big smile, people couldn't wait to hear what I had to say!

Most households in the south had calcium deposits in their water which rendered it "hard", so the filtration system pretty much sold itself! Part of my sales pitch was to pour a glass of water from the customers tap and add two drops of a softening agent to it which caused all the minerals to settle at the bottom of the glass. Once folks saw that, they would immediately ask where to sign!

Shortly after arriving in Greenville, we found out that Weezy was pregnant. I was ecstatic that we were having a baby and vowed to stop getting high so that I could be a good father to our baby just as my father had been to me.

At nights, I attended 12 Step meetings where I would "share" with the members about how freedom from addiction was all "mind over matter" and how a person just needed to "make up their mind" to "cure" their addiction. I even lied and told them that I had over one year clean because I was so afraid to admit that maybe, just maybe, I may have a problem !

They all just smiled and hugged me and told me to "keep coming back". I believed that I was nowhere near as bad as these "dope fiends" and "crack heads" who had screwed up their lives with drugs and were reduced to attending nightly meetings where they talked about how fucked up they were. I believed that all I had to do was be a little stronger and I would be just fine. The voice inside me had me convinced that I was superior to these low life junkies who had stolen from their parents and prostituted themselves for drugs.

After talking all that "good shit" in 12 Step meetings for about two months, I took my first commission check straight to the local crack dealer and commenced to smoking my brains out. I was in a strange town but within ten minutes of driving around the seediest part of town I was able to find out who had crack and where I could smoke it! I had become the guy back in New Haven's Ashmun St. Projects who smoked his paycheck up twenty dollars at a time, at a feverish pace. My appetite for cocaine had become insatiable and nothing else mattered other than how I could get more.

I had become totally self-centered, thinking only of my own selfish desires. Never mind that my wife was pregnant with our first child. Never mind that we had bills to pay. I wanted to get high and nothing else really mattered to me.

After my overnight binge, I returned to my in laws home with my tail tucked between my legs and a sad look on my face. My wife and her family were rightfully disgusted with me and that further reinforced my belief that I really was a lousy, no good piece of shit!

This became my pattern for months at a time; go to meetings and talk that good shit all week, then as soon as I get paid I was off and running to find the nearest crack dealer. Sometimes I would get so caught up in my crack smoking frenzy that I would buy a "beat bag" from a street hustler and then go back to him and cop garbage again; hoping that this time I would get the real thing!

Although it had become abundantly clear that I couldn't manage my own money, I resented my wife for suggesting that she go with me to pick up my paycheck in an effort to prevent me from spending it all on crack. "I'm a grown assed man", I would scream to her. "I don't need anyone to hold my hand while I get the money that I worked all week for". I was adamantly against any idea that would interfere with my drug use. My state of denial had become so bad that I began to blame my addiction on my wife. My inner voice would insist that if she didn't nag me so much, I wouldn't smoke crack. If my boss wasn't so demanding, I wouldn't smoke crack. If the sky wasn't so cloudy today, I wouldn't smoke crack! Any reason became a good enough reason for me to continue on my quest for that elusive "bodygasm".

I became moody and sullen and kept to myself most of the time, ashamed and confused about how my life was turning out. I found myself sinking deeper and deeper into a state of despair because couldn't understand why I kept smoking this horrible substance in spite of the havoc it was wreaking in my life. Each time I spent my paycheck on crack and saw how I hurt my wife and all the people who believed in me I hated myself a little bit more. Eventually, I hated myself so much that I didn't even need the "Inner Voice" to berate me anymore. I got so used to being scolded by my wife, her family and myself, that it all seemed to blend together into a continuous cacophony angry criticism that was only abated by more crack use. When I was smoking crack, everything and everyone else ceased to exist and my mind was only focused on getting more. Every time my money ran out and it was time to go home and face the music, the heavy blanket of shame and guilt became harder to tolerate, causing me to repeat the vicious cycle over and over again.

I continued to go to 12 Step meetings to create the illusion that I wanted to do something about my problem, but spent my time there sharing about how annoying it was that my wife and her family were constantly on my back about my drug use. When I wasn't complaining about my wife's "nagging", I was trying to mimic the other experienced members way of speaking to create yet another illusion that I wasn't as sick as everyone else!

My new "drug of choice" became "fantasy" and I lived in this fantasy world where everyone else was the cause of my dilemma. If my Aunt and Uncle hadn't molested me, if I hadn't been beaten up so many times, if the Army would have given me one more chance! I spent so much time blaming my drug use on other people and situations that I didn't have time to explore the possibility that maybe, just maybe, the root of my problems might lay within myself!

CHAPTER 32

Manchild

The date of my first son's birth was quickly arriving, and I was able to "white knuckle" a couple months "clean time" to help my wife prepare for his arrival. I use the term "white knuckle" because I relied on nothing but my own will power which, I didn't know at the time, was no match for what I was up against. We decided to name him Miles Jr., and I was determined to stop smoking crack once and for all because I knew that I wouldn't be able to be much of a father to him if I continued down the path that I was on.

I made it through a few pay days without blowing my check on crack, which took a strain off of Weezy and my relationship, and used that as "proof" that I was "cured". My mood changed for the better and I was even more active at the 12 Step meetings "explaining" to the members how I was finally able to "overcome" my addiction after staying clean for two whole months! I tried so hard to exude an air of confidence at the meetings, but I was actually I was overwhelmed with fear! I knew deep inside that it was only a matter of time before I smoked crack again because the voice inside of me constantly reminded me of how good it felt to feel the intense rush of cocaine running through my veins.

Weezy and I were renting a large room in her aunt's home which we decorated with mobiles and a baby crib in anticipation of our son's arrival. I helped her get her travel bag together so when the big day came she would be prepared and enjoyed looking at cute little outfits as we shopped for our first child. I enjoyed long walks with her up and down the dirt roads of the "Woods" as she entered her ninth month of pregnancy and marveled at how much more beautiful she became as our child grew within her. Her skin seemed to glow and she became even more attractive to me as she progressed in her pregnancy. At night, I enjoyed lying in bed with her as we planned our future together and discussed getting a place of our own once the baby arrived. I was very proud of the fact that I had helped her create this new life that was growing inside of her and used that as a reason to stop smoking crack and get my life together.

My father was an excellent example of how important it is to have a father in your life and I wanted to emulate him and be there for my son also, but in the deep recesses of my mind there was a war going on. There was that soft gentle voice that told me that I could be free of this horrible addiction and live a happy, productive life, but there was also a loud, persistent voice that told me that I only needed to use the right combination of drugs and alcohol to control my crack use. "If you just make sure you get a little weed and some hard liquor to "even out" the crack", it told me. "You can just smoke 20 or 40 dollars' worth and bring the rest of your money home to Weezy!" On the other hand, I knew deep inside that no matter what combination of drugs I used; I always wound up smoking every last penny on this insidious drug that was wreaking havoc in my life.

The big day finally arrived, and as I rushed Weezy to the maternity ward I was excited that I was about to meet my first-born son! Ever since we saw the ultrasound that confirmed the fact that we were having a son, I couldn't wait to see the son who would carry on the Walcott name.

Her mom met us at the hospital as Weezy was rushed to the maternity ward. Her water had broken and delivery was imminent. As I held Weezy's hand while I stood next to her bed counting the minutes between contractions for her, I noticed a distressed look come over her face. "He's not moving anymore," she said nervously. The mid wife's face suddenly turned from excited to serious. "We have lost the babies heart-beat," she said as she pressed the emergency button on the wall.

Suddenly, the room was filled with doctors and hospital staff who were examining Weezy with a sense of urgency that told me something was terribly wrong. The doctor announced that she would have to be rushed to the operating room for an emergency C-Section as I stood against the wall of the room, dazed and confused, wondering what could have caused her seemingly perfect pregnancy to go wrong at the last minute. Weezy was rushed out of the room and her mom and I followed the entourage of nurses and doctors until we were at the entrance to the surgical suite.

"This is all your fault!" came the voice, right on cue. *"If she wasn't so worried about your crack headed ass for the last nine months, none of this would be happening!"* I had unknowingly become so self-centered that I thought I could control not only my life, but also the lives of those around me! Confused and full of a wide range of emotions, I tried to push my way into the surgical suite so that I could stay by her side, but the doctors and nurses made it clear that my presence wouldn't help the situation. Anger, fear, shame and embarrassment are but a few of the emotions that I was feeling at the moment.

As the magnitude of the situation became abundantly clear, my angry inner voice suddenly sounded weakened. Although it was demanding that we barge through the group of concerned medical staff and create a scene, it sounded hesitant, slightly less confident than it did in the past. For the first time in my life, I paused. Instead of trusting it blindly as I had done so many times before. I decided that *this* time, I would listen to the softer, gentler voice inside me.

"No!" I shouted loudly. "No! I shouted a second time. To the people in my immediate vicinity, including my mother-in-law, it appeared that I was responding to the situation with Weezy and Miles Jr. but I was actually telling the angry voice inside of me that I was NOT going to listen to it this time.

I knew deep inside that acting a fool wasn't going to make the situation any better so I decided right then and there to listen to the quiet, gentle voice inside me that was softly suggesting that I fall back and let the medical staff do what they had to do. Suddenly, it wasn't all about me anymore. It was about my child and my wife now. As I stood there in that hallway with tears in my eyes, I realized that no matter how angry or afraid I was, there wasn't a damned thing I could do to help them. I was completely powerless to change the situation and at the precise moment that I accepted that fact, I dropped to my knees, right there in that crowded hallway, in complete peace, and prayed for their safety.

Up until this point in my life, I didn't know if there really was a God, and if there *was* one, He or She definitely wasn't going to answer the prayers of a piece of shit like me! My idea of God was an angry white guy in a long white robe with a long white beard, sitting on a white throne up in the clouds somewhere casting down judgment and punishment on sinners like me. In spite of this belief, I kneeled down on the hard, tiled floor of that hospital and prayed. I believed that the only way my wife and child were going to come out of this in good health was through divine intervention.

I didn't know who or what I was praying to so I just prayed. "God, if you are out there, I beg you to help my wife and child." I said out loud. "Please God, PLEASE!" I begged. In all the tough situations I had ever been in, I never asked for Gods help. I always believed that only I could control the outcome of any given situation. As I knelt on the floor praying for divine intervention, a young African-American orderly grabbed me by the arm and said, "Stand up man, people is watching!" He said it as if I was embarrassing myself or something so I gave him an angry scowl, snatched my arm away from him, closed my eyes, and continued to pray to whatever or whoever was "out there"

The malicious voice inside of me was completely silent. Normally, it would chime in with its anger and venom causing me to act violently. All I could feel now was a calming presence that I couldn't quite put my finger on. Although I was completely powerless to "fix" the situation, I felt calm, and at peace. It was as if a comforting blanket had been placed on my shoulders and all the stress I was feeling just melted away.

After what seemed like an eternity, the doctor emerged from the surgical suite and made an announcement. "Congratulations, you're the father of a healthy baby boy! Mom and baby are just fine!" I looked up at the ceiling with tears in my eyes and shouted, "Thank you God! Thank you!" I turned to my mother-in-law and hugged her tightly as I continued to thank a God that I didn't even know for saving my wife and child.

When my mother-in-law and I were finally allowed to visit with Weezy and Miles Jr., I was elated to see Weezy lying in the bed holding our beautiful new-born son. I leaned in and kissed them both on the forehead gazed into my son's eyes for the very first time. Although he was less than an hour old, he looked back at me and I could have sworn he looked right back into mine with a little half smile on his face!

The doctor entered the room and explained to us that they didn't know why his little heart stopped beating, but he was fine now and they didn't expect any more problems. In spite of his encouraging words, I was confident that my son was going to be fine before the doctor even spoke. To this very day, I believe that the only reason my son survived was because of divine intervention.

Later on that evening, as Weezy slept in her bed, exhausted from the traumatic ordeal she had just endured, I gently lifted Miles Jr. up and walked over to the room's window sill. The sun was setting and brilliant hues of purple and pink were splashed across the evening sky in an awesome panorama of color. I slowly raised my son up and looked upon the beautiful scene before me and said to him, "Behold, the only thing greater than yourself!" just as I had seen Kunta Kinte do in Alex Hailey's movie "Roots" years ago.

CHAPTER 33

Thanks God, I'll take it from here!

I had no idea what so ever that on the day of my firstborn son's birth, I had tapped into a Power far greater than anything that I would ever experience in my life. I thought it was a fluke, a coincidence. "Things just happened to turn out for the good" I told myself. It didn't dawn on me until much later on in life how that malevolent voice within me fell completely silent when I called upon a God that I wasn't even sure existed!

Once Weezy and Miles Jr. were safe at home, I began my quest for the ultimate high again. I started out slowly, just doing a dime or two here and there, but before long, I was going on two and three day crack binges that lasted until I had spent every last dime in my pocket. My wife and her family got tired of the sad, puppy dog eyes I would give them once I dragged my tired, broke ass home, and eventually asked me to leave.

That familiar voice from within kicked in and I immediately became indignant and resentful. "*How could she kick you out after all you have done for her?*" it said. "*You took her all over the world! Champagne in France, wine in Munich. You showed her the Swiss Alps and the Black Forest, things she would have never seen if it had not been for you! Bitches aint shit! No matter what you do for them, it's never enough*" said the angry voice from within. Between the two of us, we were doing a good job of alienating me from the very people who had my best interests at heart.

I had sunk into such a delusional state of mind that I thought my wife was wrong for freeing herself and our beautiful son from a very unhealthy relationship. I suffered from a severe case of "selective amnesia" where I only remembered the good times of the past, but forgot about the havoc I was wreaking in her life now. She was a young mother who wanted the best for her son, but all I seemed to want to do was spend every last penny we had on crack. It was a wonder that she had put up with my antics THIS long! I was dragging them down and she had to let me go or her and our son would be dragged down too! I couldn't, or wouldn't see this at the time; all I could see was red! I refused to accept that it was my own behavior that was causing my problems, and I became angry and resentful towards the world.

I was in a strange state with no family or friends and felt like it was me against the world. The chip that I had carried on my shoulder for years turned into a 2 x 4 and although I didn't have the balls to put a gun to my head and pull the trigger, I lived in a way that would make you think I had a death wish.

Even though I hadn't paid a car note in months, I still had my Celica, The only reason it hadn't been repossessed was because the finance company still thought I lived in Ct. Now that I had become homeless, my car became my home. I stayed in a motel for a couple of nights, but I was "on the pipe" so bad that I reasoned if I slept in my car, I could use the motel money for more drugs.

The .38 revolver that Big D had given me back in New Haven was still under my spare tire in the trunk of my car, and I began riding around to different towns in the area robbing young drug dealers who were either naïve or cocky enough to sell by themselves. No one knew me, so I figured no one knew where to look for me. The adrenalin rush that came from sticking my pistol into the side of a scared, young "wanna be" thug was almost as intense as the high I got from smoking their drugs! I was more of a scared, desperate drug addict trying to get another hit, than I was a stick up kid.

I didn't want to kill anyone and I hate to think of what would have happened if one of them ever decided to fight back. I never took the safety off my pistol, I just acted crazy and desperate in hopes that they would just give up their drugs and money without a fight. They say God looks out for babies and fools and I truly believe that, because half the time I did stick ups, I would jump in my car and drive off; not even looking back to see if my victim was coming to retaliate. It wasn't because I was a tough guy or a thug, it was because I had thoroughly lost my damned mind!

I was working at a temp agency that distributed work assignments on a first come, first serve basis, but my drug use had gotten so bad that I always arrived late and missed out. Once again, I blamed the agency for not having work for me, instead of myself, and even developed resentment against *them*.

I became angry with everyone, including myself, as I sunk deeper into a pit of despair. I would call my wife and try to convince her to let me come back home, but she adamantly refused and insisted that I seek professional help for my drug addiction. "You are not the same man I married," she would say to me. "I don't know WHO you are anymore! To prove her right, I would begin to scream into the phone about how wrong she was for putting me out, instead of accepting responsibility for my behavior. She would always end the conversation by saying, "Please get some help!"

My inability to control her only intensified my frustration and anger until I became some one that even *I* didn't know. I no longer cared if I lived or died and began to do things that only someone who had a death wish would. I continued to do stick ups and became more and more paranoid because I knew that eventually, one of the guys I stuck up would run into me and put me out of my misery.

I was no longer allowed in any of the crack houses I frequented because once I started smoking, I would pull out my pistol and question every noise I heard, whether it was real or imagined. If someone knocked on the door, I would freak out and push the refrigerator away from the wall and hide behind it, anticipating a violent shootout.

Less than a year ago, I was driving to New York copping ounces of coke with Big D, and now, here I was in Greenville, SC, trying to sell cut up Macadamia nuts to the unsuspecting white guys who drove in from the suburbs to cop drugs! I wasn't worried about the white guys, I was worried about the angry, Angel Dust smoking drug dealers whose business I was fucking up because once someone bought $20 worth of Macadamia nuts, they usually didn't come back to that area to cop again!

The underworld in which I lurked, never lacked an abundance of addicted women who would perform sexual favors for a hit of crack, and since no sober women were beating a path to get with me, I was always more than willing to accommodate them; whether I had protection or not.

Eventually, I wound up selling my pistol for a couple of slabs of crack, which only intensified my paranoia, because now, I had no protection from anyone who wanted to settle any scores. My personality was reduced to an animalistic level where all that mattered was getting crack or figuring out the means to get more.

After about a month or so of living to get high and getting high to live, I finally got so paranoid that I decided I had to get off the streets before someone blew my brains out or my heart exploded from the massive amount of crack I was smoking.

I didn't know anything about drug programs or detox centers, but I knew that I needed to be OFF the streets before I got killed, or killed somebody. While I sat in the parking lot of a convenience store trying to come down from my last hit of crack, I came up with a "brilliant" idea. I would walk into the store and announce that it was a robbery! I wouldn't actually rob the joint; I would make my announcement, step back away from the counter, and instruct the clerk to call the police. Once they alerted the authorities, I would be arrested and taken to jail where I couldn't get any crack! Problem solved!

Well, the Greenville police department wasn't aware of my motives and took my little scheme quite seriously! As I stood there in that 7-11 waiting for the uniformed police to come with their sirens wailing, a big white guy who I thought was a customer entered the store. He casually walked over to where I was standing then suddenly grabbed me and slammed my ass on the floor face first. My first thought was that he was a Good Samaritan. I began to squirm because his knee was digging into my back, but when he smacked me in the side of my head with his .357 Magnum and said, "Police, don't move" I knew what time it was!

During the ride to the County Jail, I actually felt a wave of relief wash over me. Finally, I was off the streets! I was out of control and needed to be locked up like the animal that I had become. Now that I was in jail, I figured I could just explain my situation to the judge and get sent to some nice rehab program with tennis courts and Palm trees! Unfortunately for me, the court system didn't agree with my logic; I was charged with attempted robbery and eventually sentenced to two years in prison.

CHAPTER 34

County Jail

When I arrived on the cellblock, I kept to myself. I didn't know anyone at all, so I went into "isolation mode" and spent most of my time reading on my bunk or doing push-ups. I shared a 6 x 6 cell with a skinny, longhaired, white guy named Ben, who read the bible most of the time and did a lot of praying on his knees. He tried to engage me in conversations about Jesus, but I told him that I didn't want to talk about God and God could care less about me! He didn't push the issue, but asked me if I minded if he prayed for me. I told him," God don't give a fuck about me and when I die, I am going to hell, so don't waste your time!" I believed in my heart of hearts that if there was a God, He had forsaken me due to the animalistic way I had been living.

He explained to me that he was wrongfully accused of burglarizing a neighbor's house and I believed him because as we all know; no one in prison is guilty! Feeling the need to impress him, I told him I was in for robbery, conveniently leaving out the "attempted" part!

There was a big, fat, dark-skinned dude who looked like Biggie Smalls in my cellblock who would give me cold, hard stares when I was out of my cell. I would stare right back at him, not too defiantly, but just long enough to let him know I wasn't "soft". I had seen his kind before and knew that if you showed any sign of fear, dudes like him would use you to build their self-esteem at your expense. The way he carried himself, I believe he actually thought he was Biggie Smalls! He and his little entourage of "yes men" would sit around the table bragging about the amount of drugs they sold and I would just look at them and imagine the frightened looks on their faces when I stuck my pistol upside their foreheads and told them to "run that bundle" I had noticed him and his friends bullying the smaller guys since I had been there.

No one knew me and if someone would ask where I was from, I would say, "Not from around here" I was all alone with not even one friend so I played the hard silent type, hoping no one would fuck with me.

The cell blocks at County jail were two tiered. On the upper tier were about ten two-man cells. The lower tier had about the same amount of cells with a large shower/bathroom and a common area with tables at which the inmates played cards, wrote letters and ate their meals on.

The food at County Jail wasn't bad at all! The servings were healthy and the menu was pretty diverse. I expected a big hairy guy in an apron to serve me slop with a long handled spoon like in the movies, but the food actually arrived in trays on a food cart and was dispensed by the guards. Once an inmate received his tray, he sat at one of the round, metal tables that were bolted to the concrete floor along the length of the far side of the cellblock. Four round, metal seats were welded to the center post of each table rendering them immovable. At the end of the row of tables was a 2 gallon aluminum coffee pot that sat on a small metal shelf bolted to the wall filled with hot water for people who drank coffee, tea or hot chocolate

Now that I wasn't smoking crack anymore, my appetite had come back. I looked forward to each and every meal and never left a scrap on my tray. Ben, my cellmate, wasn't a big eater and usually gave me half of his tray during meals which made him ok in my book!

One morning, while we were eating breakfast, the fat dude who had been giving me hard looks all week, came over to the table and snatched the bacon off of Ben's plate. I gave him a long, hard look as he stood over our table munching away on my cellmate's bacon. "Fuck you lookin' at, bitch nigga" he said to me, spitting some of the crumbs in my face and all over my food. I put both hands on the table, preparing to get up and Ben grabbed my arm and said, "Don't! It aint worth it, man" Again, I acquiesced to the softer, gentler voice inside my head. I noticed a few of Fat Boy's" friends gathering around in a show of force, so I sat back down. After all, it wasn't *my* bacon! I guess he viewed me sitting back down as a sign of weakness because all of the sudden, he snatched my bacon too!

Sensing a fight about to begin the guys at my table and the surrounding tables began to get up and get out of the way, but I just sat there calmly. I picked up my tray and held it out to him. "You want my eggs too?" I said with a smile on my face. "If I wanted them, I woulda took 'em" said "Fat Boy" as he walked away with a cocky look on his face.

I got up from the table, tossed the rest of my breakfast in the trash can and returned my tray to the "Chow Cart". As I walked up the stairs to my cell, I could hear Fat Boy and his friends snickering and giggling at the "punk" who just backed down from the class bully.

I sat on my bunk and felt the rage rising up inside of me. The voice was on his job, asking me if I was just going to let that shit ride like a little punk or DO something about it. There was also a voice inside me that was telling me that "we" were here to find help for "our" problem. It quietly whispered to me that these guys were not worth it. Of course I ignored that voice, and plotted my revenge.

I was all alone and outnumbered, so I couldn't just fly into a rage and get my ass kicked. I lay back on my bunk with my hands behind my head as I watched my heart beat cause my tee shirt to flutter as I felt the rage building inside of me. It wasn't even about the bacon. It was about releasing the pent up rage that I had inside. I was angry with myself for fucking up my life with drugs and my insane scheme to get locked up in the county jail. I was angry with my wife for not letting me come home. I was angry with the Army, the skinheads, my aunt and uncle and Big Al. I was angry at the world and "Fat Boy" was just the excuse I needed to act a damn fool. I didn't know what I was going to do yet, but one thing I had convinced myself of was that I was going to do *something*!

When the guards brought the "chow wagon" around for lunch, I walked slowly down the stairs towards the chow line and casually surveyed my surroundings. The guards seldom came into the cell block except for when they counted us six times a day or did a strip search when someone lit up the occasional joint. "Fat Boy" and his three goons were at the front of the line as usual and I could feel my heart begin to beat faster as I allowed my rage to build up again.

Once they got their trays, Fat Boy and his entourage walked past me with smug looks on their faces, but I kept my eyes forward and didn't feed into their taunting glances. When my turn came to get my tray, I sat down at my usual spot and ate slowly and methodically. Ben could see that I was acting differently than usual and tried to quote a bible passage about turning the other cheek, but it fell on deaf ears as I plotted my revenge.

Like clockwork, Fat Boy and his friends finished eating first and began their usual game of spades at their table. As they sat there laughing and playing like everything was cool, I casually walked over to the aluminum coffee maker and unplugged it. During the ten or fifteen steps it took to get to their table, I could feel the hot metal burning my hands but that didn't stop me because the adrenalin had taken over. As I raised it up over my head, I could see the incredulous look on Fat Boys face as the scalding hot water leaked out and dripped down my arms and chest. Before anyone could react, I slammed the metal urn against the back of his buddy's head in an explosion of hot water as I let out an animalistic growl. A torrent of hot water splashed all over the cowardly quartet and the cellblock erupted into excited shouts!

The hot water only stunned Fat Boy and his crew and as I stood there watching them writhe from the scalding water, I realized that it wasn't over yet. "Get that motha fucka" screamed Fat Boy as he and his motley crew regained their composure. I had already planned for this moment and immediately took off running towards the shower room.

One of the ways inmates earned time off of their sentence for good behavior was by performing cellblock maintenance. These jobs were few, and highly coveted. This was, after all a small county jail and not the "Big House". I knew that the mop bucket, with its industrial sized wringer was kept in the shower room and that's exactly where I was headed. I could hear them shouting, "We got you now, bitch nigga", as they naively thought I was running away from them. When the first of the crew rounded the corner and entered the shower room he was met full force with my first blow. I swung the heavy plastic mop wringer as hard as I could, and when the mop wringer made contact with his face and upper body, he fell back and landed on the back of his head, unconscious. His face was a bloody mess and I thought I may have killed him. After 1.5 seconds of remorse, I raised the wringer waiting for the rest of his crew.

Fat Boy and his two other accomplices stopped their approach and reassessed their plan of attack when they saw their friends face busted wide open as he lay on the floor unconscious. I stood there holding the mop wringer in a defensive posture, waiting for their next move. "Come on mother fuckers" I screamed at the top of my lungs. "You want some more bacon you fat mother fucker?" I shouted as I approached them. The fear I saw in their eyes gave me enough confidence to go on the offence, smashing the heavy-duty plastic wringer into each of them in a frenzy of blood and screaming. I knew from experience that most bullies cower in fright when their victims stand up to them and these guys didn't let me down. When I realized they weren't even fighting back, I tossed the mop wringer across the floor but continued punching "Fat Boy" as he lay on the floor balled up in a fetal position like the coward that he was.

By the time the ten guards in riot gear entered the cellblock, Fat Boy and his friends were lying in a bloody heap by the main door, screaming for a "C.O.". The rest of the inmates in the cellblock were laughing riotously as they watched the "neighborhood bully" and his gang meet their match.

When the guards entered the cellblock with their batons and tear gas guns at the ready, I immediately calmed down and lay on the floor waiting for the inevitable "beat down" they gave inmates who started trouble. Surprisingly, they were rougher with Fat Boy and his friends than they were with me! Fat Boy and his friends tried to play the victim role and struggled with the guards as they plead their case. "He attacked us for no reason" cried Fat Boy. "Why are you cuffin' us? We were mindin' our own business", said another. The guards had actually watched the whole thing play out on camera earlier and knew these punks had it coming.

I offered no resistance as I was handcuffed and led away to "seg". My chest was still heaving from the physical exertion and adrenalin rush. I had just released an intense amount of rage and the tears streaming down my face were evidence of that intensity.

I was being escorted down the hallway by two guards, one black, and one white, on each arm. The white guard said to his colleague, "Take him to the bathroom". *"Oh shit, here it comes"* I said to myself. I had heard about the beat downs that the guards gave unruly inmates, and I hoped it wouldn't be too bad. When we entered the bathroom, the white guard told me to stand in front of the wall and spread my legs. He told me that he was going to put the handcuffs in the front of me and not to make any sudden moves. As he released the handcuffs, I groaned from the burns I received on my hands and forearms from the scalding hot water. "Wash your face man, you look a mess" he chuckled in a friendly tone. "You shoulda seen the other guy" I chuckled back. There was blood on my shirt and face, but none of it was mine. Miraculously, I didn't have a scratch on me! The black guard handed me a few paper towels and I washed my face and gulped the cold water from the faucet. *"I guess I aint getting' a beat down after all"* I said to myself, relieved.

When we reached the area of the jail known as administrative segregation, the guard instructed me to enter the windowless cell. After he secured the door he told me to stick my hands back through the meal tray slot so that he could remove the handcuffs. I noticed a metal cot next to a toilet/sink combination and was actually relieved that I would finally have some privacy. As the guard removed my handcuffs, he looked me in the eye with a sly grin on his face and said, "About time someone put those assholes in their place!" As he clipped his handcuffs back to his belt he said, "I'll bring you a mattress in a few minutes".

A day or two later, a social worker stopped by and interviewed me. I had calmed down by now, and was able to carry on a decent conversation. I explained to him that I wasn't a troublemaker and that I needed help for my addiction. I asked him if there was anything he could do to help me and he recommended an in-patient drug program called Metamorphosis. "I will give you a recommendation" he said, "but don't get your hopes up, you have to be interviewed by the director of the program, and he has the final say"

"Seg" was great! I had a cell to myself, and the guards brought my meals right to my door. By now, guards from each shift knew me as the guy who put foot in the ass of the bully and his crew, so I enjoyed a bit of celebrity status. They gave me a bible, some magazines and a pencil and paper, which I used to write letters to Weezy. I missed her and my newborn son terribly and vowed to get my act together once and for all.

A couple of days later, I was interviewed by a huge white guy named Jim, the director of the Metamorphosis program. Jim stood at least 6'5" and was built like an NFL football player. He sported a short crew cut and wore a small diamond stud in his ear. I was intimidated at first when the guard escorted me into the small interview room, but Jim's calm demeanor instantly put me at ease.

He asked me a bunch of questions about my past that I easily answered, but when he asked me if I was an addict I paused and became tearful. He waited a few seconds and then asked me again. By now the tears were streaming down my face as I thought of the horrible mess I had made of my life. For the first time in my life, I looked into the eyes of another human being and admitted that I was an addict. As I wiped the tears and snot from my face with the tissue he handed me, I humbly answered, "Yes! Please help me!"

CHAPTER 35

Metamorphosis

A few days later, Jim stood before the judge with me and I was remanded to his custody, converting the rest of my time to probation. Of course, this was contingent upon me remaining in treatment and abstinent from drugs. Metamorphosis, or "Meta" as we called it, was a wonderful program! It was located about two blocks away from the County Jail in a peaceful, wooded area. Although I wasn't physically in jail anymore, the sight of the Alachua County Jail through the stand of majestic pine trees was a constant reminder of what was in store for me if I decided to get it twisted again!

The program was housed in an off-white clapboard covered, ranch styled house that had been converted into an in-patient, co-ed drug program. The six males' and four females' sleeping areas were separated by a large living room and kitchen area that had three dingy looking couches and a few chairs. Off to the side was a small office that the staff used for individual counseling. Outside, there was a large screen house where we ate our meals and lounged.

Within days of arriving at Meta I began to feel hopeful that once and for all, I could stop smoking crack and begin a better life. The clinicians in the program were great. They helped me gain insight into the disease of addiction and told me that anyone can recover if they follow certain steps, the first one being admitting you are an addict. I was relieved to find out that I had a disease and not a moral deficiency, because I had begun to believe that I really was just a "piece of shit". In spite of the education I was receiving about addiction, I continued to believe that I could stop if I just tried hard enough.

During one of my first groups, I learned that Jim had been a heroin addict for many years, but got clean and was now the executive director of a state funded drug treatment facility! Knowing this gave me some much needed hope, because at that point in my life, I was completely hopeless! I thought that once a person became an addict they stayed an addict until they died or went to prison! To hear tales of this "gentle giant" who stopped using drugs and became a productive member of society amazed me. I vowed to become just like Jim and dreamed of some day running a drug program myself!

In typical addict fashion, I went from one extreme to the next. I went from feeling like a "piece of shit", to feeling superior to the other residents of the program within a week's time. I figured that the majority of the residents were down on their luck drug addicts who needed a place to stay till there next welfare check came. They were the dregs of society as opposed to me, who was still physically fit from six years of exercise in the Army and much more articulate than the other residents whose bodies and minds were emaciated from years of drug use. I looked down on the other residents with contempt, while conveniently forgetting that I had been sleeping in my car and going for days without eating or washing a short time ago.

Most of the residents were high school drop outs who didn't speak as well as I did, so I dominated the group therapy sessions to the point where I would notice my peers rolling their eyes or shaking their heads during my "informational" speeches. Eventually, even the facilitators of the groups had to start interrupting me so that the other residents could get a word in edgewise. In spite of the fact that I hadn't completed high school either, I never the less considered myself superior to the other residents in the program. I learned much later on in life that when I allow myself to feel inferior or superior to others, I am heading for trouble!

Jim suggested I keep my mouth shut for a few days and listen. "Take the cotton out of your ears, and put it in your mouth" he told me. I followed his suggestion and sat back and allowed the "country bumpkins" to talk about feelings and being abused and other "bullshit". I "knew" that the solution to addiction was to just man up and do the right thing and I believed that anyone who really wanted to stop using could do so if they were strong willed enough. I wasn't afraid to voice my opinion either and when Jim got wind of my philosophy, he dropped in on our group to debunk my theory!

"Miles", he said in a very calm voice while holding up a box of Ex-Lax. "Since you believe your own self will can control what your body does, I want you to take four of these Ex-Lax tablets, remain on that couch and show us all how your will power can keep you from shitting your pants!" After the all of the laughter (including my own) died down, I realized that maybe I didn't have all the answers, but I wasn't going to let anyone *here* know that. I needed to feel superior to the other residents in order to feel good about myself!

One day, a woman named "Melony" was sharing to the group about how she had prostituted herself to get drugs. She was weeping as she spoke of how that behavior made her feel and I couldn't wait for my turn so I could show the group how much stronger and smarter I was. When my turn came to speak, I began to talk about how I would *never* do some of the things I heard other people doing no matter how bad I wanted to get high. I started talking about how I used to rob drug dealers when I needed more drugs, but before I could finish my "dissertation", "Melony" jumped up and tore me a "new one"!

"Who da FUCK do you think you are, Miles? You in here just like the rest of us!" she screamed tearfully. I was expecting the group leader to make her shut up, but he sat there and allowed Melony to continue. "You come in here with all ya big, fancy words and try to act like you better than everybody else, but you a fuckin crack head just like the rest of us! You came from the jail just like the rest of us!" she screamed at the top of her lungs. "It don't matter if you were robbing drug dealers or sucking dicks for a hit, you aint no better than anyone else here! You need to come down off that high horse of yours!"

By now, the group leader had risen to his feet and was trying to calm Melony down, but before he could, she continued with her tearful lecture that had probably been building up since my arrogant ass arrived.

"If you have all the fucking answers then why was YOU in the county jail, Mr. Know-it-all? If you knew so fucking much, you wouldn't be in here with us!" At least we know we are addicts, you don't have a fuckin clue! If you keep thinking like you thinkin', you gonna be RIGHT back out there smokin' crack again!" *"Yeah, right!"* said the Voice.

As Melony sat back down on the couch, the room fell silent. I sat in my seat digesting what she had just said to me and realized that she was absolutely right! I was too arrogant at the time to admit it to the group so I just acted remorseful and even apologized to the staff and residents for my insensitive behavior. Deep inside, I still believed I was stronger than the average drug addict and vowed to "show them" that I could stay clean without their stupid 12 Steps!

After 60 days in the program, we were allowed to get jobs. The staff would conduct classes for us on how to budget our money and balance a checking account. The goal was for us to save our money so that we could get a place to live when our six months at Meta were over.

The first week I was on "Work Status" as they referred to residents who were eligible to become employed, I landed a job at Arby's. The fact that I was able to land a job so quickly further reinforced my belief that I was superior to the other residents because some of them had been on "work status" weeks before me and hadn't landed a job yet.

I was hired as a manager trainee and my ego swelled to gigantic proportions and so did my self-centeredness. Although my wife was raising our son with no financial help from me, I used my extra money to buy nice clothes and fancy sneakers. Now that I was off drugs, my insecurities kicked in and I needed to dress up my outsides to hide the scared, insecure person that was inside of my body.

Although we were separated due to my own unacceptable behavior, "We" held her responsible. *"We don't need her,"* said my inner voice. *"A handsome guy like you can find another woman easy!"* I was too immature and selfish at the time to realize that even though my wife and I were separated, I was still obligated to provide emotional and financial support to my child.

I learned my job quickly and became the model employee. The manager, a big, fat, red nosed, "Good Ole Boy" from the south named Roy, would occasionally give me a ride back to Meta, and during the ride we would listen to old school country and western music as he spit chewing tobacco out of his cars window and told me how hard it was to believe that a "good kid" like me ever got caught up in the drug scene. I downplayed my drug use and just told him that I had gotten into a drunken fight and didn't use street drugs at all. I was still ashamed of my past so I decided to keep that part of it a secret.

I had pre-judged him as a closet Ku Klux Klan member who only hired me as the "token black guy"; but Roy took a special interest in me. He taught me all the ins and outs of running the restaurant and trusted me with the keys to the joint as well as the combination to the safe. He even invited me to his house to play horseshoes occasionally, while his wife made the crispiest, tastiest, fried chicken I have ever tasted. Before long, I was promoted to full time day shift manager and my ego swelled to enormous proportions.

By now, I had been off crack and all other drugs for six months. I walked around Meta like my shit didn't stink and took all of the credit for the good things that were going on in my life. I really believed that I had stayed clean this long because I had a stronger mind than the "losers" in the program and I was beginning to believe my own lie about not having a serious drug problem. In spite of the fact that I was living in a state run drug program and could be tossed back in jail for so much as one beer, I still thought that I wasn't as "bad" as everyone else.

One Sunday, after returning from church services, I entered the house and noticed a cute little toddler sitting on the couch in the main room. There was something special about him but I couldn't quite put my finger on it. As I walked by, I stopped and took a second look at him and continued on my way to my room so that I could change. I noticed that the few residents and counselors who were present had funny looks on their faces, but paid no attention to them until I saw Weezy exit Jim's office. Once I saw her, I put one and one together and realized that the cute little kid on the sofa was my son! I hadn't seen him since he was a few weeks old and felt a heavy wave of guilt wash over me as I picked him up with tears in my eyes.

I expected Weezy to be impressed with the fact that I was off drugs, but she really didn't have much to say to me. As we sat and talked in the parking lot, I begged Weezy to take me back. "I'm done with the crack", I told her. "Please take me back" I pleaded. I had put Weezy through a lot over the last year and she now had a child to think about. "Complete this program" she said, "And we'll see". Those were the words that came out of her mouth, but what I heard was, "No! I don't want you anymore." My total self-centeredness and lack of patience wouldn't allow me to hear her words. I wanted what I wanted, and I wanted it now. It was either my way or the highway!

Chapter 36

Relapse

I was eligible to take weekend passes now and I couldn't wait to spend my first one with Weezy and Miles Jr.! I planned on taking her out to dinner and then, maybe, if she was game, spend the night with her!

During the week leading up to my weekend pass, Weezy wouldn't accept my calls. She was too busy working and taking care of our son, but the evil voice inside my head convinced me that she had found someone else and didn't want me anymore. *"It's over" it told me. "You might as well move on"* It's amazing how easily I allowed myself to become convinced to give up on the woman of my dreams. The persuasive entity that inhabited my mind and body was too powerful to resist as I lost all hope of ever getting back together with my wife.

As Friday approached, a "brilliant" idea was introduced to my mind! Now that I didn't smoke crack anymore, I could get a motel room and pick up a cute hooker and have a ball with her!" I didn't deserve a good wholesome woman like Weezy anyway, so why not pick up an "easy" woman who I could use for my own selfish desires?

I told the staff at Meta that my wife was going to pick me up after work on Friday and we would spend the weekend together before she dropped me off on Sunday evening. I even told my manager, Jim, that I was looking forward to spending my first weekend in a while with my wife and son . . . insinuating that we would be having some long awaited sex!

When my shift ended, I made my way down to Porters Quarters and easily picked up a cute young lady who didn't look like she had been "out there" that long. I gave her $40 to cop some crack for herself and we caught a cab to a nearby motel.

On the ride over, she was very flirtatious and seductive. She rubbed my upper thighs in the back seat of the cab and promised me an evening of sexual pleasure that I would never forget. I was filled with desire, and once we entered the room, I immediately began to undress. The woman got undressed also and I was impressed with her curvaceous body. Her skin was smooth and light brown and she had an amazing set of breasts that seemed to be on the verge of bursting out of her sheer bra.

She got on the bed and began to fondle my manhood as my hands feverishly explored every inch of her body. She began to kiss my chest and slowly moved down until her lips were tantalizingly close to my groin. Then she suddenly stopped. "I need to take a hit first, baby" she moaned. As she leaned over to grab her pipe and a hit of crack, exposing the tightest little brown booty I had seen in a long time, I anticipated how good it would feel to ravage her body.

She sat upright in the bed and placed the rock in her glass pipe, then glanced over at me as I watched her. "Baby, you sure you don't want some?" she asked. "Nah baby, I'm good" was my reply. I was fine and in control as she lit the pipe and inhaled the smoke, but as soon as she exhaled, an overwhelming desire to smoke crack came over me.

"Let me hit that shit" I said to her. She must have thought I was talking about her booty, because she told me that as soon as she went into the bathroom and freshened up, we could do anything I wanted.

As I listened to her run the water in the bathroom, I broke out in a cold sweat as I feebly tried to resist the temptation. When I couldn't take it anymore, I grabbed a piece of crack, put it in her pipe and lit it. As the "bodygasm" that I missed so much began to envelop my body, tears began to roll down my face. Before the "bodygasm" could reach its peak, it suddenly began to wear off. I felt as if the voice that had always remained inside of my head had suddenly materialized into a hideous demon that was sitting on the side of the bed with an evil smirk on its face.

"I got you now, sucker!" said the familiar voice. *"I knew you would be back!"* As I continued to cry, the hideous demon taunted me as I took yet another hit of crack, searching for that ecstatic feeling I felt back in New

Haven when I took my first hit. Years later, my best friend Howie would tell me that Satan baits the hook according to the taste of the fish, but at that point in my life, I was oblivious to the evil spell that I was under.

"What's the matter baby?" said the hooker as she reentered the room. I said nothing as I continued to light the pipe with trembling hands. She tried to distract me from smoking by putting her head between my legs, but I closed my legs and turned away from her, lost in a crack smoking frenzy. I had become the Yale employee from Sherry's house back in the Ashmun St projects. Sex was the last thing on my mind as I franticly attempted to recapture the crack's elusive "bodygasm".

There was only about two or three hits left, and as my companion reached for some, I growled at her like a rabid dog would growl at a puppy who attempted to take a morsel of his food. I could see her getting dressed out of the corner of my eye but ignored her as I tried unsuccessfully to reach nirvana. She left the hotel room in a huff, leaving the door open, but I remained naked on the edge of the bed waiting for the ecstasy that the crack kept promising me.

A car door slammed, snapping me out of my stupor. I got up and walked to the door naked, my manhood shriveled up like a turtle hiding its head and closed the room door. I had enough money left for a cab ride back to Porters Quarters to buy a few more pieces of "rock", as they referred to crack in Florida. As I put my clothes back on, I looked into the mirror and didn't recognize the person in the reflection. I saw a crazed crack fiend with sweat rolling down his face, desperately longing for another hit of the Great Lie that crack cocaine is.

Even though I still had a couple hours left to keep the room, I left the key on the bed when I left because I knew deep inside that as soon as I copped some rock I would find the nearest crack house and get "glued" to my seat. I decided to walk back to the "hood" because paying for a cab would be a waste of good crack money.

As soon as I arrived in Porters Quarters, a young crack dealer approached me. "Whussup playa?" he asked. He could tell by the wide-eyed look I had that I was in search of crack. "Gimme forty dollars' worth" I replied. He pulled out a slab of rock the size of a Ritz cracker and snapped off a forty dollar piece. I was in such a rush to smoke that I took the piece and started to walk away without even paying. "Fuck you doin' playa?" he shouted. I turned around and dug into my pocket as I realized I didn't pay and pulled out two twenty-dollar bills. "My bad, man".

As I walked down the small side street, I noticed a woman who looked like she smoked crack and asked her if she knew where we could take a hit. She told me to follow her and we went inside a clapboard house that looked like actual slaves had lived in it at one time. The house was so dilapidated that I could see daylight through the walls. It was more shack than house. Two inch long cockroaches competed for space with me on the greasy table that we sat at. I kept my crack in my hand instead of on the table because I feared that the king sized roaches would scurry off with what little crack I had left!

I took hit after hit and wasn't even coming close to the euphoria that I so desperately wanted. The only effect the rock was having on me was that my heart beat like the piston on a racecar and my mind body and soul craved MORE! I was smoking frantically, like the guy who didn't go to work when I first set out to become a big time drug dealer in the Ashmun St Projects. I had promised myself that I would never get to that point, but here I was; a geek monster smoking like it was going out of style! I had set out to become Nino Brown, but wound up becoming Pookie!

After the last hit was smoked, I abruptly stood up and exited the shack. I needed more money and had to come up with an idea quickly because the hunger had returned. In the past, I would simply use my pistol and stick up the nearest young boy who had some crack, but now, without a pistol, I was clueless.

It was dark now, and the streets were almost deserted. The same young boy who I had copped from earlier approached me from behind. "Hold up playa, I got some good shit for ya!" I knew I didn't have any money so I told him I was straight. "Just take a look at it, playa" he persisted. "I told you, I'm straight, man" I replied as I kept walking. The teenager, who couldn't have been any more than sixteen or seventeen, jogged up to me and insisted that I take a look at his "product".

I intentionally stuck out my left hand and let him place a rock about the size of a red and white peppermint in my hand as my right hand remained at my side. I appeared to be checking out the weight of it and then suddenly smashed the fist of my right hand into the side of his face. He was out cold before he hit the ground and I took off running, crack in hand, towards the "slave shack" I had just left minutes ago. I literally ran right out of the loosely laced, shell-toed Adiddas I was wearing, but continued to run in my socks until I arrived at my destination.

I burst through the door of the shack without knocking, startling the frail woman who sat at the table scraping the residue of her pipe with a wire hanger. She looked me up and down noticing that I wasn't wearing any shoes with a puzzled look on her face until I showed her the rock that I had just . . . acquired. While we smoked, I wasn't able to enjoy my high because I kept expecting the young boy and his friends to burst through the door, pistols blazing. After each hit, I would glance nervously at the door, but my paranoia didn't stop me from taking hit after hit until the crack was gone.

When I was done smoking, I took a few minutes to "come down" and then stood up to leave. I was convinced that once I exited the shack I would be killed in a hail of gunfire, but my craving for more crack gave me the courage to go back out into the night in search of more drugs.

As I walked down the street in my stocking feet, I expected every car that drove by to be filled with shooters seeking retribution for the strong-arm robbery I had just committed. I had no idea how or where I was going to get any money, so I walked aimlessly around the downtown area.

"Look at you, you piece of shit" said the voice inside my crack filled brain. *"Walking around like a damn fool with no shoes on! You were clean for six months and were on your way to getting back together with your wife and child, but you threw it all away for a piece of ass that you didn't even get! What a fucking loser"* As I "listened" to the ridicule emanating from within me, I gave up on myself. I believed that I really WAS a loser. I accepted the fact that I would be a crack head for the rest of my life, and never amount to anything.

I had lost all hope in myself, and we all know that a person who has no hope can be dangerous to themselves and others. I was lost and turned out and didn't care about myself or anyone else. All that mattered was the next hit.

As I walked the streets of Greenville that night, with no shoes on, and a crazed look in my eyes, I could hear the automatic locks of peoples cars clicking as I crossed the street. I had reached the point of no return and thank God I didn't have my pistol anymore because I would probably be doing "ten to twenty" if I did!

I entered the Arby's restaurant at about 10:30pm as they were about to close and hopped across the counter. The cute young college girl who was working the cash register looked at me in amazement as she noticed my tattered socks. "Miles?" she said as I walked towards the back where the safe was located. I ignored her and entered the manager's office where the company safe was located. Due to my disoriented state of mind, it took me a couple of tries before I got the safe opened. Once I had it opened, I took all the cash on hand and stuffed it into my jeans pockets. As I hopped back over the counter and made my way out, the employees that I had trained looked at me incredulously as the day shift manager walked out of the restaurant with the day's receipts, wearing nothing on his feet but dirty, worn out socks!

I had at least a thousand dollars in my pockets. *"We can smoke all the rock we want now!"* I said to myself. I no longer viewed the malicious voice inside my head as a separate entity; I just figured it was an undesirable part of my personality that didn't like me too much! Yes, dear reader, I was completely off my rocker!

As I approached another part of town where I knew I could cop some rock, I could feel the anticipation building inside of me so fast that my stomach began to growl as if I hadn't eaten in days. The mental aspect of my addiction was manifesting itself in physical form as my heart rate increased and my bowels released an unusual amount of flatulence.

I noticed a car with two men in it pass me and slow to a stop about a block away. The car turned around and passed me again and I could tell the two guys were staring at me hard. I stuck up my middle finger at them and shouted, "Get the fuck outta here, you fuckin' faggots!" thinking they were trying to pick me up.

Suddenly, squad cars came screaming down the street from both directions and the two guys I had just given the finger to, jumped out of their car, guns drawn. "Get on the ground mother fucker" they shouted. I was high as a kite, but I knew better than to try and fight the police, so I followed their orders and got on my knees. They slammed me to the ground, face first as one of them put his knee on my neck. I wasn't fighting back, but they took no chances as they handcuffed me. One of the cops went through my pockets and removed the cash I had stolen before they threw me into the back seat of a patrol car.

As I lay in the back seat with my face on the seat, I could feel the dirt and gravel that was stuck to my sweaty face scratch me as the car turned corners and hit bumps in the road. We arrived at Arby's parking lot and the female cashier walked up to the rear of the patrol car accompanied by a uniformed policeman. "That's him" she said, and walked away shaking her head.

I just lay there with my face down, feeling ashamed of myself and embarrassed that I was once again getting arrested because I was allowing this cunning and baffling addiction to ruin my life. Roy, the owner abruptly appeared at the squad cars rear window and let loose a torrent of expletive laced screams as his star employee lay in the back seat of a police car for stealing the contents of the company safe!

"I hope you rot in jail you piece of shit! After ALL I done for you, this is how you repay me?" He had tears in his eyes as he screamed at me, oblivious to why I would do something like this. As he chastised me through the window of the squad car, I balled up into a semi fetal position and began to cry uncontrollably as I wondered why I would behave in such an insane way after doing so well for the last six months. The amount of shame and guilt inside of me multiplied exponentially as I wished for death. *"I can't spend the rest of my life like this,"* I told myself. *"If there is a God, please strike me down this instant and release me from this pain and agony that I have brought upon myself!"*

As the squad car left the parking lot, I began to scream at the top of my lungs. "Why, why, why!" I wanna die, I wanna die, I wanna die!" I screamed over and over again, spit and snot spraying from my mouth and nose. The cops were telling me to shut the fuck up, but all I could do was scream and beg God or the devil to please take my life.

When we arrived back at the county jail, I was placed in the "Psyche Unit" and placed on suicide watch in a padded cell with a paper robe and a metal cot. I had become catatonic and lay there for days, refusing food and water. Whenever a guard would speak to me, I just stared off into the distance or turned my back to them and squeezed my eyes shut, praying for death.

Even though I was physically locked up in jail, I retreated further into the prison of my mind where it was safe and warm. I had no desire whatsoever to interact with anyone in the real world because I had lost everything and everybody that meant anything to me. The purpose of me moving to Greenville was to get my act together, but all I had done was make my life worse!

Unable to soothe the pain in my mind with drugs, I resorted back to the drug of my childhood . . . fantasy!

Oblivious to the world around me, I prayed to the devil because I knew for sure that if there really was a God, He wanted nothing to do with a wretch like me! "Oh mighty Prince of Darkness, please take my life and I will serve you for eternity!" Anything had to be better than the living hell that I found myself in. I retreated into a world of fantasy within my fractured mind where the Devil magically transported me out of jail with a suitcase full of money and a suitcase full of crack. "Go forth into the world my servant, and partake in whatever decadent behavior you desire!" Old Satan told me. "Have a ball you sorry piece of shit, and when you are finished, your ass belongs to me!"

I dreamed of crack laced hotel parties and wild sexual excursions with porn stars. I spent money like it was going out of style and was the center of attention as naked women caressed my body and performed the most outrageous sexual acts on me.

I drifted in and out of consciousness; briefly returning to reality when the guards clanged my meal tray on the metal platform of my cell door. The only time I acted like I had any kind of sense was when the cellblock nurse offered me that little plastic cup of pills. I have no idea what kind of pills they were but they facilitated my return to oblivion.

Even in the deep, dark recesses of my own mind, I was unable to escape the evil clutches of my deep-seated, self-hatred. Throughout my disassociation from reality, the negative spirit within me would periodically rip me away from my fantasy world and berate me until I drifted back to my fantasy du jour. Whenever my self-hatred reared its ugly head, I would scream at myself internally, ranting about how much of a loser I was. *"You had it all! Good wife, Army career, the love and respect of your family . . . now look at you. No wonder people always kicked your ass when you were growing up; you are a worthless piece of shit!"*

Whenever the shame and embarrassment became too much to bear, I begged the Devil to please end this miserable existence of mine. The line between fantasy and reality became blurred and I didn't know if I was really conversing with the Devil or not.

Chapter 37

The Big House

After a week or two, I went before the judge, who was flabbergasted that I was before him again! He had given me a sweetheart deal by allowing me to go to Meta when he could have easily sent me to prison in the first place. I was on two years' probation for my stupid little "faux attempted robbery", and he vowed to make sure I did every day of it in prison! I stood there with my head down and listened as he admonished me, feeling ashamed and embarrassed as the prosecutor read out loud the police report of the night I had completely lost my mind and robbed my own job in plain sight of the very employees that I had trained! This was definitely *not* the life I had planned for myself when I got my G.E.D. and embarked on my Army career!

After I listened to my charges read out loud, including the specifics about not having shoes on and screaming in the back seat of the police car, the judge looked at me over his glasses and told me that I would be dead within five years if I continued down the road I was on. He explained to me and the 20 or so guards, court workers and family members who were crowded into the small court room that it wasn't too late to turn my life around and get back on track. I saw compassion in his eyes as his voice lowered, and he kept referring to me as "son", much like 1st Sgt. Hilliard did back in Germany.

At first, when I went before the middle aged, balding, white guy sitting on the judge's bench wearing a black robe, and stern look on his face, I had him pegged for just another red neck who enjoyed sending "niggas" to jail, but his tone changed as he spoke to me with genuine compassion. I actually felt hopeful as he implored me to get my life together. When he asked me if I was going to continue to seek help for my addiction, I bowed my head and said, "Yes your honor" with a tentative voice and tears running down my face. In spite of the fact that I was about to go to prison for two years, this man's words were comforting to me. I vowed right there in that court room that I would rid myself of this horrible condition once and for all and become the man that I always wanted to be.

When I returned to the county jail, I removed my ass from the "pity-pot" and began to take showers and eat my meals. I reassured the jail house social worker that I was fine and I was placed back into the general population. This time I slept in a large bay with about 50 other inmates. Due to overcrowding, the cellblocks were all filled up, so cots were set up in the gym and the prisoners who had already been sentenced slept there. It took about two weeks to actually get transferred to prison because the prisons were at capacity also!

Cocaine was big business in the eighties and I couldn't help but notice that the majority of the prisoners in jail were either drug users or drug dealers. I found the hierarchy between the dealers and the users quite amusing. The dealers looked down on the "crackheads" with disdain, not realizing that whether you sold the shit or smoked it, you still wound up locked up like an animal! The only difference between a drug addict and a drug dealer in jail is the fancy sneakers that contrasted with your orange prison jumpsuit and more commissary items in your locker!

A major part of my fractured personality had given up, but there was a tiny part, deep inside my soul that wanted to live and enjoy life. In time, I began to pray to a God named "Whatever Is Out There". I didn't think there was really a God at all, and if there WAS one, he sat angry and in judgment of me; dispensing punishment after punishment upon me, in retaliation for the horrible sins I had committed. In spite of my spiritual immaturity, I knew damned well that I didn't need to be prayin' to no damned devil. I wasn't sure if God or the devil even existed, but just in case they did, I wanted to be on the right side!

One day, I was called to the "admin' section over the loudspeaker. "Inmate Miles Walcott report to admin. Inmate Miles Walcott, report to admin. I was kinda confused because the only time an inmate was called to admin was when they received additional charges or someone posted their bond. I knew for sure that I didn't have new charges and being a sentenced prisoner, I knew I for damn sure that I wasn't getting bonded out; so what could they possibly want me for?

As I entered the admin wing with a puzzled look on my face, a sheriff's deputy walked over to me. "Are you Miles Walcott?" he asked. "Yeah, what did I do now? I asked with a silly smirk on my face. I knew I hadn't committed any other crimes (that they knew of) so I figured there must be some kind of mistake. "Apparently, you didn't do enough" said the sheriff, with an equally silly smirk. "You've been served" he stated, as he handed me a manila folder filled with official looking papers. He smiled and walked away as I stood there going over the contents of the folder.

Weezy had filed for divorce and had me served in jail! As I read the papers and realized what they were, a deep sadness tried to take over and make me drop to my knees crying, but I had to put on a front in front of the guard because I had a reputation as the silent, tough guy ever since I kicked "Fat Guy" and his friend's asses. "Wow, talk about kickin' a man when he's down" I joked to the guard as he escorted me back to the dorm. "I don't want the bitch no more anyway," I said, trying to appear macho, when right beneath the surface, I was crushed! I knew deep down inside that I deserved this, but my already shattered personality and nonexistent self-esteem felt obliterated as I read court documents that I interpreted as saying that "You fucked up so bad that your wife doesn't even want you anymore!"

After a day or two, I became at peace with the fact that Weezy had went above and beyond the call of duty and taken far more than the average woman would have. I signed the papers and gave her an uncontested divorce, which was probably the most mature decision I had made in a very long time! I had a tough guy image to protect, and basically chose not to feel the pain of rejection, so I stuffed those feelings deep down in to my psyche, where they festered for years.

I actually looked forward to being transferred to one of South Carolina's numerous state prisons, and getting away from the riotous atmosphere of the county jail. In the "County", as inmates referred to the jail, there was a volatile mixture of different gangs from around the area. The majority of the prisoners were teenagers and loud as hell! They never seemed to sleep and carried on loud conversations well into the night, even after the cells were locked. Guys on one end of the cellblock would yell down to guys on the other end as if they weren't going to see each other first thing in the morning. Eventually, someone would scream out, "SHUT THE FUCK UP!" and they would bring it down to a "quiet roar"

At times, it sounded like I was in the monkey house at the Bronx Zoo! The older inmates spoke of state prison as some sort of peaceful utopia where cats just wanted to do their time and come home. Sure, there was the occasional fight at the "State", but it wasn't a mad house where people got shanked every day the way prisons are portrayed in TV and film.

They never told you in advance exactly when you were leaving, I guess to prevent you from planning an escape, but I looked forward to my departure with anticipation as if I was getting an up grade on a cruise!

The day for my transfer to state prison finally came and I felt like a kid on Christmas morning when the guard kicked the corner of my bed at 4a.m. and told me to grab my belongings and report to the front entrance of the "dorm"

I sat in my seat on the prison bus that drove all over South Carolina's countryside dropping off one or two prisoners to the many prisons that dotted the country side. Our hands were free to eat the bag lunch we were provided, but our ankle shackles were locked to a bolt in the floor of the bus. As I looked out the bus's window in awe at the diverse South Carolina landscape, my dreams were of a happy life without the shackles of addiction.

I was going to do my time and when I got out, get some type of training or college and live a happy productive life! For the first time in my life I felt hopeful about the future.

I was sent to a minimum-security prison compound in the middle of a swampy area on the South Carolina-Georgia state line. A chain link fence with loops of barbed wire across the top surrounded it, but other than that, it didn't look like a prison at all. There were no towers with shot gun toting guards in them, but it was common knowledge that if you tried to escape, the guards had the right to shoot you. If you had the balls to escape, you would have to forge through 10 miles of swamp and snakes to get to the nearest hick town.

The compound had six barracks style units that had windows instead of bars. Each unit housed about 25 or 30 inmates. There was a dining hall, a medical building and an administration building also. Besides the barbed wire, it resembled a small Army post. Smack dab in the middle of it all was a recreation area or "rec" yard that had sets of weights and a horseshoe pit, but the full-length, regulation sized basketball court is what caught my eye.

This particular prison was designated for criminals convicted of what were considered to be non-violent crimes, such as drug possession, auto theft and the like. The South Carolina Department of Corrections was very generous with giving out "good time", which was time off of your sentence for good behavior, so the majority of prisoners here avoided fighting as much as possible because a fight could cost you as much as six months extra on your sentence. Five years if you hit a guard! No one at this prison had more than a two-year sentence and dudes didn't want to extend their all ready short stay here!

The highlight of the day was the evening basketball games that were played after evening chow. The mid-level drug dealers who had what seemed like and endless supply of commissary items such as cigarettes, cigars, cakes, cookies, soups and toiletries, would "sponsor" five man teams that competed against each other in an unauthorized but tolerated basketball league.

Each of the teams "coaches" would bet each other cash and commissary and divide the "loot" amongst their players after each game, of course keeping the lions share for themselves. The first hour of "rec" was called open court, where anyone who wanted to play could run half court "pick-up" games. It was here that I showed off my exceptional basketball skills.

I was about twenty-four or twenty-five years old and in spite of my recent drug use, I was in tiptop shape. I dominated every game, performing powerful dunks and fancy dribbling skills and it wasn't long before I caught the eye of the "coaches". They offered me all the Newport cigarettes I could smoke, and all the cakes and snacks I wanted if I played on their team. Their offers were tempting, but I held out a few days waiting for the best offer.

Guys would ask me where I was from and when I told them Connecticut, they would almost always say, "Where the fuck is Connecticut?" I would use undetectable sarcasm and explain that Ct. was right above New York and watch as they nodded their heads in understanding. Eventually, my nickname became New York, apparently Connecticut just didn't sound "cool" enough! It gave me a great sense of pride when I heard the spectators yell, "Give it to New York" in a clutch situation!

The Florida Department of Corrections provided me with "three hots and a cot" but I needed money to buy toiletries, smokes and the occasional honey bun. My family practiced tough love and didn't coddle me by sending me money every week like some of the other inmate's families did. Like my Mom said, "You made your bed hard, now you gotta sleep in it!" She didn't leave me for dead though, she sent me underwear and socks which I was grateful for, but that was about it.

I had a little hustle where I would write letters for inmates who couldn't write, but that was slow money. I would only write two or three letters a week earning a pack of smokes here and there or a cake, but that was no match for the "loot" the "Ballers" and "Shot callers" were offering.

I wound up playing for a dude named Flex who was so confident in my skills that he even pitted me against the other "coaches" best players in special 1:1 games that drew the whole compound including the guards.

I was able to get a job working in the chow hall as a kitchen helper, which subtracted time off my sentence. Anyone who took on an extra duty would get additional time off for good behavior calculated into the time that the state automatically gave out.

Every day after breakfast, I would stay behind with a few other inmates and helped sweep and mop the floors and wash pots. It broke up the monotony of the day and I enjoyed certain perks, such as extra leftovers and deserts from the night before that I was allowed to bring back to my dorm to be eaten at night while we watched TV.

Even though I was in prison, I enjoyed my time there. It was kind of like living on an Army post, except we got locked in at night. I wasn't on crack anymore and being sort of a celebrity ball player on the prison "rec" yard made me feel good about myself. Between my "earnings" from basketball and letter writing, my commissary locker stayed pretty full. I had finally made it to the pros! (Insert tongue in cheek)

On Wednesdays, a list would be posted on the dorm wall with everyone's "good time" totals and release dates. Your release date changed every week based on how much "good time" you had accrued, and my release date was rapidly approaching.

I wound up serving a year and a half on my two-year sentence and was released with $100.00 cash and a bus ticket to Greenville, SC. As the guard drove me to the Greyhound bus depot that was about five miles from the prison compound, I felt the breeze from the open window caress my face as I vowed to remain crack free and get my life back together.

Once I arrived in Greenville, I stayed at a homeless shelter for three or four days until my mother and father agreed to purchase a bus ticket for me so that I could return to Ct. They were very leery about helping me because they knew how crazy I had been acting since I got out of the Army. "I don't want any shit from you when you get up here, Son" My father warned me. "It's time to put that bullshit down and be a man!"

I was convinced that if I stayed in Greenville, I would go back to smoking crack, so I made the decision to leave my first born, man child until I could get my act together and be the father that he deserved. At the time, I had no idea that wherever I went . . . there I was! If I didn't have something stronger than the sweet serenade of the devilish desires from within, I was destined to fail.

CHAPTER 38

The Prodigal Son Returns . . . Again!

I hit the ground running once again when I returned to Ct. Within a week; I was hired at Walgreens Pharmacy on Whalley Ave., and was actively looking for something more lucrative. My parents allowed me to live at their house, but there was no hero's welcome this time. Mom and Dad sat me down and explained to me that at the first hint of drug use, I would be asked to leave. My father and I were to sit down at the kitchen table each time I got paid and manage my money together. We would deposit a percentage of my check into a dual savings account that was to be exclusively used for an apartment. This wasn't an indefinite stay at the "Walcott Mansion" and my parents reminded me that a real, able-bodied man supported himself. Once I had enough saved for an apartment, it was agreed that I would become independent. "You can come by once in a while to eat" my father said. "ONCE in a while!"

My father and I put twenty or thirty dollars a week of my salary into an envelope, for gas money and expenses during the week, and I agreed to put receipts for any money spent back into the envelope each time I made a withdrawal. He also encouraged me to send money to Weezy each time I got paid to help with Miles Jr, but he left that up to me. "Taking care of your son is between you and Weezy." He told me, "That boy aint ask to come here. Make sure you do right by your son"

Depending on how much I made that week, I was expected to pay on a sliding scale for my room and board! No adult children lived under my parents roof for free! Even if you were unemployed, you were expected to at least do your fair share of the chores in the house.

I worked the third shift at Walgreens, unloading pallets of merchandise and putting it on the shelves. I got off at 7a.m. and my dad didn't have to be at work till 9a.m. so he allowed me to drive his sporty Dodge Daytona. This was a significant show of love on my father's part, because anyone who knew Charlie Walcott, knew that he was notorious for not letting anyone drive his cars! He kept all of his cars meticulously clean and took excellent care of the engine and maintenance; that's why his cars always lasted for years.

Although my parents were showing me tough love by monitoring my whereabouts and enforcing a curfew ("You aint gonna be comin in and out of my house at all hours of the night"), the threat of being homeless if I smoked crack was enough to keep me on the straight and narrow.

After about three months, I had enough money saved up to pay for a nice efficiency apartment and moved into a nice little spot on Edwards St., which was on the "artsy" side of town, by Peabody Museum. In my own "infinite wisdom", I figured that if I didn't live in "the hood" I would be less likely to smoke crack. The place was furnished with a kitchenette table and a pullout couch, so along with the end tables and kitchen utensils my mom gave me; I had a pretty cool bachelor pad!

My father surprised me by giving me all the money I had paid him for room and board back to me! "Get yourself some new clothes," he said with a proud smile on his face. "And don't forget to send some money to Florida for Miles Jr. Even though I was an adult, my dad wasn't finished teaching me how to be a man, and I appreciate that to this very day!

I began going to local 12 Step meetings, and was amazed at the many "success stories" who attended them. Guys who used to be on the street corners begging for change in between heroin nods or crack hits, were pulling up in brand new cars and wearing fresh gear. One dude, who used to be a notorious dope fiend, was at the meeting sharing about closing on a new house and getting a big promotion at his job!

The same guy, who I had looked down my nose in disgust at when I first got into the drug game, had over two years clean now, which I thought was a miracle! He had a certain "glow" about him that let me know he had found peace and serenity. The same guy who I judged a few years ago as I sold him drugs, was now picking me up to go to meetings and treating my broke ass to coffee! He was living proof that a person could become free of addiction, and live a happy, productive life!

Even my cousin Lynne who had been on coke for years, had gotten clean and graduated from nursing school all the while raising her three children in an immaculately furnished apartment on Prospect St. The more 12 step meetings I attended, the more miracles I witnessed; but I still refused to believe that it could happen to me.

Occasionally, experienced members were asked to tell everyone how long they had been "clean" from drugs. One of the purposes of this was to let newer members know that freedom from active addiction was possible. I claimed three years clean, even though I had more like a year and a half. My self-esteem was so low and my personality so shattered that I felt like I needed to lie in order to be accepted. I had a deep-rooted need to be accepted and thought I would be more accepted by lying about my clean time. After attending the meetings for a while, I realized that the members with the least amount of clean time were showered with love and attention from the moment they entered the door!

I picked up on the Recovery "lingo" quickly and when I "shared", I did so in a way that insinuated I had more Recovery than I really did. I'm sure the older members could tell that I was full of shit because they would occasionally pull me to the side on the smoke breaks and suggest that I "take the cotton out of my ears, and put it in my mouth!" Learn to listen and listen to learn, they gently told me.

Just like at the Metamorphosis drug program, I believed that I wasn't as "bad" as the weak-minded folks at the meetings, and refused to believe that the spiritual principles of 12 Step Programs applied to me. I was still convinced that I could overcome my malady through sheer will-power alone, in spite of the fact that my strongest attempts at will power never lasted more than a year or two.

My parents were proud of their wayward son who appeared to have finally gotten his life together and even allowed me to use their cars to attend out of town meetings and large conventions where thousands of recovering addicts gathered and celebrated Recovery. It was at these conventions that my sham caught up with me and I felt the worst. I was attending 12 Step meetings to feel better, but because of the fear driven lie I was living, I felt worse than I felt BEFORE coming to the meetings!

At one point during the convention, over a thousand addicts from all over the country would gather in the main ballroom of whatever hotel they had rented for the weekend and have what was called the "clean time count-down". During this countdown, they would start with the folks with the most clean time and ask them to stand. Usually, one or two people with 25 to 30 years clean would stand up and the ballroom would erupt into a roar of applause. We would then count down through the years and when they got to three years clean, I had to continue my charade and stand up and cheer with the rest of the people with three years. I could see looks of sheer joy as folks proudly stood up and represented their clean time as I stood there and faked the funk!

There is a saying in the recovery community that says, "You can't keep what you have unless you give it away". It basically encourages members to share their experience strength and hope with newer members in order to show them that Recovery was possible. I thought I sounded pretty good as I parroted recovery lingo at the 12 step meetings, sharing about spiritual awakenings and conscious contact with a Higher Power, but what I failed to realize was that you can't give away that which you do not all ready possess!

I continued to attend the meetings and conventions and passed myself off as a person in Recovery for a few more months but eventually, the empty feeling I had from perpetrating a fraud caused me to slowly drift away from the clean and sober crowd.

By now, I was floating on a false sense of confidence and the fact that I still believed that all it took was willpower to resist the urge to smoke crack. I thought all this talk of Higher Powers and Fellowshipping was a bunch of bullshit for weak-minded individuals who were too weak to stop on their own!

CHAPTER 39

Chaos

My younger sister Lizan and I became close friends during my twenties. As teens, we pretty much argued and fussed all the time as teen siblings often do. However, we had a deep bond since childhood and would fight tooth and nail for each other if anyone even looked at one of us wrong!

Even though she was my younger sister, Lizan was very protective of me. "Answer ya damn phone sometimes" she would admonish me if she hadn't talked to me in a few days. "You better not be smoking that shit again!" she would say if I wanted to borrow ten or twenty dollars. I welcomed her sisterly concern and would always reassure her that I was just fine. She always showed me unconditional love, even in my darkest moments. All my sisters believed in me . . . even when I didn't believe in myself!

She didn't want her brother caught out on drugs again and wasn't going to let me go out like that. Not on HER watch! One time, she even broke the window to my apartment when I didn't respond to her calls. I had spent the night at a lady friend's house and left my dads car at my apartment while I rode in my lady friend's car with her. Liz and I were so close that if I had company, I could simply crack the door and say, "I have company" with a silly grin on my face and she would get the picture and leave, so when I didn't answer the door with Dad's car parked outside my apartment, she panicked. This was before cell phones and beepers came out so if someone didn't answer their house phone, you had no way of contacting them. I had all ready told my sister of my exploits in Florida and the poor girl was terrified of finding me overdosed or shot dead! I used to justify my drug use by saying that I wasn't hurting anyone but myself, but when my little sister broke into my house because she feared that I was back on crack again, I finally realized that an addicts drug use affects everyone who loves them!

Lizan had graduated from a Certified Nurses Aid course and was making good money doing private duty cases. I was busting suds as a busboy at one of Yale University's many dining halls. It was a good job and paid a good wage but I just couldn't see myself running a dishwasher the rest of my life. Liz was making about five more dollars an hour than I was as a C.N.A. so I began to reconsider my career options. "You would make a great C.N.A." she encouraged. "Later on, you get your nursing license and make even more money!"

I did enjoy working with people and quite frankly; working in a line of work that was predominantly female was quite appealing to me! My boss at Pierson Dining Hall allowed me to change my shift from mornings to evenings, and I enrolled in a CNA class at the Ct Business Institute located in downtown New Haven. I am eternally grateful that Lizan encouraged me to go into the health care field. I work in the human services field to this day and get immense pleasure from helping those who are less fortunate than me!

I felt a strong sense of pride as I rode the city bus in my crisp white scrubs and believed I was on top of the world. I felt as though nothing could shake my determination to stay out of trouble and carried myself with pep in my step and a glide in my stride! Nothing could stop me now! I had arrived to a point in my life where I felt I was in control of my life. I began to entertain thoughts that maybe, just maybe I could smoke crack again, safely. Now that I was in control of myself, I reasoned, there was no way I would get caught out again. The thoughts would come and go, depending on the mood I was in, but never the less, they came. I learned later on in life that it is impossible for me to control my crack use, but at this particular time in my life I truly believed it was just a case of mind over matter!

I was beginning to have a different awareness of myself in the fall of 1989 and I no longer viewed the angry voice from within as a part of my personality. I thought of it as a separate entity that wasn't a part of me at all and was hell bent on sending me to an early grave. While I was incarcerated, I read extensively on the id, ego and super ego. I knew about delusions, hallucinations and personality disorders, but this . . . anomaly, for lack of a better word, was something quite different.

At the core of my soul was something that *didn't* want to destroy my life with drugs and dangerous living. *This* part of me wanted me to be a happy, productive member of society! It was very soft spoken, kind of like that good friend who says, "I wouldn't do that if I were you!" right before you make a stupid decision. It was a constant presence that sort of operated in the background of my soul; non-intrusive, but ready to comfort me the second I called on it.

It was the evil voice that had suggested I smoke crack in the past after being clean for six months. It was THIS voice that told me to risk my life by robbing drug dealers to support my habit and have unprotected sex with prostitutes, when no decent woman in her right mind would have anything to do with me! It was also the same voice that propelled me into action whenever I felt threatened and for that reason, I allowed it to call the shots when I felt I was in danger; like the day I got arrested for assault in the American Discount variety store.

The day had started out great. I was in the "clinical" phase of my training where instead of a classroom, we met at the Veterans Administration Hospital and do actual hands on care. As I ironed my white scrubs, I had a great conversation with my dad over the phone. He was telling me how proud he was of me and to keep up the good work. My father and I were closer than ever now, and I enjoyed making him proud.

When my dad and I were done talking, I took a leisurely stroll to the bus stop with my chest poked out and my head held high, strutting proudly in a fresh pair white Nikes and my crisp white scrubs. While I waited for the bus, I flirted with a cutie pie that was waiting there also. She flirted back, and I reveled in the fact that women were once again giving me attention. When I was "smoking" women stayed away, but I was only two or three months out of prison and still in great shape and wanted to bang every girl I met!

I got off the bus three stops early and walked across the New Haven green, hoping to check out the pretty ladies as I made my way to my next bus stop. The American Discount store in downtown New Haven, had entrances on two different streets, so I took the shortcut through the store. As I exited the store on Chapel St., I inadvertently bumped a guy as we passed in the doorway. "My bad" I said apologetically, and continued on my way out of the store. The next thing I knew, the guy had grabbed me by the shoulder and yelled into my face, "You can't FUCKING say excuse me?"

As he yelled the word "FUCKING", some spit flew out of his mouth and I immediately turned from happy-go-lucky nurse's aide student to that scared soldier being accosted by the skinheads. I whirled around and punched him in the face twice before he knew what hit him. He stumbled backwards into the store and instead of leaving, I followed him inside and grabbed a piece of the metal clothes rack that I noticed sitting on a nearby shelf. He began to dig into his pocket for something and that gave me permission to go sick on his ass before he could pull out whatever he was reaching for. "Kill this motherfucker, man! Who does he think he is, putting his hands on you!" said the angry voice from within. It was as if I was suddenly possessed by an angry spirit as "Crazy Miles" began to defend the scared little kid trapped in a grown man's body.

"*Enough*" said the soft quiet voice from within me. It wasn't really a voice; it was more like a feeling that emanated from deep within my soul. I stopped swinging the piece of metal and felt my temper return back to normal and just stared at "Tough Guy". He looked up at me and took off running, so I dropped the metal pole on the floor and made my way out of the store.

In the course of the fight, I managed to cut my hand, and my once pristine uniform had blood splattered all over it. I grabbed some napkins from the hot dog vender on the corner to stem the bleeding, and walked across the street to the bus stop. "I'll tell them I fell or something," I said to myself as I thought about what I would tell my instructors.

Before my bus came, a squad car pulled up right in front of me with "Tough Guy" in the back seat. "That's him!" he yelled, while pointing his finger at me with one hand and holding his head with the other. Ten minutes ago, he was grabbing my shoulder and cussing in my face, but now that I had given him a "two piece dinner with extra fries", he was sitting in the back of the police car playing the victim! I tried to explain to the police that the guy laid hands on me first and I was just defending myself, but they told me to turn around. "You're under arrest!"

As the paddy wagon made its way to the Union Ave. Police Station, I broke out into uncontrollable tears. As we rode through the streets of New Haven, picking up other prisoners, a dude sitting across from me found it quite amusing that the tall, muscular guy who was charged with a misdemeanor, was crying as if he were about to go do twenty years. "Take it easy young blood" said the middle aged man with long, nappy, lint filled dread locks. "You'll be out in an hour man" he said, with an amused smile. I could smell his putrid, alcohol and vomit laced breathe through my hands as I held my head in my hands and when I looked up at him to tell him why I was *really* crying, I noticed his teeth were either missing or rotting in his head. Although he looked like the stereotypical "wino", there was something about his eyes that made me feel at ease. As I squinted in the dim confines of the "Paddy Wagon" to get a better view of the twinkle in this strangers eyes, he leaned forward and whispered, "You gonna be ok, young blood, trust me."

A few seconds later, we were all herded into the holding tank, or "bull-pen" as it was affectionately called. Once I was fingerprinted and processed, the guard placed me in a cell by myself. As I lay on the metal bench, waiting for the bondsman to come through, I tried to figure out why I would react so violently when I was in such a great mood. Why the hell do I "lose it" so easily? I had never even heard of post traumatic stress disorder yet, and didn't yet realize that I was re-living every traumatic event of my life each time I got into a confrontation. I carried around a complete 10-piece luggage set that was over flowing with emotional turmoil wherever I went. It would be a very long time before I would figure out how to lighten the load.

I was charged with Assault II and spent a couple hours in lock up before my dad posted my bond. "As long as it aint about drugs, I got your back" said my father. While we sat in his car, my father reached over and gingerly ruffled my hair as I sat there feeling ashamed. Even without any drugs in my system, I still managed to get myself arrested! "its o.k. Chief" my dad reassured me. "Sometimes you gotta do what you gotta do!" I told the police and my father that I was just defending myself, but I knew deep inside that I was ready to inflict some major pain on that guy until something that I didn't quite understand helped me "come down". I thought I was in control of myself but I was actually one "shoulder bump" away from a murder charge!

When I was arraigned, my charges had been reduced to Breach of Peace, to which I plead guilty and received 1 years' probation. I walked out of the courthouse relieved that I didn't get jail time and listened to the voice from within reassure me. "We aint gonna let NOBODY beat us up anymore! Anyone fucks with us has another thing coming!" I was convinced that if I didn't let "Crazy Miles" take over during altercations and confrontations, I would wind up getting my ass kicked like so many times in the past. I just got out of going to jail which called for a celebration, so I caught the bus to Winchester Avenue and got off at Doug's liquor store.

Old Mr. Doug, the kind West Indian guy who was the original owner, had retired a few years earlier. After having two strokes back to back, running the store was more than he could handle, and I found it quite amusing to walk in and find two Middle Eastern guys running the store! Mr. Doug was a fixture in my childhood and I revered him as an uncle, so I was pretty disappointed not to see him behind the counter.

I ran into Mr. Doug one day as I was dropping off a private duty patient of mines at an adult day care center. He was sitting in a wheelchair looking out of a window, facing the court yard. As I walked by him he looked up and said, "Hello there, Son!" in that familiar West Indian accent that I knew all too well. Before I even turned to see who was speaking, I knew who it was from the sound of his voice. I locked the wheels of my patient's wheel chair, walked over and hugged him as if he was a long lost uncle! The strokes had beaten him physically, but his essence and personality remained intact. We exchanged smiles and pleasantries for a moment or two until he looked me straight in the eye and asked, "Are you ok?" At the time of our encounter I had been clean for some time so I looked him in the eye and proudly said, "Yes, sir!" We both knew what he was really asking and parted with a smile. But, I digress.

It's been said that someone trying to stay off of coke should avoid alcohol, because alcohol lowers your inhibitions and decision making skills. This is undoubtedly true for most addicted people, including myself at the time, but I walked to the projects and copped two $20 bags of crack before I even popped the top of the "40oz" I had just copped from "Doug's". I was "off and running" again, damn the consequences! I was caught in a seemingly endless cycle of self-centered behavior where the only needs that were important were mines!

Webster's defines relapse as a return to a diseased state after apparent recovery, so I don't consider the many times I returned to crack in the years leading up to 1999 as relapses because I never really began the recovery process. I merely showed up at meetings and played the role of a recovering addict. I made coffee, helped set up the meeting place and even got voted in to chair some meetings because I was articulate and could "talk the talk". Problem was; I wasn't walking the walk! I wanted all the material stuff that recovering addicts worked years to obtain, but wasn't willing to do the personal work on myself that thousands of other Persons in Recovery had proven to be indispensable in *keeping* that stuff!

I wanted all the material perks of being in Recovery, such as the jobs, cars, houses, jewelry and clothes, but I was clueless that these things were mere by-products of an even larger transformation. Until I became willing to accept personal responsibility for my Recovery, I would continue the pattern of acquiring "stuff" and then losing it shortly after because I thought I could "handle it".

I even asked a few guys to be my sponsor based on what kind of car they drove! In my naivety, I equated material possessions with recovery. For the next ten years of my life I was in *refusal*, not relapse. I refused to accept any help. I refused all of the evidence that true recovery was possible and I refused to accept the fact that I could NOT control my crack use! I was what alcoholics considered a "Dry Drunk". I made no changes in my behavior or personality at all. I simply stopped smoking crack on my own will power without making any personal changes. I had all the attitudes and behaviors of a crack addict without actually smoking crack!

It's one thing to remain caught out on drugs due to a pre-existing or co-occurring mental illness, but to *know* that Recovery is possible and *still* refuse to follow the light, caused me to feel completely hopeless and despondent. What was WRONG with me? Why do I keep screwing up my life? I didn't know if there even WAS a God or not, but if there was, could He please help me? I saw Him working in other people's lives, why wouldn't he work in mine? As I sat on the pity pot, I listened to my inner self convince me that the God that I heard other people speak of in the 12 Step Meetings and churches had no time for a scumbag like me! Where I once thought of God as a fairy tale like Santa and the Easter Bunny, I now thought of Him as an angry, vengeful God who was punishing me for all my sins!

Because I willfully participated in unlawful carnal knowledge with my aunt in New York, I believed I had committed the unforgiveable. Not being in my firstborn son's life? Unforgiveable! Causing emotional pain and distress to my siblings and parents? Unforgiveable! These, and a long line of other transgressions that I was also guilty of, caused me to walk around carrying a 100 lb. duffle bag full of shame and guilt. I was a dead man walking, waiting for the day when a vindictive God, who had grown impatient with me, finally struck me down.

I was also unable to sustain any long-term relationships with women because of my drug use and volatile temper that always seemed to surface when I didn't have the money to get high and felt miserable. The old saying, "Misery loves company" certainly applied to me! My M.O. was to sweet talk my way into a woman's life and then sit back and watch it all fall apart as I allowed my addiction to rear its ugly head! My life was totally unmanageable and out of control, but I would try and control my woman's' life and demand to be treated like a king, even when I was behaving like a pawn!

I racked up a long record of domestic violence charges from having arguments that never would have happened had I not been caught in the grip of this insidious addiction. I behaved like a childish coward and had violent temper tantrums where I usually pushed and slapped the women in my life when I didn't get my way, or if, God forbid, they called me on my bullshit.

It was always all about what she could do for me, and what I needed. My woman's wants and needs came secondary, if at all. I figured that once a woman found out what kind of scumbag I really was she was going to leave me anyways, so I might as well sabotage the relationship first by either spending all my money on crack, or putting my hands on her during an argument, which always seemed to guarantee an arrest and subsequent end to the relationship.

After spending my half of the household expense money, I would get all indignant when my woman asked me for my share, I would start whooping and hollering about how I was a grown ass man and didn't need anyone questioning me about MY money. All the self-righteous screaming was just a smokescreen to divert the argument away from the fact that I had fucked up the bill money!

It is safe to say that 99% of the problems in my life could be traced directly to the self-inflicted misery that I was subjecting myself to. I never saw my father hit my mom nor even raise his voice to her so, at the time, I couldn't understand why I was so violent towards the women in my life. I learned later that if I don't love and respect myself, it's impossible to love and respect anyone else. I also learned that I was so hell bent on controlling people, places and things that if a woman stood up to me, I would use violence and intimidation to control them. If another person had done the things to me that I had done to myself, and the women I loved, I would have hunted them down and killed them!

I also reacted violently outside the home. I truly hated to fight. To this day, I abhor inflicting pain on another human being, but it seemed like I was a magnet for assholes like the guy at the American Discount store. I know now that I could have handled the majority of my disputes more appropriately, but at the time, I just felt like Charlie Brown . . . "Why is everybody always pickin on me?"

Fighting became an automatic response to any situation where I felt threatened or intimidated. Take, for instance, the day I was walking down Dixwell Avenue with my girlfriend on a warm summer's day. We were chillin' together, having a wonderful time. We had walked all the way from the downtown mall, holding hands and licking cones from Ashley's Ice Cream Shoppe like two teens in love!

I was like thirty years old and still didn't own a car because I was too busy buying BMW's and Lexus Coupes for my dealers! This dude I knew confronted me about finding my picture in his girlfriend's pocketbook. I knew exactly who he was talking about but I hadn't had any contact whatsoever with the woman in question for at least six months. It wasn't my fault that she still had my picture! As I tried to explain this to homeboy, he began to take off his Members Only jacket like he was about to kick my ass or something.

Mind you, dear reader, that this was during a period when I had a substantial amount of clean time! I had been sharing in 12 Step Meetings about how *spiritual* I felt, and how I was getting *closer* to the "God of my understanding", just like I heard other members share, but I didn't really believe the words I was sharing. They told me to "Fake it till you make it!" and faking it was exactly what I was doing, because right beneath the surface was this angry, violent guy who was always ready to fight at the drop of a hat! I used to blame my troubles on my crack use, but could not understand why I continued to get into fights and get arrested even after months, or even years of abstaining from drugs.

As Jerome took off his jacket, I waited for the precise moment when the sleeves of his jacket rendered his arms pretty much useless, and let loose with a barrage of punches that caught him off guard. As he stood there stunned, I moved in close, placing my left arm around the back of his neck and my right hand between his legs. I lifted him up to about shoulder length and then abruptly flipped him and slammed him onto the ground onto his back.

Jerome saw that the fight wasn't going in his favor, and took off running into the barbershop. Sensing that he was going in there to grab a weapon, fear took over, and I raced into the barbershop behind him. Sure enough, he was reaching for a pair of scissors as I entered, so before he could get his hands on them I smashed my body into his, knocking over bottles of hair care products and the shelves that they were on.

"You wanna STAB me, muff hugger?" I screamed repeatedly, as I pummeled his head with both fists. When I saw that he wasn't responding to my blows anymore, I jumped up, walked quickly out of the barbershop and headed down the first side street I came to. I threw my $5 faux Chicago Bulls cap and black tee shirt into a trashcan just as my girlfriend caught up with me. I resumed my leisurely walk with her, sans hat, and wearing the white tank top that I had worn underneath my tee shirt. Feeling arrogantly proud of myself, I put my arms around her waist and continued walking as if nothing ever happened.

I chuckled to myself as a police cruiser rode by us looking for a guy wearing a black tee shirt and black and red cap. The stereotype that we all look alike certainly worked in my favor *that* day! During the fight, one of the barbers had threatened to call the police, but when two black guys are fighting, it takes them at least ten minutes to respond. If you wanted the police to come quickly, you had to tell the police that two black guys were jumping a *white* person!

Even though I acted macho and said things like "He must not know who he fuckin' whiff" to impress my girlfriend, I was terrified of how easily I went from cool, calm and collected to madman at the drop of a hat. Whenever I behaved that way, it was as if I was hovering over the scene watching some strange, mad man "catch wreck". I am confident that if I were growing up in today's gun infested streets, I would surely meet an early demise!

To the judges and probation officers whom I put in charge of my freedom, I may have looked like some trouble making tough guy, but in all actuality, I was just a scared little kid trapped in a grown man's body. I was terrified of getting beat up like I did in the past, so I responded impulsively and overcompensated, when I felt threatened or intimidated. Mix that with guy who is angry at himself and every other person who ever hurt him and you have one volatile individual!

I spent the majority of the nineties smoking crack and generally making a mess of my life. I went in and out of drug programs, detoxification centers and jails. On at least three occasions, I smoked so much crack that I developed chest pains and my heart began to beat so erratically that I thought I was going to die, but as soon as I "came down" I would return to the crack like a moth to a flame.

Just like in the Army, I was living a double life. Hard working C.N.A. by day, crack addict by night. Sometimes, I would return to work the next day wearing the same dingy, white scrubs I had on when I left work the day before, because I spent the whole night smoking.

My life had blurred into one crack binge after the next. Taking a break only when I was incarcerated or in a drug treatment program. My mode of operation became as follows: Smoke crack till my life became unmanageable, either get arrested or check into a drug program, get out against medical advice well before the discharge date (because I was cured now, and could control my drug use), get a job and an apartment, get into relationships with women who were just as sick as I was, and repeat the process ad infinitum!

Still thinking that I was better than the average addict, I would brag at 12 Step Meetings about how I paid child support for my son, knowing damn well that if the court hadn't garnished my wages, I wouldn't be paying any child support at all. I resented it when the courts garnished my wages in spite of the fact that they gave me ample opportunity to pay even a fraction of what I owed. The insidious force within me always convinced me that "we" would pay child support NEXT week, but this week we needed the money to smoke crack! It meant being there for that child when he fell off the bike and encouraging him/her to try again. "Anyone with a "Johnson" can make a baby," he told me. ". . . But it takes a real man to be a father!"

In the midst of my chaotic life, I fathered my second son, Montel. His arrival was a bright spot in an otherwise dreary life. When I looked into my little boys eyes as he drank from his bottle I would enjoy a brief respite from my miserable existence. Watching him grow from an infant to a toddler was a privilege that I had forfeited with my first-born son, Miles Jr. Shortly after Montel's birth, I decided that I needed to check into a Program so that I could be there for *this* child. I had done a poor job being a father to my first son and the guilt and shame I had inside for not being there for him continued to grow exponentially.

By the time I checked into the Grant St. Partnership drug program, I had pretty much made a total mess of my life. I wasn't allowed into my parent's house anymore because of my thieving ways, which caused me to hate myself even more. I had a conscience, and it hurt me to the core of my soul to see the pained look in my mother's face as she passed me a foil covered plate of food through her front door. I wasn't allowed in the house, but she wasn't going to let her "Baby Boy" starve.

I had just gotten fired from my latest job at a local nursing home for meeting with union organizers. I told people that I needed to get myself together so I could be a father to my sons, but my ulterior motive was to have "three hots and a cot" because my latest girlfriend had asked me to leave. "I can do bad all by myself", she told me, after I returned home from my latest crack binge.

Chapter 40

The Devil in Me

I visited my parents on the night before I went into the program and announced, for the umpteenth time, that I was going to "do it" this time. My mother asked me with tears in her eyes, why someone with so much promise and potential would destroy their life the way I was doing. At that particular point in my life, I was able to function fairly normally during the week, but on paydays, I would run off and spend my entire paycheck on crack cocaine.

As I opened my mouth to speak, she gently placed her index finger over my lips and said, "Shh . . . before you answer me, go deep, deep down inside yourself and find the answer". I did as she told me to and as I looked inside myself, I brushed away all of the familiar excuses like being angry at myself for getting kicked out of the Army, losing my wife or any of the other "Top Ten" excuses for getting high. I was honestly trying to figure out why I was doing this to myself.

While I sat there in my parents den that night, I went inside my mind, honestly searching for a valid reason that could justify my addiction. Although I didn't have any drugs in my system, a voice deep down inside was telling me to hurry up and borrow some money so "we" could cop some crack and smoke one more time before I went into the program. I was sincerely ready to get my shit together that night, and knew that whatever was telling me to borrow some money for drugs did not have my best interests at heart. "Just one more bag" it told me, "And that's it!" I knew that was a big lie because I NEVER did just "one bag"

As I sat there, the answer suddenly became abundantly clear and I shuddered as I broke out in uncontrollable tears. My mom sat on the arm of the chair and hugged me tight until I could regain my composure. After a few minutes, I had finally calmed down enough to speak and she asked, "Did you find out the answer?" I looked at her with a bewildered look in my eyes and sheepishly said;" I think the devil in me".

That was the only logical explanation I could come up with other than insanity. I couldn't be insane because insane people are insane twenty four hours a day, seven days a week . . . not just on payday!

The next day, I entered The Grant Street Partnership, an amazing rehab center that was run by a living saint named John Martinez. He was also a state senator who was passionate about improving his community and lobbying the government for money to fund substance abuse programs. Some people had a different opinion about him, but all I knew was that his wife, children and the residents of Grant St. adored him, and he really put his heart into running the program. He was also one of the snazziest dressers I had ever met!

John was the executive director of the program and could have walked around in his two hundred dollar shoes and five hundred dollar suits and did nothing, but he wasn't that type of man. Although he had a swagger that was more akin to a hustler, John Martinez took Recovery very seriously. He facilitated groups and was an active member of everyone's treatment planning. An ex junkie himself, John was living proof that a person could rise from the ashes of a burnt out life and become a productive member of society! Not only was he a power of example; he was an example of the Power!

John and I developed a personal relationship after I left the program and would play chess together or discuss politics or Black History. He had more knowledge of African-American history than I did; a fact that we both found amusing. We would swap books with each other and then spend hours discussing and debating what had been written down as fact. John was very instrumental in convincing me that I could break free of the shackles of addiction and live a happy, productive life.

GSP also had an amazing therapist named Sue Feldman, who helped me explore every possible reason I could come up with to justify my using. She told me that I could spend the rest of my life feeling sorry for myself, or learn how to rid myself of the wreckage of my past and start to actually recover from addiction instead of wallowing in a pit of self-pity. She helped me understand that even though I felt partially responsible for the sexual abuse I had endured because I willingly participated, I was actually a child who was manipulated by immoral adults. She explained to me that a child is not capable of making an adult decision like that, and therefore, could not possibly be expected to bare any of the responsibility for our illicit affair.

Sue was different from any therapist or drug counselor I had ever met in my many hospitalizations because she made me feel like she genuinely cared about my recovery from this insidious illness. Her quiet, caring demeanor set me at ease during our sessions, and I loved the way she framed her questions in a way that helped me recognize that my way of approaching recovery was flawed.

Although she practiced Judaism, Sue helped me realize that the key to remaining abstinent depended on having a healthy relationship with loving and caring God without pushing her personal view of God on me. She encouraged me to develop my own personal relationship with God. "It doesn't matter if you call him Jehovah, Allah, Jesus Christ or even Bob!" she would tell me. "As long as you believe that your God is more powerful than yourself and your addiction, and you believe that He or She loves you, you will be just fine!"

Sue truly believed in me because she used her influence to get me a job as a CNA at the Jewish Home for the Aged while I was still a resident at the Grant St. program! She took a big risk on me because I could have screwed up the job and made her regret vouching for me. One thing for sure was that I had an abundance of people who believed in me, and who thought I was worthy of having a meaningful life. Now, the trick was to get *me* to believe that!

When I told my mother a while back that the devil was in me, my answer wasn't very far from the truth. Even though I bore some of the responsibility in my Recovery, I was doomed to fail if I didn't develop a relationship with a Power greater than myself. For the Devil WAS in me, and the only way to keep him from whispering his sweet serenade into the ears of my soul was to have a powerful, loving God of my understanding "in me" also!

CHAPTER 41

Coming To Believe

For the first time in my life, I completed the program without leaving before my discharge date. I was a star employee at the Jewish Home and for the first time in my life I was able to keep an apartment for more than a month or two.

Although I was still hesitant about placing my trust in a Power greater than myself, my mom, John Martinez, Sue Feldman and the many recovering addicts who attended the 12 Step meetings, had planted the "seeds" of Recovery in me. The information I needed to begin my Recovery was there, but I still insisted that I could control my addiction myself. In spite of all the undeniable evidence that Recovery was possible, I eventually "picked up" again due to my refusal to accept that I could not control my crack use.

It's been said that insanity is doing the same thing over and over, expecting different results. If that's the case, then I was truly insane! Why else would I continue to destroy my life when I had overwhelming evidence that Recovery was possible? Proof of my insanity was that now that I knew that the malevolent "voice" inside me was the devil, and the only way to defeat him was with a Power greater than him, I still refused to trust in the same God that had changed the lives of countless other addicts.

My mom always said, "A hard head makes a soft behind" and although I was sick and tired of getting my "behind" whipped, I couldn't bring myself to trust God. I shared about this lack of trust to my 12 Step sponsor Malik, and he asked me a question that was crucial to me coming to believe in God. "When you stuck your money into that slot in the door at the crack house or into the hands of a drug dealer, you *trusted* that they were giving you some real shit, right? When that hooker told you she was clean right before you went up in her "raw dog" you *trusted* her, right? So why do you find it so hard to trust in a loving and caring God who only has your best interests at heart?"

Malik was a brother that I had met in the 12 Step meetings and over the years, I came to admire how he carried himself in a dignified, yet humble way. He was sure of himself, but not cocky and was another example of how Recovery could work in anyone's life. He used to be just as caught out as me, but had found a way to become free from not only the shackles of addiction, but free from the destructive, self-centered thinking that most addicts have.

Over the many years that I had been attending 12 Step meetings, I saw addicts come, and I saw addicts go. Just like me, they would come into the meetings and talk the talk but not walk the walk. They never made any changes to their ways of thinking and eventually fell prey to the cunning and baffling disease called addiction.

Every time I returned to the meetings after a return to active addiction, there were always certain people who were a constant source of hope. These were the people who, in spite of going through the same things I had went through in life or worse, remained off drugs and were living happy and productive lives. They weren't emotionless zombies who walked around with permanent smiles on their faces; they endured the deaths of loved ones, loss of jobs and a host of other "shit" that "happens" but they all had the ability to get through these terrible experiences without using drugs to deaden the pain!

It was THESE people, including Malik that I turned to for help. I sat in many a meeting and listened to stories of people doing things more horrible than I had done, and they were living happy, meaningful lives. They spoke of robbery and murder. They spoke of neglecting themselves and their children. Women *and* men spoke of prostituting themselves and other sexually deviant behavior, but in spite of having a checkered past, they ALL found a God that loved them, cared for them, and protected them from the ravages of addiction.

I didn't believe I was worthy of such a God working in my life, but one thing had become abundantly clear; He/She was definitely working in their lives! Slowly but surely I began to believe that maybe, just maybe, it was possible that the God these people spoke of might see fit to have mercy on my tired, battered soul.

The two years leading up to my freedom from active addiction were probably the most tumultuous days of my life. I kept smoking crack, but it wasn't enjoyable anymore. I knew that my search for that initial "bodygasm" was in vain, and I also knew that it wasn't necessary to continue smoking crack. I had seen people recover from addiction with my own eyes, so I felt like an idiot every time I took a hit!

Because I continued to destroy my life with my drug use, I began to hate myself more than ever. I avoided looking at myself in mirrors because I hated what I had become. One time, during an alcohol and crack fueled rage, I hock spit into a mirror when I caught a glimpse of the shell of a man that I had become. "I fuckin' HATE you!" I screamed as I looked at myself. I had thoughts of suicide, but couldn't muster the courage to take my own life, so I lived in a reckless way, hoping someone else would do the honors.

One time, I copped some drugs from some guys with counterfeit money I had created on a color printer. Before I got halfway down the street they pulled up alongside me with their pistols out and told me to pull over. "Maybe they will kill me and put me out of my misery" I said to myself. I told them a lie about a "white boy" who had given me the "funny money" and reassured them that as soon as I saw him I was going to "fuck him up". Lying had become second hand due to the nature of my disease. I lied about one thing or another at least ten times a day! I gave them their crack back and they sped off into the night without laying a hand (or bullet) on me. At the time, I thought it was because I was such a good liar, but like they say, "God looks out for children and fools!"

I also began "flipping" eight balls of crack, where I would "bag up" a hundred dollar piece of crack, post up in a crack house and sell just enough to "re-up". Any profit I may have accumulated always went back up in smoke. I foolishly and arrogantly thought I was doing something slick because I wasn't spending my entire paycheck on crack. Its only through Gods grace that I am alive today because "flipping eight balls" allowed me to smoke crack continuously without running out of money. I subjected my heart, brain and lungs to an endless supply of poison which I hoped would kill me one day, and end my miserable existence. Not only was this a good way to have a heart attack or stroke, I was selling in neighborhoods that I didn't belong to. If any of the local dealers caught wind that I was selling on their turf, I would have surely been shot!

By now, it was about 1998 and even though I knew that Recovery was possible, I insisted on smoking my life away. I had a third son named Trevor now, who was about two years old. Although I loved ALL my children dearly, my drug addiction was preventing me from being the father that I should have been. Sure, I provided a roof over his head and fed him, but I wasn't there for him emotionally. I spent the majority of my free time chasing that elusive "bodygasm"! When I *was* in the house with him, I was too busy in the bathroom smoking to pay him any real attention.

I was losing all hope in the possibility that I would ever get off drugs and began to accept that I was destined to go on to the bitter ends and die; a drug addicted failure. I trudged through life feeling ashamed and embarrassed of myself on the inside while putting on a façade of self-confidence on the outside. The most painful part of my addiction was when I wasn't getting high, because that was when I had to feel all the negative feelings that saturated my soul with shame, guilt and embarrassment.

I was able to hold down a pretty decent job at a work program for developmentally disabled people as a Program Facilitator and even got promoted to supervising my own work site, but as soon as I got off work I made a bee line to the nearest dealer to cop some crack and continue destroying my life. Ever since my first job at U.P.S., I never had a problem getting a job, but once I did, I spent almost all my income on crack. Oh sure, I paid rent, utilities and brought food; but after that, all extra money was earmarked for the nearest drug dealer!

The summer of 1999 was a bittersweet one. My father had been waging a courageous battle against cancer and after major surgery and chemotherapy, he had apparently beaten it. My family and I breathed a sigh of relief as we watched him slowly regain his strength and weight, and celebrated the fact that ole Charlie Walcott had beaten cancer! This was one of the happiest times of our lives, and we all reveled in the fact that we would have our dad a little while longer.

One of the most beautiful sights I ever saw was the sparkle in my mother's eyes as she nursed her husband of 45 years back to health. She was a devoted wife, and she did whatever she could to make sure her man was comfortable as he recovered. It was wonderful to see moms face light up as my dad complimented her on the meal she had prepared for him, or when he said sweet, romantic things to her as he sat in his easy chair. Once, when Ma had left the living room to get Dad something to eat, he turned to me and said, "I would drink her dirty bath water if she asked me to!" I really don't think he was joking.

Dad had lost an awful lot of weight from his illness and was literally half his previous size. Plus, the heavy-duty pain medication he was on caused him to frequently fall asleep in his favorite chair while he watched TV in the living room. One night, while visiting my parents, my dad was too weak to make the walk from the living room to the first floor guest room. We had converted the 1st floor guest room into a bedroom for Pop, to keep him from having to climb the stairs to the second floor. Although I had been on crack on and off for years, I was still a pretty big guy because I was also addicted to junk food, Chinese take-out and basketball! My mom asked me if I would carry Pop to bed and of course I said yes.

While my mom opened the door to the guestroom in front of us, I stumbled slightly, but quickly recovered. I stood in the guest room holding my frail father in my arms, while my mother turned down the bed. "That's all we need is for you to have a heart attack while carrying your father and the both of you fall on top of me and crush me!" she joked. "I'd love to be a fly on the wall when the paramedics find us all piled up on top of each other in this tiny little room!"

As we both chuckled at my mom's macabre humor, our chuckles turned to laughter as my dad opened his eyes and said, "You better not drop me, boy!" with that familiar twinkle in his eyes that let you know he was just fooling' around!

My parent's home was on the way home from my job, so after work I would call and see if they needed anything before stopping by their house to check on them. When necessary, I would mow their grass and trim their hedges for them with pleasure, as my parents sat on their deck in the back yard. It made me feel good to be able to do little things like that for them because I loved them dearly and I knew they always kept their yard meticulously landscaped before Pops illness. One of my favorite pictures in the world is the one of my beautiful mom in front of her house watering her flowers!

My girlfriend and I were expecting the birth of Tamia, my first biological daughter. I had two other stepdaughters from previous relationships named LaToya and Bianca whom I loved dearly, but there was something special about awaiting the birth of a daughter that I had helped create. One of my fondest memories of my mother is of her sitting in her living room crocheting a pink and white "Blanky" for Tamia as we listened to mom's favorite R&B group "Boyz to Men" sing "Momma". "Momma, you know I love you!"

As Tamia's arrival date approached, I continued to selfishly get high without any regard for the fact that I had another child coming into this world. What was it going to take to get me to make a sincere effort at stopping this madness? I had failed miserably at all attempts to stop the madness in the past, and I was beginning to believe that I was just one of those people who were going to smoke crack until I died. My hopelessness was turning into despair as I slowly gave up on myself and started to accept the fact that I was going to die in active addiction.

The folks from the "12 Step community" continued to reach out to me, even coming directly to the crack houses that I frequented, attempting to lure me away with stories of living a happy, productive life. I resisted their loving and caring overtures and stubbornly trudged along, thinking that I was too far gone to ever taste the sweet life that I saw others living. I could no longer ignore the fact that there was a God because I had seen Him working in so many people's lives, but I thought that I had done too much "dirt" to be blessed with grace or mercy. It wasn't until a few years later when my third N.A. sponsor, Mark K. had me actually look up the definition of "grace" that I found out that it was "unwarranted merit". "That's right, Miles" my sponsor said, "We don't even deserve grace but God gives it to us anyway!" That blew me away because if I got what I truly deserved, I would be dead or in prison!

Chapter 42

The Summer of Hell

On June 6th, 1999, my beautiful daughter Tamia Alexandria Walcott was born. She had aspirated amniotic fluid into her lungs while in the womb and had to be delivered by emergency C-Section. This was the third time a child of mines had a stressful birth and of course, in my self-centered way of thinking; I asked God why he was doing this to *me*! I experienced total, complete powerlessness as I looked down at my fragile newborn daughter with respirator tubes and an assortment of wire monitors attached to her body.

Tears rolled down my face as I gently touched her tiny little hand with my forefinger and whispered to her that "It's gonna be all right, princess". When I asked the doctors if she would make it, they wouldn't commit to a yes or no answer; they just looked at me and said things like, "It's too early to tell" or "Let's wait and see".

Although I believed in an angry, punishing God, I pleaded to Him to have mercy on my innocent, guiltless baby. The funny thing about it was that I actually *believed* He would heal her in spite of my transgressions, but I didn't reach out until I knew without a doubt that there wasn't a damned thing I could do to help her!

For the first time in my life, I truly realized how helpless and innocent my children were. Once again, the angry, fearful and malevolent voice within me was immediately subdued when I called on the soft, loving "glow" that had always patiently waited for my temper tantrum du jour to subside before comforting me during my remorseful moments. As I stood in the pediatric intensive care unit, tearfully gazing down at my helpless daughter who couldn't even breathe on her own, a sudden calm engulfed me. I somehow knew that my baby girl was going to be just fine! At that precise moment, Tamia's eyes popped open and she looked directly into my eyes for a few tender moments as I felt pure, uncut joy, tenderly touch my soul!. I was beginning to think that maybe, just maybe, there was something to this loving and caring God that I heard others speak of.

After a few more minutes of communing with my daughter and an awesome Power that I could literally feel in my body, I left her to rest and made my way to the telephone to give my mom the news that her granddaughter was born. It was about 8a.m. by now and Ma was at the dining room table having her morning cup of Tasters Choice when I called. "That's wonderful" she said when I gave her the news. "As soon as I get your father situated, I will be there"

I went back to the nursery to check on my baby girl, and then went to check on her mom. She was sleeping peacefully in bed, which wasn't surprising, given the traumatic ordeal she had just gone through. Before I knew it, I was asleep in the easy chair next to her bed and didn't awake until noon, when the nurse knocked on the door. While the nurse was doing her thing, I noticed the time and decided to call my mom and see what time she was coming to see her new granddaughter.

After two or three rings, my sister Tamara answered the phone, and I could tell by her voice that something was terribly wrong. "What's wrong, Tam" I asked nervously. "We found Ma on the floor unresponsive and the paramedics are bringing her to St Raphael's now" she answered tearfully. "I'll meet you there" I said, and slammed the phone down.

All of my siblings and my dad were in the waiting room when I arrived, and I could tell by the looks on everyone's faces that my mother was in bad shape. My father, whose frail, weakened body had been emaciated from the cancer and subsequent treatment, waved me over to him. "They say your mother had a massive stroke, son" he told me. For the first time in my life, my father looked beaten. He held his head high during his courageous battle with cancer, but this was just too much for him to endure. His devoted wife of 45 years was slipping away from him and I could see an unfathomable pain in his tired eyes.

When I entered my mother's room on the intensive care unit, I felt a heavy sadness wash over me as I looked at her face. She was being kept alive by life support, but I knew deep inside that her spirit had left her physical body. As I held my mom's hand telling her how much I loved her, it felt as if a piece of my heart had been ripped out, leaving a gaping hole in my chest. I began to cry uncontrollably, begging her not to leave me, but she just lay there, limp and lifeless, while the life support system beeped and clicked in the background.

Lizan, stood beside me and rubbed my shoulders, trying to console her big brother and gently guided me back to the waiting room to rejoin the rest of the family. The doctors told us that Ma had actually suffered two more strokes since arriving at the hospital, and would never regain consciousness. We had to make the decision to remove her from life support and I tearfully stated that I would never agree to that. My sisters explained to me that mommy would never be able to have any quality of life and would basically be in a coma if we kept her alive, but I didn't want to let her go. My mom was the sweetest woman in the world. She represented love, stability and kindness and I couldn't imagine life without her.

Even though I hated to lose my mother, I reluctantly joined my family in our decision to allow Ma to "Go home". As my mom's body convulsed from being taken off the respirator, I stormed out of the hospital in pursuit of something to take the intense pain away.

My life was already a mess, but after my mother's death, I was an emotional wreck as well. I was a passenger on an emotional roller coaster that went from one extreme to another. No calm periods in between peaks and valleys, just one steep rise and fall after another. I was overjoyed that my beautiful daughter Tamia was fine, but deeply saddened over the loss of my wonderful mother. It saddened me even more, to see the pain in my brother and sisters eyes, but the most heartbreaking thing I ever witnessed in my life was the miserable look of despair in Dads eyes as he mourned the loss of his soul mate. My parents had been together forever, and raised five children together! They took their family on vacations to Cape Cod, Philly and enjoyed romantic cruises together. They were both retired and were enjoying their golden years together in the beautiful home they had purchased. My mom had selflessly nursed my dad back to health during his bout with cancer, and they had been enjoying a period of relief now that he was on the mend:

and now she was gone! The light in my father's eyes had diminished, and all that was left were two hollow, glazed over orbs that took the place of his once sparkling eyes.

After witnessing the painful, dejected look in my father's face, I proceeded to do what I had become accustomed to doing whenever I felt deep emotional pain (or joyful happiness for that matter . . . ANY excuse was sufficient) and went on a three day coke and alcohol fueled binge at a crack house on Winchester Ave. I had purchased an "Eightball" of crack which I divided into a smoke stash and a "sell" stash; which virtually allowed me to smoke continuously . . . 24/7.

No matter how much crack I smoked or liquor I drank, my mother was still gone! Getting high wasn't going to bring he back! The drugs could no longer mask my pain and I was left feeling even emptier on the inside. I told the other addicts at the crack house that I had just lost my mother, expecting sympathy, but of course they just gave me superficial condolences as they waited for another hit. My life was completely out of control, but I enjoyed a false sense of control as I made my fellow addicts wait patiently for another sale to come through, so I could crack open another bag and dole out another couple of hits to them!

They sheepishly avoided my eyes as I lit the pipe with tears running down my face; lost and turned out, without my mommy to run to when things got too tough. The drugs just weren't working for me anymore. No matter how high I got, I couldn't erase the intense emotional pain that was wreaking havoc on my soul.

After my binge was over, I walked the two miles from Winchester Avenue to my parent's house in Hamden, with tears streaming down my face. The thought of never giving my mom a hug or kissing her cheek was unfathomable. "How could you leave me Ma?" I said out loud. "What am I gonna do without you?" The puzzled stares that I was getting from folks on the street didn't faze me one bit. No amount of macho bravado could hold back the torrential tears streaming down my face! I had just lost the woman who loved me from day one and didn't give a damn who saw me cry!

It was mid-day, and there was a fair amount of people on busy Dixwell Avenue. I felt "lost and turned out" and needed my dad and the rest of my family. I had an intense desire to be in my family's presence, so I picked up the pace. I continued to plead out loud with God, my mother and whatever else was "out there" to PLEASE bring my mother back as I made my way to my parent's house.

"*Look at you! Crying like a little bitch!*" The voice was back with a vengeance! It was attempting to make me feel ashamed of crying, but I wasn't trying to hear it today. "Shut da FUCK up!" I screamed out loud. "Leave me alone! Leave me the FUCK alone!" I shook my head back and forth, trying to expel the madness from my head but it was relentless. "*She probably died because your sorry, crack-head ass broke her heart!*"

Although the "voice" emanated from within, I answered it out loud, in exactly the same fashion a person who suffers from schizophrenia yells at his demons. I was a sad sight, walking alone, down the busiest street in New Haven, screaming as if someone else was walking with me.

The sadness I was feeling and the turmoil from within threatened to overcome me and drive me insane, so I decided that I would now feel anger. I was in control of my emotions, yet had no control at all. Crying one moment, scowling the next, this was truly one of the darkest times of my life.

I walked into my parent's house looking a hot mess. My eyes were red and swollen from crying, but I had an angry deranged look on my face. I had been wearing the same cloths for three or four days and smelled like shit! The house was full of friends and family, but I stormed past everyone and demanded to be told where my dad was. Someone pointed upstairs so I took the stairs two at a time and burst into my parent's bedroom and stood in the doorway looking like something the cat dragged in. My father was sitting on the side of his bed, beaten and weary. He motioned for him to sit next to him and I did. I looked at him with a confused look on my face, sort of waiting for his direction . . . some sign that it was ok to cry. My father, who had just lost his soul mate, and had his own feelings to deal with, put his arm on my shoulder and said," Let it out, Son! Let it out before it kills you!"

I let out a bellowing, mournful howl from the bottom of my soul that drowned out all the chatter from downstairs, and began to cry harder than I had ever cried in my life. My body convulsed in emotional agony as I cried, like a child, on my father's chest. "That's right son, let it out" my father said, as he cried himself. I continued to release my pain in deep, guttural cries for another ten or fifteen minutes until I couldn't produce another sound, and lay there, quivering in my father's embrace.

By now, my sisters had all came upstairs and comforted their father and brother as we all mourned the loss of our Queen!

I arrived at my parent's home on the morning of my Mom's funeral bright and early. I had decided the night before that I was going to be at my best, to support my family members on this somber day. After I helped my father put his suit jacket on, he dusted my shoulders off and began straightening my tie for me. My dad looked me straight in the eye with a dejected look on his face that I had never seen before that sent a chill through my whole body. It was the look of a man who had lost all hope. "I'm sorry Son," he said with tears in his eyes. "I can't do this without her." After a brief silence, my father and I embraced, and I knew exactly what he meant.

Although it was a warm June morning, the sky was overcast and foreboding. My whole family formed a circle on my parent's front lawn and held hands. At least four generations of Walcott's had gathered, from our patriarch, Charles C. Walcott Jr., to my niece India and her unborn child. The scene was surreal and seemed to be orchestrated by an unseen conductor because as soon as we began to pray, the songbirds began to chirp on cue, and the bright morning sun was filtered through a small stand of pine trees down the block; casting gentle rays of sunlight on the exact spot we were standing. While we stood there, waiting for my sisters Lizan and Tamara to escort dad to his place in the circle, a warm breeze danced ever so gently through the midst of us. The quiet chatter we were having came to a halt as Tamara announced that Daddy would like to start the prayer.

My father was never much of an openly religious man, but during the last few years of his life, I watched his spirituality grow tremendously. He would spend hours reading the bible and even asked me to purchase a Holy Q'uran for him to study. The suns warmth on my neck and the soft gentle words my dear old dad was saying seemed to rejuvenate my spirit and give me a confidence that I hadn't felt in years. It felt as if God Himself was speaking vicariously through my father! I glanced around the circle at the tearful faces of my loved ones and decided that today; I would be the strong shoulder for them to cry on.

The funeral for my beautiful Mother, Barbara Sarah Walcott, was standing room only! It gave me great pride to look around and see so many people in attendance. The ushers were guiding the overflow of mourners downstairs to view the services on closed circuit television in the church hall! Community Baptist church on Shelton Avenue is one of the largest congregations in the city and the huge crowd that came to pay their last respects was evidence of how loved my dear mom was!

When the time came, I carefully escorted my devoted father to view mom's beautiful face one more time. Dad was still weak from his battle with cancer, and needed an aluminum walker to get around with, but being the proud man that he was, today he insisted on using the metal crutches with the wrist supporters; more dangerous, but also more dignified. It felt good to be able to assist my dad on his trip to the altar. The last time Charlie and Barbie Walcott had been to the altar together was in 1955 when they embarked on a happy marriage and raised five children together.

I supported my dad's weight as he leaned over and placed a gentle kiss on his wife's lips. "I'll see you real soon" he whispered as he tenderly kissed her and placed his hand upon hers.

The next couple of months are hazy to me. I continued to get high, but it just wasn't the same anymore. It seemed like my body was so numb from grief that I couldn't even feel the drugs anymore. I watched my father steadily decline in health as he lost his desire to live. On August 19th, just two months after the loss of his soul mate, my father passed away in his sleep. Well, at least his body died, his spirit had died two months ago at my mother's funeral. The doctors said that the cancer had returned, but I know that my father died from a broken heart.

Now that I had lost both my parents, I allowed myself to slip even deeper into the pit of self-despair. I used drugs harder than I ever used before now, but no matter how much I drank or smoked, the pain wouldn't go away. I even began spending my rent money on crack again. With an eviction pending and being on the verge of being homeless, I turned to a friend of mines who got high also. He and his girlfriend rented a condo on the New Haven/East Haven town line and invited my two children, their mother and I to stay with them until I got back on my feet.

They charged us next to nothing to stay there, but instead of using this as an opportunity to save money to get a new apartment, I spent every available penny on crack! I justified my drug use by saying that I wasn't just using crack, I was selling it but the bottom line was that I made absolutely NO profits! I only made barely enough money to "re-up" to keep my insatiable appetite for crack fulfilled.

The garage to my friend's condo was clean and had a carpet on the floor. We had heat, a television and refrigerator hooked up which allowed my sick, twisted mind to rationalize that our living arrangements were adequate; in spite of the fact that we were living in a GARAGE! A garage is a place to store cars and tools; not to raise your children!

When I wasn't at work, I was running the streets searching in vain for a respite from the enormous pit of pain that dwelled within me. I began to abhor crack due to the havoc it was wreaking in my life, but couldn't muster the strength to break free of the talons of its grasp. The only time I was ever able to enjoy a reprieve was when I embraced the soft, gentle voice that had always been inside me. The voice may have been soft and gentle, but my experience with it showed me that it was also much, much stronger than the angry, destructive voice that always seemed to lead me into even more pain and misery. In spite of possessing this vital information, I still insisted on ignoring the peaceful voice and following the evil one.

Eventually, the Department of Children and Families got wind of our living situation and swiftly revoked the privilege of raising my children. Trevor was only three and Tamia was barely one year old. Apparently, DCF frowns on children and families living in garages! They placed my precious children in foster care and that STILL wasn't enough to stop me from using! I became enraged at DCF for taking my kids even though I knew my life was out of control and my babies were in better hands. I had to blame *somebody*. Luckily, they were placed with their maternal grandmother, so at least they weren't with total strangers.

Chapter 43

Spiritual Awakening

It was December 1999, and I was driving my rusted out Chevy Blazer to the DCF building for my first supervised visit with my children. The trucks heater was broken so I had to use my hat to wipe the frost from the windshield in order to see. "Ole Betsy" wasn't even registered or insured because I had "better" things to do with my money!

When I entered the visiting room, I became embarrassed at the fact that I had abused the privilege of raising my children so bad, that I wasn't even allowed to visit them without a social worker present. My spirit was so filled with anger and resentment that I wasn't even able to acknowledge that I had neglected my children. In spite of the fact that we were living in a garage, I felt that I had been doing "what a man was supposed to do". My dysfunctional way of thinking prevented me from seeing how inappropriate it was to have my family living in a garage and how unmanageable my life had become.

When my babies were escorted into the visiting room, my heart became heavy as I suddenly realized how much my precious little angels needed their father. Tamia, who was only one year old, was afraid to come to me because she barely knew me. Trevor, her three-year-old big brother, reassured her by saying, "Its ok Mia, its daddy!" My beautiful little girl trusted her big "brudda" and took a few tentative steps towards me. I could see the puzzled look on my child's face as she struggled to remember who I was, so I just held back my tears, smiled and said, "Hi, sweetie!"

It was finally beginning to dawn on me that something was terribly wrong with this picture. They had only been in foster care for a few weeks, but all ready, my daughter barely knew me, and her three-year-old brother had taken over the role as her "protector". I held back my tears because I didn't want to cause my babies any distress, but during our visit, I began to ask myself some serious questions.

After a few awkward moments, Tamia warmed up to me and before I knew it, she was bouncing all over my lap and hugging me the way she used to. We enjoyed a delightful hour of pure love, as I my innocent children and I began the healing process.

When the visit was over, I took the elevator to the ground floor with the Social Worker and my two angels. As I helped him place my babies in the car seats in the rear of the state vehicle, Trevor and Tamia realized that daddy wasn't coming with them and began to cry. After they were both strapped in, I kissed my darling children and told them that Daddy would see them soon. As the Social Worker warmed the car up and strapped himself in, I stood outside of the state vehicle that my children were in and saw the distraught faces of my two children as their little arms reached out for their daddy!

The sound of their crying was muffled because the car windows were up, but I could see the look of sheer terror on their faces as they realized that daddy wasn't coming with them. The sight of my poor little babies crying like that shook me to the very core of my soul. Never before in my life had I felt such pain and despair. My children were my pride and joy, but I was allowing my drug use to prevent me from being their father.

Going to prison, living in squalor, not even the death of both of my parents was enough to make me feel this kind of pain. Having my children taken away from me two weeks earlier wasn't even enough to make me stop smoking crack, but when I saw the pain in my innocent children's eyes as the DCF worker drove away, I decided right then and there that ENOUGH IS ENOUGH!!!

I walked slowly back to my rusted out truck devoid of any feeling other than utter despair. I felt empty on the inside, and all I could think of was the looks on my children's faces as they pulled out of the parking lot. I couldn't even muster up the strength to cry as I sat in my cold assed truck and stared through the windshield at some seagulls circling in the distance. At times, they seemed to just hover in the sky as the cold winter air sustained them in flight.

The DCF building was across the street from the "Long Wharf", an area of wetlands, tidal marshes and a stretch of muddy sand. In New Havens heyday, it was a bustling shipping port, but with the construction of Interstate I-95, it had become a drop off point for oil tankers and a dock where the Amistad replica ship was anchored.

When I was about 12 or 13 years old, my father and I would don rubber waders and walk 100 feet out from the shore and fish for harbor blues, a smaller version of the Big Blues that New England is famous for. "That's far enough!" he would shout to me as I waded as far as I could in the waist deep water to get the optimal distance when I cast my line. Everyone knew that after about one hundred and fifty feet or so, the sand dropped off sharply, forming a channel for the oil tankers to sail in and out of the harbor. "If you drown, your mother will KILL me!" he joked. Some of my fondest memories as a kid were of my dad and I fishing together. It was during these times that I felt closest to him and had his undivided attention.

I started my rusty old Chevy Blazer and headed over to one of the parking areas of the Long Wharf. It was late in the afternoon, and the sky was grey and overcast. In spite of the frigid temperature, I got out of my truck, walked over to a wooden bench and sat down. As I sat there with my arms stretched across the back of the bench, I stared across the harbor in deep contemplation. As I pondered my dilemma, visions of my children's distraught faces kept flashing through my mind.

I had made a complete mess of my life with my drug use and failed miserably at every attempt to stop using. My children had just been taken away from me, I was basically homeless. A few weeks earlier, I had lost my job because the director of the program had caught me sleeping numerous times while on duty. On top of all that, I wished I were dead. I wouldn't say that I was suicidal in a sense that I planned on cutting my wrists or some other form of suicide, but I was living the reckless lifestyle of someone with a death wish. Buying crack with counterfeit money and selling it in neighborhoods that I wasn't from were not activities that someone who wanted to live should partake in! I think it's pretty safe to say that I had finally hit rock bottom!

One thing had become abundantly clear to me; left to my own devices I would fall flat on my face again if I tried to do this on my own. I knew that there was some "thing", some "power" that was helping others because I had seen first-hand how it had transformed the lives of people at the meetings. Some of the most destitute, and "caught out" addicts had become happy, productive members of society and they attributed it to this mysterious "God" of their understanding!

I believed in a God; but I believed He was an angry God, sitting in judgment, doling out punishment to horrible sinners, like myself. In spite of what I believed, I couldn't ignore the fact that the folks at the 12 Step meetings had this loving, caring and powerful God, who loved them and gave them the strength to overcome their addiction.

The intense hopelessness that had been weighing down on me for the last few years was beginning to acquiesce to something much stronger than anything I had ever felt before. I couldn't quite put my finger on it at the time, but this powerful feeling began rumble deep within me and I could tell that it was just getting started.

Suicide was no longer an option directly or indirectly. I never really wanted to die in the first place, but if my life continued in the direction it was, I knew that I would literally wither and die. I thought of Trevor and Tamia in the custody of D.C.F. I thought of Miles Jr, Montel and my other two daughters, LaToya and Bianca, growing up with a "ghost dad" who was only a father in name only. Plus, I had a host of nieces and nephews that needed a positive man in their lives. I knew this all along, but lacked the power to break free from my addiction's deadly grip. Now, I was beginning to feel something stirring within me that was akin to a glorious sunrise after a long, dark night.

As I sat there on that cold, wooden bench in the frigid December air, I looked up into the dark, grey clouds and asked the God of my friends to help me. "Please, God" I prayed out loud. "Please, please, please help me!" I didn't really know how to pray, but I knew that if there really were a God, He would hear my prayers. This wasn't one of those, Please help me get out of this mess" prayers, where I went back to using after the present crisis passed. It was a sincere admission that I was willing to do whatever I had to do to get clean; and stay clean!

As I sat there praying, the sun momentarily peeked through a break in the clouds, its warming rays caressing my body, but also warming my soul. Some would say it was a coincidence, but I think not! Before the clouds could cover the sun's rays again, a sudden calm came over me. I no longer felt sad or depressed. I didn't even feel the anger I had towards DCF for "taking" my kids away (I knew now that I had *given* them away). All I felt was a serene, tranquil feeling as I breathed an emotional "sigh of relief". It suddenly dawned on me what that beautiful feeling was that was welling up inside of me at an exponential rate. The glow that was growing within me was God's love in the form of hope!

I started up my old rust bucket with a smile on my face because I knew exactly what I needed to do.

I drove to my buddy Rocky's condo with a determined spirit. The malevolent voice from within was completely silenced, and I was totally focused on the soft voice that I used to dismiss as weak and insignificant. It didn't really "speak" to me with words; it was more like a gentle, comforting feeling that made me feel safe. When I listened to this voice, the angry, insidious voice was instantly muted; as though it was afraid to utter a word!

When I arrived at the condo, I knocked on the door at least five times before Rocky came to the door. He had that wide-eyed look that crack addicts have when they have just taken a hit, and it made me feel nauseous. Normally, I would have asked him if he had any more, but today, the thought of smoking crack was revolting! "Whussup man?" he asked in a nervous tone. "I am goin' to get some help, dawg" I replied, as I headed towards the garage. "I got a couple bags left, you wanna hit?" he said as he followed me to the garage. "Nah Dawg, I'm done with that shit" Hardcore crack addicts like us rarely offered someone a hit; but we NEVER asked twice! My buddy headed back up the stairs as I thanked my newfound God for giving me the strength to resist the offer.

I immediately began packing my truck with my belongings. Not concerned with being neat, I began cramming everything into my truck, until it was completely full; even the passenger seat! Other than my parents mahogany bedroom set, all my worldly possessions fit into the back of my Chevy Blazer; an obvious example of how unmanageable I had let my life had become!

I said goodbye to Rocky through his bedroom door, thanked him and his girlfriend for letting me stay there and asked if I could leave my small fridge and bedroom set there for a few weeks. "No problem, dawg" he yelled back from inside his room. I caught a whiff of the unmistakable odor of cocaine smoke coming from under the door and hauled ass out of there like a bat out of hell. I closed the garage door, jumped in my truck and put the pedal to the metal as I drove towards my sister Tamara's house.

As I crossed the Veterans Memorial Bridge back into New Haven, I smiled inwardly as I imagined a life without drugs. Although I had told myself and my family that I was quitting, many times before, I had never felt as confident as I did since I asked this "Power" greater than myself for help. I had no idea if this loving and caring God that I had heard others talk about was going to help me, but I only had two choices: believe or die!

My sister Tamara, like my other two sisters, would do anything to help her little brother, short of enabling me. All she wanted for me was to see me get off drugs and live up to my full potential. "You are so talented" she would lecture me. "Why are you letting all that talent go to waste?" She owned two houses, and I was her unofficial painter and odd job guy. Plenty of times, when I had no idea how I was going to pay my rent or buy food, Tamara would save the day with an apartment that needed painting or a fence that needed to be put up. She was old school like my Dad. She wouldn't just give me money I had to earn it! Like Charlie Walcott used to say, "There is no such thing as a free lunch!"

After mom and dad passed away, Tam and I became tighter than we ever were. We always enjoyed a close bond, but with the passing of our parents, we seemed to grow even closer. During my last incarceration, which was only for 90 days, but seemed like an eternity, Tam was very supportive and helped me keep in touch with my children by way of three way calls. In my mother's absence, she became sort of a surrogate mother in addition to being a great big sister!

I pulled my truck into her driveway, and sat there, experiencing the feeling hope coursing through my body. I had a long ways to go in my Recovery, but knowing that my sisters and brother were in my corner was going to make my journey easier.

Tam came to the door as I got out of my truck and greeted me with her usual cheerful greeting. "What's up?" she said to me with a smile on her face. No matter how deep I was in my insanity, Tamara always greeted me with sincere love and affection. She practiced tough love with me, but never left out the "love" part!

"Hey Sis, I need a big favor!" I said as I hugged her. Her facial expression changed as she anticipated my usual request for a "couple of dollars" and she became serious. "Before you even ask, I aint got NO money to loan you!" "No, Sis" I explained. "I just need you to let me park my truck in your driveway while I take a little trip for thirty days"

I didn't have that wide eyed look that I normally had when I came to borrow money, and was actually quite calm and collected since my conversation with God a little while earlier. "What kinda *trip* are you talkin' about?" she asked with a puzzled look on her face. Ever since I communed with my newfound God at the waterfront, I knew exactly what I needed to do to get my act together. Well, at least I knew what I needed to do *first*!

"I'm going into treatment in the morning Sis, and I was wondering if I could leave my truck in your driveway till I get out?" My truck wasn't registered or insured, and if I left it parked on the street it would surely get towed away. I had made this announcement plenty of times in the past, but this time something was different. This time, I was excited about getting clean. In the past, I looked at getting clean as having to deprive myself of something that I loved to do, but this time, I looked at getting clean as a glorious occasion that would give me freedom from this treacherous illness I voluntarily acquired! Of course, addiction is a physical disease, but it's also a spiritual disease that can be overcome with a Power that is greater than the disease. So far, I have only found one "Power" that is greater than addiction; the power of God! Finally, I intuitively knew deep down inside that my crack smoking days were over, and I felt a joy in my heart that I had never felt before!

Tamara could sense my excitement and told me that it would be no problem leaving my truck in her driveway. My big sister and I enjoyed a long hug on her porch as we both cried tears of joy! I told her my plan, as we walked into her house. "You are gonna be just fine" she told me. "Now come in the kitchen and help me peel these potatoes so we can have some potato salad with dinner!"

I enjoyed a lovely meal with my sister, her children Tse' and Prince and her husband Peanut, as we talked about new beginnings and how powerful God was. "He was always there" my sister Tam explained. "He was just waiting on you to call!"

Later on that evening, Tam brought me a piece of chocolate cake to go with my coffee, and hugged me tightly. "You can do this!" she told me with a sparkle in her eye! "You know where the towels and linen are, getcha self cleaned up and get some rest; you have a long day ahead of you tomorrow!"

As I drifted off to sleep on my sister's couch, I thanked this God that I didn't fully understand yet, for giving me the power to make my first intelligent decision in years! I didn't understand God yet, but like my mom used to tell me," You don't have to believe in God yet . . . just believe that I believe!"

The next morning, I was up bright and early and began calling every rehab facility in the state! In the past, when I would make half-hearted attempts to get admitted into a program, I would secretly hope there were no openings. This time, every molecule in my body wanted to "go in-patient" because not only did I want help, I basically had no place to live! After the fifth or sixth call, I slammed the phone down. "Fuck" I shouted in frustration. Every place I called had either a long waiting list or wasn't accepting new clients at the time. I was beginning to get discouraged but my sister told me to just pray about it. I told her I would pray, but inside I was already beginning to doubt that I would be able to get the help that I needed. The moment I began to get discouraged, that old familiar voice chimed right in! "You don't need any stupid program! You can do it on your own." It said. I knew that was a damn lie and immediately began to pray.

My idea of prayer at the time was, "God, please help me!" nothing more, nothing less. I was told by the folks at the 12 Step meetings to K.I.S.S. or "keep it simple and quite frankly, I didn't have any experience at prayer. The only time I ever prayed in the past was when the proverbial "shit" hit the fan. As I sat at my sister's kitchen table wondering how in the world I was going to get into a drug program, an idea entered my head. I didn't have a good track record at having good ideas, but this one seemed like it would work.

I hugged and kissed my sister good-bye on December 26th, 2000 and began walking towards New Haven Hospital. As I walked down Chapel St. in the cold December air, a vision of my children's faces flashed in my mind. I could vividly see their faces in the back seat of the DCF car, from their arms reaching out for their father, down to the tears streaming down their cheeks! I became angry at myself for putting my babies through that, and vowed to never let it happen again. Just the thought of my children in the back seat of that DCF car gave me the courage to do what I was about to do once I got to the hospital.

I could "hear" my father's voice telling me that "Your children didn't ask to be here, be a man and take care of them" I knew he was just trying to motivate me to do better, but each time I neglected my duties as a father, I chipped away a little more at what little self-esteem I had left. "If a real man takes care of his children", I told myself, "Then I must not be much of a man!" I felt hopeful that I could finally "be a man" and do what I needed to do to get my children back and be the man I needed to be, but I knew I couldn't do it alone.

The DCF worker assigned to my case had told me exactly what I needed to do in order to get my kids back. "It may take a year to 18 months to get them back" she said, "but if you get substance abuse treatment and remain drug free along with securing clean and safe housing for you and your children, it can be done". The thought of not having my children for up to eighteen months was unbearable and I prayed to the God of my mother to help us all get through the difficult times ahead. I prayed to my mother's God because I didn't believe any kind of benevolent God would give a damn about a "piece of shit" like me. Coming to believe that a Power greater than myself could restore me to sanity was a process, not an event.

I entered the emergency room at New Haven Hospital and told the triage nurse that I wanted to kill myself. She asked me if I had a plan to kill myself and I told her that I was going to jump off of the Quinnipiac River Bridge. I had thought of doing so many times and felt that if I kept getting high I would eventually become so hopeless that I just might try it. I knew that if I told them that I had a plan, they were obligated to give me help and I was immediately taken to the back and strapped by my wrists and ankles to a gurney. I felt a wide range of emotions as I lay there in the hallway strapped to that gurney. Tears streamed down the sides of my face and pooled in my ears as lay on the gurney thinking about my children, my recently deceased parents and the mess I had made of my life with drugs.

A kind nurse came by and wiped my face with a tissue and told me everything was going to be just fine. Somehow, I believed her and smiled through my tears as I was wheeled to the psychiatric intensive care unit.

A psychiatrist did an intake interview with me and the next day, I was transferred to the Yale Psychiatric Institute.

CHAPTER 44

Rehab

When I arrived on the unit, the first thing I noticed was a middle aged white man with long dirty hair who looked like he hadn't shaved in years. His fingernails were also long and dirty and although he wore clean hospital pajamas, he smelled like he hadn't had a shower in weeks. As I walked by him, I frowned at the repulsive body odor that emanated from him. He stood by a window mumbling and laughing to himself with a crazed look in his eyes and I wondered to myself what kind of drugs he used to end up in such a state.

The brightly lit unit was buzzing with activity as hospital staff scurried about and patients in blue hospital pajamas tried to get their attention as they walked by. The social worker who had escorted me there asked me to have a seat on one of the vinyl couches that sat face to face in the middle of what appeared to be the T.V. room. As I approached the back of one of the couches, a cute, blonde haired girl turned her head and gave me a cheerful greeting. "Hi! My name is Sally," she said as she smiled at me with a perfect set of pearly white teeth. She had a pair of piercing blue eyes and a little too much bright red lipstick on, but besides that, she looked like she was in far better shape than the "nut" that was standing by the window mumbling to himself.

"'Sup" I said as I rounded the corner of the couch and sat down. She held her hand out for me to shake it and I noticed that she had white gauze wrapped around both wrists. I looked at her bandaged wrists and asked, "What happened?" "Oh, this?" she said as she looked at her wrists. "I fell on some glass the other day" she casually replied. "Damn, she must fall on glass a lot!" I said to myself as I noticed the rows of scars that ran up the length of both her forearms.

The cute white girl with a little too much red lipstick looked innocently into my eyes and said, "So, you wanna fuck me?" My jaw dropped and my left eyebrow rose as I looked at her incredulously. Before I could articulate an answer, a big, African-American orderly came over and said, "That's enough, Sally. I think you need to go to your room for a little while until you can act more appropriately" Sally got up off the couch and turned to me, "I'll see you later, sexy" she said in a seductive voice as she winked her eye at me. Then, without missing a beat, she turned to the orderly and shouted at the top of her lungs, "FUCK YOU, ASSHOLE! I WAS JUST BEING FRIENDLY!" and stormed away.

As I sat there dumbfounded at what had just transpired, the tall orderly put his hands on the back of the couch, leaned over and whispered, "Stay away from her unless you wanna catch the A.I.D.S." I nodded my head slowly and turned to the television, pretending to watch it. Inside my head, I was becoming angry. "They think I am fucking CRAZY" I said to myself. "I may have a drug problem, but I aint crazy!"

Shortly after, a pretty, brown-skinned nurse in pink scrubs that were just tight enough in all the right places walked over to me and asked if I was "Miles Walcott". I answered yes, and she coolly instructed me to follow her to the examination room where she took my vital signs. As she adjusted the blood pressure cuff on my arm, I said to her, "These people are crazy! Are you sure I am in the right place?" She smiled and told me that the doctor would be in shortly and that I could express my concerns with him. She frowned as she read my blood pressure and said, "Your blood pressure's a little high." "It always gets like that when I am around a woman as pretty as you!" I said with a sly smile on my face. She ignored my corny attempt at flirting and continued with her exam. My mind had become so deluded by the cloud of addiction that I actually thought she would be actually be interested in a suicidal, drug addicted patient in a psychiatric facility!

After checking my blood sugar, she asked me if I had diabetes. "No" I said, becoming alarmed. "Your sugar is a high too. The doctor will be in soon" she said, and turned around to leave. As I checked out her behind in those tight medical scrub pants, I nervously joked that perhaps my blood pressure would go down once she left!

A few minutes later, a short, balding white man, wearing a lab coat that barely concealed his Santa Clause like belly entered the exam room and introduced himself to me. "Hi, I am Dr Summerhoff, what brings you here?" I told him that I needed help with my drug problem, but assured him that I wasn't crazy like the rest of the folks here. He smiled and proceeded to ask me some questions about my drug use.

Dr. S: "Have you ever gotten arrested while under the influence?

Me: "Yes"

Dr. S: "Have you ever had unprotected sex under the influence?"

Me: "Yes"

Dr. S: "Have you ever committed an act of violence or had an act of violence committed against you while you were on drugs?"

Me: "Yes"

Dr. S: Have you ever thought about, or attempted suicide while under the influence of drugs?"

Me: "Uh, yes"

Dr. Sommerhoff proceeded to ask me a few more questions regarding my drug use and then looked at me with a serious look on his face. "Hmmm . . ." He said with a chuckle, ". . . sounds pretty crazy to me!" He gave me a playful smile to ease the pain of the truth he just spoke to me. He then turned to my chart, giving me a chance to ponder our brief conversation.

At first, I was deeply offended. My initial instinct was to ask him who the fuck he was calling crazy, but as I sat there and contemplated the way I had been behaving over the last 15 years of my life, it became abundantly clear to me: I *was* crazy! Who else but a crazy person would do the things I had been doing? I had put my drug use ahead of the welfare of my children and myself. My whole life had become centered on getting high or finding ways to get high. I finally realized that if I kept going down the road I was traveling, I would end up back in jail, in and out of institutions like the one I was in now . . . or dead.

"You're killing yourself, Mr. Walcott" the doctor announced sternly, as he turned back towards me. "You smoke crack, you're over-weight, your blood pressure is out of control and your glucose level is also dangerously high! You're a heart attack or stroke waiting to happen. If you keep living the way you have been, you'll be dead within six months!" Dr. Sommershoff's words stung sharply and I began crying. At first, the tears rolled slowly down my cheek, but as his words sunk in, I began sobbing uncontrollably; rocking back and forth on the cold, stainless steel examination table while I held my arms crisscrossed on my chest and balled my fists up as tight as I could hold them. Dr. Somershoff put a firmly placed a hand on each of my shoulders and looked me in the eye. His stern countenance softened, much like First Sgt. Hilliard's did that day back in Germany, after my drunken fiasco. His voice softened as he spoke directly to my soul. "Listen to me son" he said softly. "The blood pressure and diabetes can be controlled with medicine and changes in your diet, but you have to stop using drugs; IMMEDIATELY!

His voice raised a couple of octaves as he spoke that last word, and I looked back into his eyes. Suddenly, that warm, safe feeling that had enveloped me after enduring the pain of watching my children being driven away by the DCF worker washed over me again. In retrospect, I believe that at times like this, my God was speaking directly to me! I knew deep inside that I *could* stop using, get my act together and live a happy, productive life; without the use of drugs, but I didn't know *how*!

I began to wonder how folks like Malik, and countless other apparently hopeless addicts were able to stop using and lead happy productive lives. I had witnessed first-hand, many people who had been the dregs of society become happy, productive members of that same society and I began to believe that I too, could do the same! In spite of the horrible mess I made of my life, I finally had the spark of hope that I needed to come up out of the muck and the mire that my life had become and finally break free of the shackles of addiction; and that feeling of hope came from seeing living proof of people recovering from this insidious disease when I went to 12 Step Meetings!

Once I completed thirty days at The Yale Psychiatric Institute, I was discharged after convincing the psychiatrist (and myself) that I no longer wanted to die! I couldn't wait to embark on my new journey! Finally, I was going to get my life together and be the man I always wished I could be!

I hit the ground running, submitting job applications to every employer I could think of. I knew that the sooner I became employed and had my own apartment, the sooner I would be able to regain custody of my precious children. The pain of having them removed from my custody hurt me deep inside my soul, but that quiet voice inside me, that I was beginning to listen to more and more, reassured me that as long as I did the right thing, we would soon be reunited. I had always thought that it was my right to raise my kids, but I now realized that raising my children was not a right, but a privilege . . . a privilege that could be revoked if I abused it!

Tamara, one of my biggest supporters, hired me to paint her house. She paid me a handsome fee, but in small increments, because we agreed that having a large sum of money in my pocket at one time probably wasn't such a great idea for someone new in Recovery. Tam had become the spiritual "leader" of our family since our moms passing and she always had encouraging words and a hug for me whenever I saw her. Knowing that my sisters still loved me and hadn't given up on their brother provided my self-esteem with fertile ground to grow in.

As I unpacked my clothes and placed them in the dresser in the spare room of Lizan's apartment, she looked at me and said, "I don't know what it is, Miles, but there is something different about you this time. You have some sort of glow about you and although you've said you were done getting high a thousand times before, I *believe* you this time!" Lizan's belief in me reinforced my own fragile self-esteem which I had all but destroyed over the last 15 years of my life. I know now that cultivating ones self-esteem is absolutely vital to sustained Recovery. The bottom line is this; "People who feel good about themselves usually don't abuse drugs". In a sweet display of sisterly love, my baby sister opened her home to me as I embarked on my road to Recovery not truly knowing if I was done getting high or not! In retrospect, she believed in me before I believed in myself! I am forever grateful for the love and support of my sisters in addition to taking care of the needs of their own families!

Prior to going "In-Patient", Lizan and I had a loud argument at her home one night that centered on my irresponsible lifestyle and the poor choices I had been making. Of course I responded defensively and angrily due to the deep state of denial that I was in. At the time, I was unwilling to accept that I was destroying my life and the lives of my children too! The argument deteriorated into a shouting match and not having much of a defense for my decadent lifestyle, I resorted to an expletive laced name calling tirade that I wont even repeat here. After the argument, I was sure it would be years before we spoke again. My sister was only expressing her frustration at watching her older brother's life go "down the tubes", but all I could hear was that she wanted me to stop "dating" my beloved girlfriend . . . Crack Cocaine! In spite of my irresponsible behavior, Liz was actually one of my biggest supporters and only wanted the best for her big brother!

CHAPTER 45

The Transformation

I had been complaining at the 12 Step Meetings lately about how frustrating it was trying to get an apartment with bad credit and was just about to give up. "This recovery shit just ain't working" that familiar voice would tell me. "God doesn't give a damn about you" it whispered to my soul. The same voice was also reminding me how good a nice hit of crack would feel and how it would alleviate my frustrations, but I chose not to listen to that malicious voice and have faith in a God that I wasn't even sure existed.

Malik pulled me to the side one night, after I had just shared openly about my ambivalence about a Higher Power's existence and spoke softly to me as I scowled in the church parking lot, smoking a cigarette. In order to regain custody of my precious children, I needed to have an apartment and so far, I had been rejected by every landlord I applied to . . . even the Housing Authority! You know your credit sucks when the projects turn you down!

Malik asked me if I remembered where he had come from so I took a second to reminisce. Back in the day, Malik was your stereotypical, undesirable drug addict. The kind of person that you wouldn't rent an apartment to *or* hire as an employee! Now, he was a college graduate who had his own private counseling practice. He was a productive member of society and you could tell by the "glow" that surrounded him that he was truly happy and enjoying life!

As we stood outside in the church parking lot, Malik asked me, "Do you believe in God, my brother?" I took a drag of my cigarette and began to cry. "I don't know" I said between sobs. "I want to believe, but it seems like He doesn't hear my prayers! I need an apartment so I can get my kids back and I keep getting turned down! ". Malik placed his hand on my shoulder, looked me in the eye and said, "Until you believe in God, my brother, believe that *I* believe! Believe that the same God who rescued me will rescue you too!" He told me that I needed to learn how to turn *my* will over, and let *God's* will be done.

Malik explained to me that I needed to *practice* faith, not just *talk* about it. He promised me that the more I trusted in God's will instead of my own, the stronger my faith would become. "Hold on, my brother" he told me. "Don't get high no matter what and believe in a God who loves and cares for you . . . everything else will be fall into place!" Malik taught me how to stop praying for "things", like jobs, apartments and automobiles and pray instead, for strength, patience, wisdom and understanding. Everything that happens is either a lesson or a blessin', my wise mentor explained; learn to be grateful for both!

He explained to me that God wasn't in the business of punishing His faithful; He only wanted what was best for us. It was only because of our choices that we became addicted, but God's grace and mercy could free us from those shackles.

I knew how far Malik had come in his Recovery, and I wanted the same for myself. I wanted the nice home, the nice job and the nice car, but I had to do some "footwork" in order to achieve them. "If you want what I have" he told me, "You gotta do what I do!"

I never was a very religious person and I said so to my friend Malik. "This aint about religion!" he exclaimed. "It's about spirituality! It's about practicing spiritual principles such as honesty, open-mindedness and willingness in your life; it's about becoming more God centered instead of self-centered!"

I asked Malik what the difference between religion and spirituality was because I always thought that they were one in the same. He looked at me with a sly grin on his face and said, "Religion is for people who are afraid to go to hell, my brother; spirituality is for people who have already been there and made it back! Now get off the pity pot and stop feeling sorry for yourself! If you take one hundred steps into the forest, it's gonna take one hundred steps to get back out!"

Malik went on to explain that the 1st Step of The Program wasn't just admitting that we were powerless over drugs; it meant we were powerless over people, places and things also! It meant that we had to stop trying to control everything and everybody and learn how to turn our will and our lives over to Power greater than ourselves! "That doesn't mean to sit back and wait for God to do everything", he explained. "It means do the very best you can and leave the rest in His hands! He will either give you what you need, or give you the strength to live without it!

I realized that there was a lot of truth to what he was saying to me. For most of my life, I had been trying to control everything and everyone around me. The women in my life, the drugs . . . hell, I even tried to control how I felt! Every time I lost control (which was quite often) I lashed out in anger and frustration; only to add more shame guilt and embarrassment to that which was already overflowing within me. It was no wonder why it was so easy to get the "fuck-its" and obey that "lower power" that had been whispering sweet nothings in my ear for all these years! I was finally starting to understand why I was always a ticking time-bomb waiting to explode. Being a control freak combined with the pain of the multiple traumas I had endured throughout my life ensured that I was always one step away from exploding into a temper tantrum at any given moment. Every single arrest I ever had wasn't from trying to get away with breaking the law; they were all a result of my reaction to losing control!

"Stop trying to control everything, my brother, and turn control over to God! You'll save yourself a whole heap of pain and misery!"

In the past, I would catch domestic violence charges or get into "bar fights" and just blame it on the alcohol, but I had been free from alcohol for over year now and found myself still getting into fights with men on the streets and even the woman in my life! I could no longer blame it on the liquor and finally had to accept the fact that I was a "control freak" who threw childish temper tantrums when I didn't get my way or someone hurt my feelings!

Although I wasn't on drugs anymore, I still had the mentality of an addict. I wanted what I wanted when I wanted it! I still had an overwhelming desire to control everyone and everything around me and I got very upset when I didn't get my way. I had learned how to turn my cravings to get high over to God, but that was about all I was ready to relinquish control of! I was like, "God, I need you to help me stay clean, but I can handle everything else!"

As a result of my self-centered behavior, I was constantly at odds with the world. It was either "My way, or the highway" and God help anyone who didn't agree with me! Even though I wasn't getting high anymore and claimed to be "Clean & Serene" when I shared at meetings, I was still in a constant state of rage just below the surface, and it didn't take much to unleash the devil inside me. Oh, The Voice was still there, but it knew I had turned my addiction completely over to God so it didn't try to talk me into using drugs anymore. The evil entity that was still within me hadn't gone anywhere; it just laid in wait until the opportune moment when it could rear its ugly head! It just wanted me to be miserable or better yet; dead. If it couldn't get me to destroy myself with crack, it would try to destroy me by any means necessary!

One of my best friends, Howie, used to say, "Satan baits the hook according to the taste of the fish". What that meant to me was; "If I don't turn myself completely over to a Power Greater Than Myself, Satan would find our weak spot and tempt us there. For some, it could be promiscuity, for others, it may be excessive shopping; the list goes on and on. The bottom line is; as long as the behavior causes unmanageability in our lives, Satan, The Devil, The Voice, Addiction or whatever you want to call it is completely happy!

For me, it was my unwillingness to turn my will completely over to God. As long as I held on to the illusion that I could control everything, I would continue to become frustrated and angry; and that anger could surely cause unmanageability and even death.

For instance, one afternoon, when I had about one and a half years clean, I was driving my rusted out Chevy Blazer down Whalley Avenue. Trevor was about five years old and we had just gotten ice-cream from the corner store. As we approached the corner of Whalley Avenue and the Boulevard, a grey Honda Civic pulled away from the curb and I had to swerve quickly to avoid hitting it, causing my son's ice cream to fall from his hands and land on the floor of my truck.

When we arrived at the light, I threw my truck into park, exited my vehicle and stormed over to the car that had just cut me off. "What the fuck is your PROBLEM" I screamed, as I prepared to smack the crap out of whoever was driving. Not only did they almost cause me to have an accident in my unregistered, un-insured vehicle, which would have caused me big problems with the police; I self-righteously needed to vindicate the fact that my son had nearly smashed into the dash-board when I slammed on my brakes!

Before I even reached the jerks car, Marijuana smoke mixed with a "chemical-like" aroma that I couldn't quite distinguish, emanated from the raggedy Honda and hit me in the face, infuriating me even more. Since *I* wasn't getting high anymore I expected everyone *else* to stop too!

As I arrived at the rear of the vehicle, a kid no more than seventeen pulled out a 9mm pistol and pointed it out the window at me. A cold chill an up my spine as I realized that I was about to be shot in broad daylight; in front of my son! My anger immediately subsided as intense fear took over. I slowly back-pedaled my way back to my truck in silence as the young boy leaned out of the car window with an angry scowl on his face. "That's right Old Skool, back da fuck UP!" he shouted as the beat up Honda sped off.

I got back into the driver's seat of my truck and sat there, stunned. I could vaguely hear Trevor asking me if I was ok from "far away", but my mind was still stuck on the fact that I had almost gotten my head blown off seconds ago because of my self-centered, arrogant behavior. As I sat there in the middle of the street, squeezing my steering wheel with a glazed over look in my eyes, a blaring car horn snapped me back into reality. My heart was still pumping a mile a minute, but I was able to pull myself together and drive away.

I decided right then and there that if I didn't stop trying to control people and behaving like an angry child every time I got upset, I was going to wind up dead or in prison. I decided that it was absolutely imperative that I turn my will completely over to God whether I fully believed in Him or not. I didn't have time for internal theological or intellectual debate; it was either believe now . . . or die!

I had gotten arrested for fighting and domestic violence in the past, and the judge would always order me to attend anger management classes. This experience taught me that I didn't have an anger management problem at all! I finally realized that if the police showed up or if someone pointed a gun in my face, I could manage my anger quite well! My problem was that I had a *choice* management problem! When I lost control of a situation, I *chose* to act out in an angry, violent fashion; but only if the odds were in my favor! When I accepted the fact that I couldn't control any given situation or person, I was able to relinquish control immediately. It suddenly became abundantly clear to me that if

I didn't stop trying to control people and behaving like an angry child every time I got upset, I was going to wind up dead or in prison, whether I used drugs or not!

In spite of the fact that I was no longer using drugs, there was still an evil spirit within me that lay dormant until my weakest moments. Once it sensed I a weak moment, it pounced upon my spirit like a lion pounces upon the slowest gazelle. "What's the point of not using drugs?" I asked myself, "Only to die from my total self-centeredness?" My experiences in life taught me that I couldn't defeat this "lower" power on my own, so I finally surrendered my will and my life to a benevolent, loving Power that was much greater than myself and the evil entity that wanted me dead!

After that day on Whalley Avenue, when my son almost witnessed his father's violent death, I experienced another spiritual awakening. I prayed that God Himself would cover me with his grace and mercy. I asked Him to protect me from myself and that wicked entity that had preyed upon my soul for most of my life. I prayed for protection from myself because I knew now that I couldn't blame everything on the devil. A lot of the pain and misery in my past had been self-inflicted. I made the choice to put that pipe to my mouth. I made the choice to continue down that dark and dreary road called Addiction" It was me who chose to jump out of my truck that day and almost have an early demise. The devil only had power over me with his sweet sounding lies once I had made the ***choice*** to do wrong!

Now, for the very first time in my life, I had made a choice to turn my will *and* my life over to the care of a loving and compassionate God. Never before in the history of Miles Preston Walcott had I been willing to *totally* submit to a Higher Power! In the past, I had submitted time and time again to a "*lower power*" only to fall flat on my face over and over again until the day I saw my life held in the hands of a seventeen year old, angel dust smoking kid.

At the precise moment I made the decision to "turn it over" to my God, a feeling of serenity ten times greater than the one I felt that gloomy day on the Long Wharf a year ago enveloped me. I immediately felt impervious to "The Voice" that had plagued me since childhood. I decided that from this point forward, I would listen to that soft, gentle voice that I had always ignored. The voice that never told me a lie, the voice that always had my best interests at heart, the voice that I now was the voice of GOD!

CHAPTER 46

The Miracles

It was during this period of early Recovery that I needed tangible evidence that God existed. I was trying to completely surrender my life to Him, and He, in His infinite wisdom, knew how fragile my faith was. As I developed my relationship with God and incorporated spiritual principles into my life, I began to notice what I like to refer to as "The Miracles". The Miracles were events that I would have NEVER expected; not even in my wildest dreams! "The Miracles" defied the laws of probability and let me know that besides the "Lower Power" that had dragged me through the muck and the mire, there was also a Higher Power that could make my life better as well!

One of the most obvious miracles was the fact that the desire to use drugs had been miraculously lifted! In the past, thoughts of my next hit would consume my mind beginning the moment I woke up, but now that the obsession to use had been lifted, I was able to focus on the business of Recovery. I wasn't even aware of it yet, but the binding shackles of addiction had been removed and the Miracles began to come in rapid succession!

The mere fact that my sister Lizan had offered me a safe, drug free place to stay during this vulnerable time of my life, was a miracle in itself and further proof that a Power greater than myself was at work. Trust me when I tell you that after that loud argument we had a while back, she was the last person I expected to offer me a place to live!

My sisters already had relationships with God and they all encouraged me to pray. The only problem was that up until this point in my life, my only idea of God was an angry, malevolent deity whose only desire was to pass out punishment to the sinners of the world. If He did exist, He surely didn't have time for a sinner like me! My spiritual beliefs vacillated between this "Angry God" and the "Santa Claus God" . . . a sort of imaginary friend who people referred to, but deep down inside, they knew He didn't really exist!

When I realized that the desire to use had been lifted as a result of my feeble, yet sincere prayers, I decided that this "God" that my mother and sisters prayed to might not be so angry after all! My prayers began to be more sincere, and slowly but surely I began to believe that maybe, just maybe, there might be a God after all!

"The Miracles" continued to happen in rapid succession! Lizan decided to move to South Carolina and the apartment she rented in a very nice section of New Haven suddenly became available. Her landlord, who didn't know me from a can of paint agreed to rent the apartment to me without doing a credit check or even checking to verify that I even had a job! He even told me that I could pay the deposit a little at a time each month!

Imagine if you will the intense joy that I felt at finally being able to have a place of my own! I had been turned down by every landlord that I applied to and had been denied by the projects, but thanks to the spiritual guidance of folks like Mark K, Leon H, Denny K, Malik W and Sam A., I didn't give up! They all encouraged me to not quit before the miracle happened and now I saw what they were talking about!

After my visits with Trevor and Tamia, I would always sit them on top of my rusted out Chevy Blazer and promise them that soon, we would all live together. As we enjoyed the last few minutes of our visits, the three of us would dream of Dora the Explorer comforter sets for Tamia and posters of Michael Jordan on Trevor's bedroom walls. It was such an awesome feeling knowing that I was finally able to make good on my promises!

I am eternally grateful to the folks from the 12 Step Fellowship who donated some really nice things for our new apartment; a leather love seat and sofa from Cordell P., pots and pans from Cynthia S. and a brand new Hewlett Packard computer from my man Robert B. who owned his own landscaping business now! My Aunt Diane gave us beautiful bedroom sets for the kids and my older sisters Tamara and Kandi continued to give me odd jobs at their rental properties to supplement my income.

I had about nine months clean now and it was time for me to go back to court to attempt to regain custody of my children. My DCF worker, who had told me that it would take a year to eighteen months for my children to come home, was so impressed with the apartment and my clean urines that she advocated to the judge that my babies be returned to my custody immediately! It was as if God Himself had taken out a big ole pot of miracles and dumped them right on my head!

The first night my children came home was a very emotional one for us all. We had been separated for nine months and being re-united once again was a joyous occasion; almost like Christmas Eve! We ate dinner together at the practically brand new table that Lizan had left for us and a feeling of "family" settled over me as I watched my precious gifts from God enjoy their new home!

As I tucked them into the bed that first night, Trevor, who was about five years old at the time, looked up at me and said, "Thanks for coming to get us daddy, I love you". I told my son that I loved him also and solemnly swore to him that we would never be separated again. I kissed him and his sister goodnight and told them how much I loved them. I went into the living room, sat down on the couch and surveyed my surroundings. I had come a long way from living in my buddies garage and it suddenly dawned on me how blessed I really was. As I sat there and cried deep, cleansing tears of joy, I made a solemn vow to God that I would never forsake Him, myself or my children again; and to this day, I have kept that promise.

The miracles didn't stop there though! I celebrated one year clean on December 27th 2000, and shortly after that I was hired by the state of Connecticut Department of Mental Health and Addiction Services as a Mental Health Assistant. Suddenly, I was making more money than I had ever made. We were all ready enjoying a higher quality of life than we had ever experienced due to me being clean and focusing on family and God but it sure felt great to be able to buy nice things for my kids and take them on family trips.

I had been quite the "rolling stone" in the past, but now that I wasn't a slave to my addiction anymore, I was able to begin the healing process with my other children. Miles Jr., Montel, Bianca and LaToya had also suffered because of the poor choices I had made, but now, we were becoming close again as we spent more and more quality time together. My family playfully referred to my house as "The Daddy Day-Care Center" because on any given weekend it was normal for me to have all of my children and their friends over for food, fun and family time.

Based on the stellar example of my dad and the positive men in "The Fellowship", I was learning how to become a father all over again. I had gotten lost along the way, but God has a way of putting loving and caring people on our paths as long as we are open-minded and willing to remain teachable!

As I continued to stay clean and rely on the Power within me, I found myself doing things that I never did before. I became actively involved at my children's school, attended almost every one of Montel's basketball games and basically began "showing up for life". I had been a "Ghost Dad" for a very long time, but now I realized that I actually loved the responsibility of raising my kids! I even became a Biddy Basketball coach at the Farnham Neighborhood Corporation and coached my son Trevor's team until he entered Junior High! With the help of God, The Fellowship and my beautiful family, I had began "giving back" to the society that I had taken from for most of my adult life!

Up until this point in my life, I had held down many jobs, from dishwasher, soldier and landscaper, to Certified Nursing Assistant, painter and Residential Counselor; but my favorite occupation of them all had become "Father"! I remembered my own dad saying, "Those kids didn't ask to be here", and I strived to become the best dad that I could possibly be. I used to think that raising my children was my God given right, but I now knew that it was actually a privilege that should never be abused!

I also found out that I loved being a responsible, productive member of society and I took particular pride in being a hardworking, conscientious employee. For years, I had only done just enough to get by, but now, I always went above and beyond the call of duty and prided myself on having an impeccable work ethic. My dad always said," I don't care if you are the sh*t shoveler at the circus, as long as you are the best sh*t shoveler they have!" Well, as a direct result of having a loving God in my life and a strong desire to be the best that I could be, I was promoted to day shift supervisor at my job within three years!

So, if anyone ever tells you that miracles don't happen, tell them about the recovering addict with a criminal record and a G.E.D. who lost the desire to destroy his life with drugs, became a loving, responsible parent and got promoted to a supervisory position at the state of Connecticut's Department of Mental Health and Addiction Services!

Those who know me personally understand that I am not being arrogant or boastful regarding my successes; I am merely attempting to give hope to the hopeless! I want the world to know that miracles do happen if we allow the God that resides in us all to lead our lives and also truly believe that this Power greater than ourselves can restore us to sanity!

CHAPTER 47

Miles to Go

During the summer of 2008, while enjoying my 8th year of Recovery, I was blessed with the opportunity to take my family on a week-long vacation to Martha's Vineyard. The days leading up to our trip were filled with excited anticipation of our first Family vacation together since my parents had taken my siblings and I over 25 years earlier! My two older sisters, their children, my children and I rented a house in the" Inkwell" section of "The Vineyard", which was a miracle in and of itself! Not even in my wildest dreams would I have ever thought that my family and I would be vacationing in the same place that president Obama vacationed with his family! I realized that I had finally grown up and I loved it! For the first time in the history of Miles, I loved life! The obsession to "use" had finally been lifted and I was free, enjoying life on life's terms! Not only was I living a drug-free lifestyle, more importantly, I was doing the "inside work" that allowed me to enjoy that lifestyle; for what's the point of getting clean and then being miserable because I still held on to that addictive mentality? That vile, cunning voice that had plagued me for years was finally silenced and God's "voice" was now my beacon of light as I navigated life!

While my family and I rode the ferry across Long Island Sound towards Martha's Vineyard, the most remarkable sunset I had ever witnessed in my life filled the summer sky before me. As my family members enjoyed its splendor, I walked alone to the far end of the ferry and peered out across the ship's bow, in awe of God's majesty. The most amazing shades of brilliant color blazed across my view and I felt as though I was in the presence of God Himself!

Tears of pure, unadulterated joy ran down my cheeks as I thanked my Creator for every second of the amazing journey I had been on for the last forty years of my life; for without the sometimes self-inflicted pain I had endured, I would not be able to appreciate the magnificence before me! Although I had miles to go on my road to Recovery; I thanked God All Mighty that I was miles away from whence I had come!

The End . . . . well, actually . . . The Beginning!

EPILOGUE

My own personal experience has shown me that Recovery from active addiction, along with developing a relationship with a Power greater than myself is a journey, not a destination. During this journey there will be trials, tribulations, disappointments and set-backs. Don't get me wrong, long periods of abstinence is great but many folks view long periods of sobriety as victory and relapse as failure but the bottom line isn't when your last drug use was; it's how are you living today? I have known folks with multiple years of sobriety who beat on their wives and actually sell drugs to people in Recovery, but I have also watched folks with mere days of sobriety do some of the most loving and caring things I have ever witnessed!

Although watching a loved one struggle with the disease of addiction may be a painful, frustrating predicament, please understand that the active addict may have prior experiences and trauma's that may prevent them from stopping their drug use right now. This in no way exonerates them from the pain and misery that they inflict on their families but it is important to know that the addict needs love and hope to break free from their self-imposed prison. If you or someone you know suffers from this insidious disorder call on the God of your understanding to guide them back to the light.

I don't believe anyone makes a conscious decision to become so addicted to drugs that they commit robberies or prostitute themselves; these negative, anti-social behaviors are only symptoms of a deeply rooted spiritual illness whose only relief can come from a loving and caring God.

"The Devil in Me" was the title that I originally wanted to use for this book, but I felt that it had a negative connotation to it that contradicted the message I was trying to convey. That message is a message of hope. Hope for any addict or survivor of trauma who feels trapped in the endless cycle of pain and misery that comes with active addiction. I decided to go with the title "Miles to go . . ." because recovery is a journey; not a destination. Although I have come a long, long ways from where I used to be, I have miles to go in my recovery. I also thought it would be pretty cool to incorporate my name into the title!

I may not be the best I can be yet, but at least I aint the worst I can be anymore! For the last thirteen years of my life, I have been striving for spiritual progress . . . not perfection.

I will never forget the feeling of intense joy I felt when I first realized I was free! Free from the self-inflicted bondage I had imposed upon myself. However, I must never forget how horrible I felt in my deepest darkest moments of despair. For as soon as I forget . . . those dark times shall surely return. miles p walcott